British Financial Institutions:
Savings and Monetary Policy

Kevin W Wilson
BSc, MSc, PhD
Research Fellow, Manchester
Business School and Consulting
Analyst, Charlton Seal
Dimmock & Co., members of the
Stock Exchange

Pitman

PITMAN BOOKS LIMITED
128 Long Acre, London WC2E 9AN

PITMAN PUBLISHING INC
1020 Plain Street, Marshfield, Massachusetts 02050

Associated Companies
Pitman Publishing Pty Ltd, Melbourne
Pitman Publishing New Zealand Ltd, Wellington
Copp Clark Pitman, Toronto

© Kevin W. Wilson 1983

First published in Great Britain 1983

British Library Cataloguing in Publication Data

Wilson, Kevin W.
    British financial institutions.
    1. Financial institutions—Great Britain
    I. Title
    332′.1′0941   HG186.G7

ISBN 0–273–01627–X
        0–273–01628–8 (pbk)

Text set in 10/12 pt Linotron 202 Times, printed and bound
in Great Britain at The Pitman Press, Bath

To Ann and John Wilson

Acknowledgements

There are a number of people who have assisted in the preparation of this book. Of the many academics who have provided creative comments, John Sparkes and John Bridge deserve special thanks. In addition, the professional opinions of Peter Hayes, Geoffrey Lipscombe, Richard Briston and Howard Jarman were of particular importance in the preparation of the final draft. Finally, an army of capable typists have shared the tedium of refining the finished product. In this latter case, I am particularly grateful to Margaret Wilson and Margot Kneppers. I am, of course, fully responsible for any errors of omission and commission which remain.

Kevin W. Wilson *)
October 1982

* He was my great - great grand father
  (Peter K. Wilson)
  That's funny: He's still alive, we are waiting
  for his departure.

Preface

The literature concerned with the financial system in the UK has in the past tended to concentrate upon the banking system, with comparatively little consideration devoted to the analysis of non-bank savings institutions. This book represents an effort to remedy this situation in some way by placing equal emphasis upon banking and non-bank financial intermediaries (NBFIs).

The term 'financial intermediary' is used frequently throughout the text because it is considered to provide a more precise description of the activities undertaken by the institutions discussed in Part One. Accordingly, Chapter 1 is concerned with introducing the reader to the concept of intermediation and describes how the changing financial system reflects the willingness of different organizations to cater for the revised saving propensities of individuals. In addition, the essential distinctions between the banks and non-banks are discussed and the impact of changing savings patterns assessed.

Chapters 2 and 3 continue in the definitional vein, concentrating upon the NBFIs. The former concentrates upon the major investment institutions and the latter on the leading deposit takers in the UK. The chapters seek also to highlight the different functions fulfilled by these institutions and provide an insight into the almost bewildering variety of financial instruments created as a natural part of those functions. The distinction between public and private sector intermediaries is made clear and the reader is kept constantly aware of the theoretical consequences of financial diversification.

In deference to the conventional approach to investigating the financial system, the banking intermediaries are described and discussed in Chapter 4. It will become apparent to the reader that the focus of monetary policy has traditionally been upon the banking system. Chapter 5 therefore describes the experience of the banks in the context of a decade which was characterized by a shifting economic philosophy, culminating in the application of controls upon banking activity and, later, a new liberalism in the conduct of monetary policy. In particular, the development of monetary targeting is assessed.

Part Two is concerned with an analysis of the theoretical consequences of the growth of non-bank intermediaries. Chapter 6 defines simply the terms and concepts involved in the study of monetary economics with reference to the essentially descriptive material contained in Part One.

Chapter 7 discusses further the implications of the growing importance of non-banking institutions by drawing upon the research conducted so far. Although the relative lack of attention received by the non-banks in the UK is evident from the proportion of research emanating from the USA, the chapter also considers the major pieces of research conducted in this country and assesses their contribution. The major focus of attention throughout is upon the definition of money and the efficient conduct of monetary policy.

The final chapter draws the descriptive and theoretical contents together in an analysis of the UK financial system in the 1980s and draws attention to the points of contention which still exist, in spite of an extensive report upon the financial system presented by the Wilson Committee. In particular, the chapter concludes with a discussion of the competition for savings and an overview of monetary policy and offers some reasons for its constantly changing emphasis, and in some cases, ineffectiveness.

The text is intended for those undertaking banking and finance options in universities, polytechnics and colleges and banking courses concerned with monetary theory and policy. It is also anticipated that the subject matter will become increasingly relevant to those concerned practically with the management of building societies, pension funds and trusts and other relevant institutions.

Kevin W. Wilson
October 1982

Contents

Part One **The increasing significance of non-banking financial institutions**

Introduction

Although considerable space is devoted to outlining the basic features of the UK banking system and the implications the conduct of monetary policy has had upon its recent development, Part One of this book is concerned primarily with describing the nature of financial intermediation and provides a description of those non-banking institutions which have assumed this role in the economy. Deliberate emphasis is placed upon non-banking financial institutions in order that the stage may be set for a careful consideration of the theoretical problems posed by their increasing importance.

The non-banking institutions are divided into investment and deposit taking classifications for the sake of convenience and are described according to the functions they seek to fulfil and the nature of their particular business. Throughout, an effort is made to set those institutions in the macroeconomic context. The banks are then introduced in order that the reader may be able to identify the major distinctions between non-bank and banking activity. Part One concludes, in Chapter 5, with an overview of monetary policy in the 1970s and the spectre of monetary targeting.

1 The growth of financial intermediaries

1 The concept of intermediation

Financial intermediaries perform the function of transferring funds from persons with an excess of money (surplus units) to persons who require extra funds to fulfil their expenditure or investment plans (deficit units). They are responsible for channelling savings to investment and consumption purposes and without them many of the funds in the economy would remain idle. In a developing economy, persons require an increasing number of alternative ways of holding wealth and financing complicated transactions. In order to facilitate this requirement, certain intermediaries 'innovate', i.e. develop alternative financial facilities and instruments, in order to finance further exchange. In so doing, these institutions fulfil an entrepreneurial role which enables economic growth to take place.

There is no doubt that it is the non-bank intermediaries rather than the banks which have created the major impetus for innovation in the British financial system since the Second World War. The reasons why will be discussed in Section 3 of this chapter. For the moment we can assume that because they have been largely responsible for innovation in the financial system, NFBIs are directly responsible for the proliferation of financial instruments (methods of holding wealth) that we see today, ranging from investment, share and deposit accounts with building societies to the complicated life assurance policies offered by the insurance companies[1].

This acceptance that intermediaries are the primary vehicle for change in a financial system was implicit in the work of Goldsmith (1969). He attempted to measure the structural development of a financial system in terms of what he called the 'financial inter-relations ratio'. Goldsmith believed that the ratio of total financial assets to total real wealth in an economy and the distribution of those financial assets are primary aspects of the financial structure of an economy. He extended his analysis to develop a ratio of financial intermediation in order to be able to compare the different financial structures of different countries. The greater the proportion of total real wealth held in the form of financial assets the

---

1 Many of the different financial instruments are discussed in Chapter 2, where a distinction between transferable and non-transferable financial instruments is also drawn.

greater is said to be the degree of intermediation. It follows that the more those assets are *not* held at banks the greater the presence of non-banking intermediation.

Goldsmith is one of many researchers who have attempted to account for the growth in the number of financial instruments which exist. It may be appropriate for the reader at this stage to stop and count the number of alternative places he or she can store money. The number of institutions and individuals willing to hold money is in itself enormous, the methods they have devised to entice savers to use them in preference to a competitor is bewildering. So Goldsmith considered that measuring the number of financial instruments was a valid indicator of the age and sophistication of a financial system. Others have concentrated upon the range of instruments provided. For example, according to Revell (1973) the number of financial instruments in an economy depends upon

'the extent to which some units are in financial surplus while other units are in financial deficit. The greater the reliance of economic units on their own saving, whether that of the current period or of the past period held in the form of financial assets, the lower the value of financial claims issued during the period [and hence the less intermediation resulting]; the smaller the reliance on their own saving, the higher the value of financial claims issued. In the second place the net value of financial claims issued will be higher if a large proportion of funds is channelled through financial intermediaries with their multiplier effects on the value of claims issued rather than direct from surplus unit to deficit unit'. (p. 15)

By intervening between deficit and surplus units, intermediaries fuel the growth in the number of financial instruments since every transaction facilitated requires a double entry. Thus if a building society were to receive a deposit from one unit and that deposit was used to provide a mortgage to a second unit then two claims, a deposit account and a mortagage arrangement, will have arisen, whereas if the transaction had taken place directly between the deficit and surplus units a simple IOU would have sufficed.

Although evidence concerning the proliferation of financial instruments can be used as a method of comparing the development of financial systems and their structure, we need to concern ourselves with the reasons behind these developments in the UK. In the UK financial system, individual, private and public concerns require funds to finance their activities, whether it be the everyday working capital for a small firm or a multi-million pound loan to finance investment in sophisticated equipment for the telecommunications industry. In both cases an agent is required to direct funds towards some purpose and there are basically two types of institutions responsible for doing so, the banking and non-banking financial institutions.

The banking institutions are specified by the Bank of England as follows

> (i)   *UK banks:* including London clearing banks, Scottish clearing banks, Northern Ireland clearing banks, accepting houses and other UK banks.
> (ii) *Overseas banks*: including the UK branches of American banks, Japanese banks and others.
> (iii) *Consortium banks*: i.e. banks which are owned by others but not controlled by one in particular. One of the shareholders must be an overseas bank.

As far as the application of monetary policy is concerned, the 'banking sector' usually refers to those banks 'listed' by the Bank of England, of which there were over 350 in 1980. Of these, 96 banks are 'recognized banks' in that their bills are eligible for discount at the Bank of England. The Non-Bank Financial Institutions, (NBFIs), can be conveniently described as those institutions whose financial liabilities are not regarded by the Bank of England as money. These include building societies, local authority treasury departments, life assurance companies, superannuation funds, unit trusts, investment trusts and other specialist intermediaries[2]. It is obvious that there is an official distinction between banks and non-banks and this distinction needs to be clarified for two reasons. First, it is confusing that a financial instrument issued by a building society (such as a deposit account) is not included in the definition of money by the Bank of England, yet if a similar account were opened with a commercial bank the money supply would register an increase. Secondly, it is also confusing that banks can act in an intermediary capacity and yet the non-banks are often referred to as 'the intermediaries'. We turn our attention now to these considerations.

Banks, non-banks and intermediation

The motivation for an institution to engage in banking is determined by the profit arising from the excess of marginal revenue over the marginal cost of lending further cash. The motivation for acting as an intermediary is the differential between the cost of attracting savings and the price charged for providing transactions or investment funds. Indeed, as we will see later, monetary policy operates by bearing directly upon these motivations,

2 The Trustee Savings Bank, formerly a member of this group of institutions, officially attained banking status in 1981.

seeking to influence the prices and flows of financial assets in the economy. The distinction between banks and non-banks is most apparent if we precisely define an intermediary. A financial intermediary is an institution which issues financial claims on itself to surplus units (savers) in order to obtain funds either to purchase other financial claims (investments) or to lend directly to deficit units (spenders). Those who demand money for transactions or investment purposes may therefore borrow at a rate of interest. This role of a financial institution is distinct from that of a bank which acts primarily as a repository for transactions cash creating further cash for transactions where necessary. In Ascheim's words (1961) 'commercial banks are *creators* of loanable funds, whereas financial intermediaries are *brokers* of loanable funds'. (p. 115)

There are two identifiable types of intermediary in the financial system consistent with the definition adopted by Burns (1969). First there are primary intermediaries, i.e. those that issue securities directly to surplus spending units and purchase securities directly from deficit spending units. For example, a building society issues shares and deposits to savers and makes loans directly to borrowers in the form of mortgages. The secondary intermediaries issue securities primarily to (and/or purchase securities primarily from) other financial intermediaries. Thus an insurance company, because it invests in stocks and shares, is acting as a secondary intermediary. The distinction is concerned with the contact between savers and borrowers: if this contact is one step removed or shared in any way by a number of institutions then they are regarded as secondary. In practice, it is the deposit institutions, like the building societies, which are primary because they act alone in facilitating exchange.

The reader will no doubt be aware that banks also engage in intermediation as previously defined. However, the intermediation undertaken by banks is said to have declined relative to the non-banks since the war. This is reflected in the relative growth of the non-banks and is certainly the case in the USA, as Goldsmith (1958) discovered. It is more appropriate in this respect to distinguish between bank lending and saving with the banks. Certainly, the proportion of saving diverted through the banking system has been reduced by effective competition from the NBFIs. Less severe has been the competition for lending opportunities since most of the non-banking institutions tend to be specialists in particular types of financing activity which the banks have hitherto tended to avoid. Nevertheless, the rate of growth in banking activity has lost ground compared with the non-banks for three basic reasons. First, the commercial banks are heavily constrained by regulations which have tended in the past to only apply to banking activities. Secondly, the banks have traditionally regarded the intermediaries as insignificant competitors. Thirdly, the amount of debt issued by respective governments, (which are a special type of intermediary since they can influence the transactions of others whilst being in deficit themselves), has increased enormously in the past decade[3]. The inter-mediaries have been active in taking up this increased debt, using the funds obtained from savers. An increasing public sector borrowing requirement (PsBR) therefore invites the growth of non-bank intermediaries.

Because banks and non-banks both facilitate exchange the distinction between them is often blurred. As a consequence it is better to distinguish theoretically between banks and non-banks by concentrating on the concept of money and its creation. Money is both a store and measure of value and a medium of exchange. The critical factor distinguishing the commercial banks from the non-banks in this respect is that the demand deposit liabilities of the former circulate as a generally accepted means of payment whereas intermediary deposits do not. It is sometimes argued that a cheque drawn on a demand deposit is not money but merely the promise to pay cash at a later date in final settlement of a debt. However, this argument ignores the fact that persons frequently exchange a cheque for goods and express their wealth with reference to demand deposits without the necessity to convert to cash. Furthermore, a note promises to pay the bearer the value of one pound, so in a sense a note is precisely the same as a cheque. Clearly, the distinction is invalid because of the fiduciary note issue and the general acceptance of a book entry as the final payment of a debt.

It is necessary at this stage to distinguish properly between money and credit. The extension of credit is the same as the creation of a debt, as Hawtrey (1919) pointed out

'The practice which we have attributed to the dealers of setting off one debt against another may be described as the use of *credit* as the means of payment. Debt and credit are different names for the same thing. That which to the debtor is a debt, is to the creditor a credit'. (p. 3–4)

A banker, he continued, is someone who deals in debts or credits to facilitate exchange. If money alone were used to facilitate exchange then there would be no need for persons to accumulate debt and therefore no credit would exist. Credit is therefore the natural consequence of matching payments in a complex economy. Of course, the financial instruments created by all financial institutions are in lieu of a debt and we can therefore conclude that they all, bank and non-bank alike, create credit. The distinction between bank and non-bank rests on the assumption that bank credit has assumed the characteristics of true money. Thus when a bank creates a loan (grants credit) for an individual he immediately incurs the debt. The transaction financed by the loan provides to someone an inflow of income (in payment for their product). The depositing of this

3 See Chapter 2, Section 2, for a breakdown of the holding of public debt by selected financial intermediaries.

income with a bank registers an addition to total money stock. Clearly the creation of credit by the bank has added to total money stock. This conclusion relies on a belief in circular flow of income and the fact that banks enjoy a monopoly of money creation.

On the other hand, the non-banks cannot assume this importance. They have neither a monopoly on the creation of money nor an assurance that, as the process of exchange takes place, the funds will eventually return to their own tills. When they create credit, it does not influence the stock of money because, it is argued, their credit instruments are unacceptable as a final means of payment. Consequently non-bank credit does not create money and the NBFIs are regarded purely as credit institutions in the financial sector. They, in fact, turn over the money created by the banks.

Revell (1973) also differentiated between the monetary claims issued by banks and the non-monetary claims of intermediaries and argued that it seems logical to assume that intermediaries dealing in non-monetary claims cannot play any significant role in the monetary process. The counter argument is that the difference between the financial instruments issued by banks and non-banks is one of degree, since they both facilitate exchange and share the attribute of a store of wealth. The essential distinction of liquidity (see page 125) is being eroded as certain non-bank financial instruments (e.g. building society deposits) assume a position of near-money. Another important aspect of the debate is that intermediaries may increase the turnover or velocity of circulation of money in order to generate business for themselves. Thus the activity of the non-bank financial intermediaries may directly influence the velocity of circulation of money which, as we shall see in Chapter 5, directly impinges upon the monetary theory which underpins the conduct of monetary policy.

There are other operational distinctions between non-bank intermediaries and banks apart from the theoretical argument concerned with the concept and creation of money. First, non-bank intermediaries tend to cater for specific needs in the economic system. They have acquired considerable expertise in the gathering and interpretation of the information required to fulfil their own particular function. This information concerns the identification of surplus and deficit units (savers and investors) in the economy and acting as a catalyst by which the transfer of funds may take place. In this capacity the intermediaries are effectively supplementing the market and ironing out inefficiencies in the system, which facilitates exchange. It has not been until relatively recently (during the past twenty-five years) that the commercial banks have diversified their own activities either by direct expansion or by the acquisition of existing intermediaries. This is seen as a response to the declining share of the deposit market held by the commercial banks but some would argue that they have left it too late. Although the commercial banks are sophisticated organizations, the intermediary function often requires specialized knowledge and personal contacts which take time to develop. Consequently, in 1980 the share of the personal deposit market held by the commercial banks was as low as 34 per cent, as indicated in Table 1.1 (page 10).

Table 1.1 illustrates the relative shares of the personal deposit market held by the clearing banks, building societies and saving banks (National and Trustee). Although the personal deposit market is but one sector of the total saving in the economy it is the sector where the competition between the banking and non-banking deposit institutions is most intense. It is obvious that between 1968 and 1980 the share of the market held by the commercial banks declined from 46 per cent to 34 per cent. It is also noticeable that this share increased in the early 1970s from 40 per cent to 45 per cent as the banks sought to reverse the trend, but has since stabilized at a lower level. The argument offered by the commercial banks for their declining market share is that they are heavily constrained by legislation and that the non-banks are in some cases given an unfair competitive advantage[4]. Certainly, when the functions of the most important inter- mediaries are reviewed in the following chapter it will become obvious that certain fiscal advantages are afforded them. Nevertheless the debate still continues, particularly as a result of the second distinguishing charac- teristics of the non-bank intermediaries.

A second distinguishing characteristic is that in general the lending activity of the non-banks is extremely restricted. For example, under the Building Society Act (1962) these institutions may only lend by way of mortgage on property. Moreover, the role of reserves is quite different between banks and non-banks, with the intermediaries being allowed to lend money subject to the constraint of a minimum liquidity ratio which is required for contingent withdrawals. On the other hand, the banks' reserve ratios are stipulated by the monetary authorities and hence their reserves are traditionally held for quite different reasons. There is therefore no reason why the reserves held by the intermediaries and the banks should comply either in size or content because they fulfil different roles for each institution. For example, in a non-bank intermediary ownership resides in the holders of its deposit liabilities (for example shares and deposit accounts in building societies). The difference between the value of assets and liabilities is reflected in the accumulated reserves of the non-bank and these reserves are used to cushion the effects of unforeseen contingencies such as a fall in the value of certain assets.

The role of reserves in the banking system is quite different. The aim of the regulations imposed upon the listed banks is not primarily to safeguard the interests of savers, which is a secondary consideration, but to create the appropriate economic climate through monetary policy. These reserve

---

4 See the evidence presented to the Wilson Committee (1980) by the clearing banks, in Vol. 1, Wilson Committee, HMSO, London, 1977. See also Chapters 3 and 8.

Table 1.1 Shares of the personal deposit market—£bn (%)

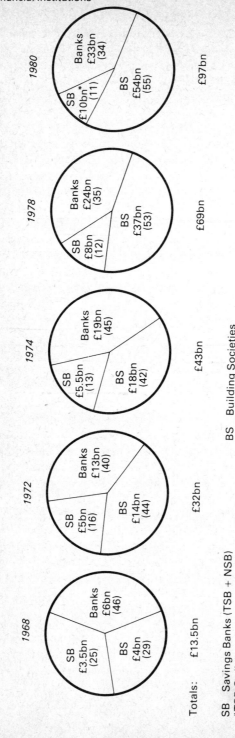

	1968	1972	1974	1978	1980
Banks	£6bn (46)	£13bn (40)	£19bn (45)	£24bn (35)	£33bn (34)
SB	£3.5bn (25)	£5bn (16)	£5.5bn (13)	£8bn (12)	SB* £10bn (11)
BS	£4bn (29)	£14bn (44)	£18bn (42)	£37bn (53)	£54bn (55)
Totals:	£13.5bn	£32bn	£43bn	£69bn	£97bn

SB   Savings Banks (TSB + NSB)   BS   Building Societies
*TSB Ordinary departments excluded from 1980 figures

Source: Lloyds Bank Economic Bulletin and Economic Progress Reports

assets were prescribed by regulation in order to facilitate control of the money supply, a topic to be discussed in Part Two. According to Duck and Sheppard (1978) a reserve asset can be described as

'. . . any financial asset or group of assets in the form of which the commercial banks are obliged by decree to hold a certain proportion of their deposits. This proportion is usually specified as a minimum'. (p. 2 (Footnote))

It should be noted that clearing banks, as distinct from other listed banks, are required to deposit a percentage of their total deposits with the Bank of England. They carry no interest and act as a control device upon the lending activity of the clearers quite separately from the minimum reserve asset ratio which is applicable to all listed banks. Previously the reserve asset ratio was required to be a minimum of $12\frac{1}{2}$ per cent of 'eligible liabilities', though the system of monetary control was revised in August 1981[5]. Finally, there now exist prudential controls upon the banking system in order to preserve its stability and the ability to suffer loss and change, as well as the monetary policy ratios. Very often the aim of regulations imposed upon banks is to discriminate between borrowers. For example the Government may wish to discourage lending to individuals whilst encouraging lending to corporate bodies for investment purposes. In this case the Bank of England would issue lending priorities to the listed banks, relying upon their co-operation in the knowledge that they are aware of the powers of the central bank. Another aim of the regulation of listed banks is to prevent those banks from attracting depositors away from the non-bank financial intermediaries whose lending may on certain occasions be accorded high social priority, such as that of the building societies. For example a maximum to the banks' deposit rate was imposed in September 1973 with the aim of conferring a competitive advantage on the building societies for they were then able to offer a higher interest rate to small savers (£10,000 and under).

It is more likely, however, that regulations on bank activities are imposed in order directly to control both the supply and direction of money and credit. We shall not delve into the intricacies of monetary management at this stage. It should be remembered however, that the money supply is influenced by the lending activity of banks. If they lend in order to facilitate a transaction then the expenditure involved will add to total national expenditure and the loan given by the bank creates an inflow of funds into the banking system once the transaction is complete. When the total deposit liabilities of the banks, which constitute the money supply, are summed they will have increased as a result of the banks' lending

5 Eligible liabilities comprise sterling deposits (except those with a maturity over two years) minus lending to other listed banks and loans not callable to discount houses plus net sterling certificates of deposit.

activity. It is by concentrating attention directly upon the lending activity of banks that the authorities seek to control the money supply. Indeed this procedure has been likened to 'birth control'[6].

The precise methods by which the authorities seek to control the activities of the listed banks are confusing in their variety. A synthesis will be provided in Chapter 4, but it is sufficient at this stage to recognize that they seek to achieve the aforementioned desired results. It is argued by the banks that the regulations merely direct business away from them into the hands of the non-banks. While this is undeniable it is also the case that the creation of money is controlled in this way. The problem then becomes one of identifying the difference, if any, between the financing of transactions by the banks and the non-banks, since the former are supposed to create money whilst the latter are said merely to create credit. It was this diversion of business to the non-banks which was first mooted by the Radcliffe Committee (1959). This committee, which was the first in this country to identify the important growth in non-bank activity, concluded that monetary policy should seek to control the money supply (which was not well defined at that stage) *and* the liquidity of the non-banks. Monetary policy, it was argued, must therefore operate on two closely related planes: one whereby the money creation by the banks is controlled, and a second where the liquidity and therefore credit creation ability of the non-banks is similarly restrained.

It will be apparent when an analysis of each intermediary is undertaken that a practical distinction between the listed banks and NBFIs rests upon the nature of their asset portfolios. However, there is a more fundamental distinction concerned with the liquidity of the financial liabilities created by the different financial institutions. It is through the routes of liquidity and acceptability of those financial instruments issued by the non-banks that we gain access to monetary theory at a later stage. Liquidity is defined as the ability to transform wealth holding into any form without loss of face value or delay[7]. Thus, if a person holds wealth in the form of a house there is likely to be a delay in realizing its cash value or if one surrenders a life assurance policy there will be a loss of face value as selling costs are incurred. On the other hand, cash can be exchanged for anything without delay and without loss of face value. Cash is therefore the ultimate liquid asset.

There is therefore a spectrum of liquidity for all financial instruments determined by the time taken to convert to cash and the loss of face value on conversion. Thus, not only must we distinguish between the banks and the non-banks on functional grounds but also on the grounds that

6 See 'Monetary Policy and Regulations Imposed on Listed Banks', *Midland Bank Review*, Summer 1979.

7 The latter, delay, will be particularly important in an inflationary situation, since the later one receives cash on redeeming a financial asset the less that cash is worth in real terms.

non-banks create financial instruments varying in liquidity whereas the banks create money. It is the fact that the banks' financial liabilities are accepted as the final settlement of a debt that provides the greatest theoretical distinction between them and NBFIs. This distinction is crucial to our understanding of the nature of our financial system, the definitions of money and credit and the conduct of monetary policy.

Finally, it should be reiterated that intermediaries are often constrained by legislation in conducting their lending activities. Apart from having to be licensed as deposit-taking institutions some intermediaries are allowed only to provide finance for specific purposes, which is why the building societies hold over 90 per cent of their assets in the form of mortgages when other lending opportunities may, at times, be a more profitable proposition. Similarly the savings banks, before recently, were required to invest their funds in specified securities and the insurance companies compelled to provide an insurance fund for the safety of depositors[8].

Despite these considerations it would be mistaken to assume that the banks do not have to compete with the NBFIs because they are dealing in different markets. The savings of the personal sector, which reflects all household saving and the saving of the unincorporated business sector, is the primary source of funds to the non-banks and certain listed banks. Since the extent to which banks create money and non-banks create credit is restricted to the amount of funds they can attract, they must compete for a slice of personal sector saving. The legal and tax advantages enjoyed by certain intermediaries and the regulatory barriers which impede banking excursions into other activities actually increase the necessity of the banks to compete for funds. Thus the contention offered by some authors, that the superior liquidity of bank liabilities implies that they do not have to compete with the non-banks for funds, is questionable.

2 The growth of non-bank savings institutions in the UK

The propensity to save

In economic theory the propensity to save is important on two counts. In the Keynesian model, saving is regarded as a leakage from the circular flow of expenditure and income through the economy. As a consequence, the reciprocal of this leakage from the flow of income to expenditure is used as a theoretical measure of the impact on national income of variations in autonomous expenditures, better known as the multiplier. The second important aspect of the propensity to save is that saving provides a source of funds which can be directed towards investment purposes. The exact

8 See 'The Licensing and Supervision of Deposit Taking Institutions', presented to Parliament by the Chancellor of the Exchequer, HMSO, London, Aug. 1976.

offsetting of investment and saving in the economy would achieve a stable though not necessarily a full employment equilibrium.

The Keynesian model (1936) of income determination considered saving to be a residual. The theory concentrated on the demand for money and incorporated the theory of liquidity preference. However, this theory was developed by Keynes in order to connect the rate of interest to saving in his model. Thus, because persons preferred liquidity to illiquidity one would have to pay for the latter by offering savers a rate of interest. The rate of interest was therefore the opportunity cost of liquidity. If interest rates rose, persons would sacrifice liquidity and save more, thereby demanding less money to hold for transactions purposes. The consequence of this theory was that the demand for money was inversely related to the rate of interest. However, the demand for borrowing by industry is also inversely related to the rate of interest and this presents a paradox. The higher the rate of interest the more persons would save but the less borrowers would invest. If however, savers and investors were free to bargain the result would be an equilibrium rate of interest. Indeed, the classical view of the rate of interest is that it is solely determined by changes in savings and investment throughout the economy.

It is now considered, however, that saving is not merely the residual factor in the income flow. Persons save for a purpose in much the same way as they desired liquidity for transactions, precautionary or speculative purposes in the Keynesian model. If we accept that saving is a purposeful exercise it follows that persons are willing to exercise discretion as to where they deposit their savings depending upon which savings medium best suits their needs. It is necessary, therefore, to understand why persons save, how saving has changed over recent years and the role played by the intermediaries in this process.

As a purposeful act, saving is necessarily a feature of a developed, high income, economy. The extent to which persons are able to save will depend upon their income, for there is a minimum amount of consumption we all need to make to stay alive. It is not until incomes rise sufficiently for there to be some discretion in what is to be done with the excess of income beyond the subsistence level that saving, in the present sense, can take place. This saving may be motivated by different desires: either in order to yield a return to the individual now (in the form of interest) or in the future (say in the form of a pension) on the one hand; or to accumulate sufficient funds to facilitate a larger than normal expenditure e.g. house purchase, on the other. Saving may also be motivated by the desire to take advantage of a specialist facility, such as the tax benefits which could accrue from investing in unit trusts with life assurance cover or saving with a credit union. Finally, persons may save in order to accumulate a contingency fund to be drawn upon in hard times; for example, if a person expects to be made redundant at some future date or if inflation requires a larger contingency reserve to pay occasional bills. Indeed, Friedman has argued that saving in the form of non-liquid financial assets may increase in inflationary times. This 'flight from cash' arises as the opportunity cost of holding cash increases, because inflation acts like a tax on holding cash and persons invest in alternatives in order to maintain the real value of wealth. However, unless the rate of inflation is below the prevailing rate of interest, a financial asset will offer a negative interest rate. The motivation to save then becomes one of loss minimization rather than the maintenance of real wealth. In the extreme case of hyper-inflation, persons normally opt out of financial assets altogether and hold wealth in the form of assets which appreciate with the rate of inflation such as houses or, in the Brazilian case of the early 1970s, in Volkswagen cars!

The growth of the NBFIs must be considered in the general context of the reasons why people save, especially since, as we will see in the following chapter, the intermediaries tend to cater for specific saving needs. It follows that, if one can identify the changing needs of savers in a high-income economy, one may make pronouncements concerning the future development of the financial system as well as providing an explanation for the prominence achieved by non-banking institutions in the British financial system.

Personal saving in the British economy

Falush (1978) and Townend (1976) have demonstrated that the savings ratio of the personal sector has increased throughout the 1970s. Table 1.2 indicates the general trend in savings from 1966 onwards. Clearly, the savings ratio has increased gradually over the period, exceeding 10 per cent since 1972 and maintaining double figures thereafter. At the same time, it is apparent from column (3) that saving by the personal sector in the form of Total Liquid Assets (TLA) has also gradually increased[9]. The most important conclusion to be drawn from this table is that the amount of saving in the form of non-bank liquid assets has increased enormously each year, reaching a peak of £9.5 billion in 1980.

Personal sector saving is one of the most important sources of new funds for the whole economy. The funds go towards financing private sector investment and for financing the Public Sector Borrowing Requirement (PSBR), which is the amount the government and other public agencies need to borrow to fulfil their expenditure plans. The acquisition of public sector debt by the private sector, as we shall see later, takes place primarily through financial intermediaries such as pension funds and national savings banks.

---

9 These include: Notes and coin; National Savings; tax instruments; Local Authority Temporary Debt; deposits with banks, building societies and other financial institutions.

Table 1.2 Changes in personal sector saving 1966–1980

Years	(1) PDI £bn	(2) Personal savings ratio	(3) Total Liquid Assets TLA +£bn	(4) Deposits with banking sector +£bn	(5) (3)–(4) +£bn
1966	26.6	9.1	1.0	0.3	0.8
1967	27.8	8.5	2.0	0.7	1.3
1968	29.8	7.9	1.7	0.7	1.0
1969	31.7	8.1	1.2	0.3	0.9
1970	34.8	8.9	2.5	0.8	1.7
1971	38.7	8.5	3.7	1.0	2.8
1972	44.6	10.4	5.0	1.8	3.2
1973	51.2	11.6	6.0	3.4	2.6
1974	60.5	14.0	5.0	3.0	2.1
1975	74.9	15.4	5.9	1.0	4.9
1976	86.3	14.9	5.8	1.3	4.5
1977	96.8	13.8	8.6	0.6	8.1
1978	111.9	14.4	10.7	3.2	7.5
1979	134.7	14.1	14.2	6.2	8.0
1980	158.7	15.3	15.8	6.3	9.5

(1) PDI Personal Disposable Income.
(2) Personal saving divided by PDI.
(3) TLA Total Liquid Assets acquired by personal sector.
(4) Personal sector deposits with banks.
(5) Deposits by the personal sector with building societies, National Savings Bank and other non-bank financial intermediaries.
Sources: Economic Trends; Financial Statistics.

Saving by the personal sector is the difference between personal disposable income (income after tax, national insurance contributions and net transfers abroad), and personal sector current expenditure on goods and services. The personal sector is defined as individuals resident in the UK but also includes unincorporated businesses, such as sole traders, partnerships, private trusts and charities. At the end of the 1970s personal sector saving exceeded £17.6 billion, which was 41 per cent of all saving in the economy. Generally, it is the consensus view that the increase in personal saving represents an effort by individuals to maintain the real value of their wealth under inflationary conditions.

According to Falush, it is evident that inflation, high personal tax rates and the diminution of the market values of certain wealth holdings (see Chapter 2, Unit Trusts and Insurance Companies) has impinged directly upon the propensity to save. Furthermore since, as already stated, higher incomes lead to greater saving, one would expect that a more equal distribution of wealth should lead to lower saving overall. It seems that the rapid rise in incomes throughout the 1970s, particularly as the Retail Prices

Index has been used as the benchmark for pay settlements, has swamped the expected impact of the redistribution of incomes upon the propensity to save. As a result, we have witnessed in the 1970s an upward shift in the propensity to save in the UK in spite of the fact that inflation has at the same time eroded the real value of saving.

Although authors such as Coghlan and Jackson (1979) have advised caution in reaching this conclusion, there is no doubt that the level of saving has increased. However, it is the distribution of this saving throughout the financial system which impinges directly upon the growth of the NBFIs since they exist by their ability to attract a slice of total personal saving. They share with the banks the common objectives of encouraging thrift, mobilizing saving and providing finance for specific purposes. Previously we have concentrated upon the distinction between the banks and non-banks but both are similar in so far as they are powerless in influencing the general level of interest rates in the economy. They both rely upon an ability to reconcile the competing objectives of borrowers (who want to borrow at low cost) and lenders (who want to maximize their rate of return). It is their respective abilities to mediate between borrowers and lenders on competitive terms which determine the distribution of savings throughout the financial system.

Table 1.3 demonstrates that the non-banks have been increasingly successful in attracting the savings of individuals and unincorporated business. Clearly, it is not unusual for the building societies to attract over one half of total personal saving and the National Savings movement has also become a more important force in this competitive situation in the later period.

The final column demonstrates the importance of contractual savings with life assurance and superannuation funds which on two occasions has exceeded total investment in liquid assets (1966 and 1969). This demonstrates that saving cannot be regarded as a 'homogeneous' product and that one must clearly distinguish between contractual and non-contractual savings. The former imply a contractual payment by individuals over a period of years, the latter are at the individual's discretion. Non-contractual saving is the most likely to respond to variations between the rates of interest offered on deposits by the competing financial institutions. This is strikingly illustrated by reference to 1977 in Table 1.3. The banks' share of the total amount invested in liquid assets by the personal sector fell to a low of $6\frac{1}{2}$ per cent. This reflects the fact that bank interest rates dropped to 5 per cent in October 1977, their lowest since 1964. Similarly, the recovery in the share of deposits achieved by the banks from 1979 reflects the high rates of interest prevailing throughout that period.

The competition for personal sector funds is vitally important. The personal sector is by far the largest holder of liquid assets in developed economies such as the UK and USA. Dorrance (1978) estimated that

Table 1.3 Proportion of personal sector total liquid assets accounted for by selected NBFIs and the banking sector

Year	Deposits of banking sector %	Building societies deposits %	National Savings (1) %	Other FIs (2) %	(LASF) TLA (3)
1966	24.7	72.3	−4.2	0.9	122.8
1967	37.1	54.8	6.5	−0.9	69.4
1968	41.2	46.1	4.8	−0.1	92.7
1969	26.7	76.7	−9.7	−0.2	132.8
1970	32.4	58.5	4.3	0.4	69.6
1971	25.7	52.9	16.5	0.1	54.1
1972	35.5	42.9	16.7	—	49.4
1973	56.7	35.7	5.2	0.3	47.3
1974	58.9	39.1	1.4	1.2	73.4
1975	16.7	70.3	7.1	3.5	76.9
1976	22.7	56.8	10.2	3.9	95.8
1977	6.5	68.6	14.9	6.9	72.1
1978	30.2	45.3	14.2	5.8	68.7
1979	33.2	46.4	17.3	2.5	61.8
1980	34.1	46.1	16.8	2.1	65.4

(1) Excluding savings banks deposits other than ordinary accounts of the National Savings Banks and Trustee Savings Banks.
(2) Including National Savings Bank investment accounts, National Savings Certificates, and Trustee Savings Banks New Department until September 1979.
(3) LASF (Life Assurance and Superannuation Funds) assets are not included in TLA. The figure given is ratio of non-liquid assets acquired to total liquid assets in any year.
The figures do not necessarily sum to 100% because of the exclusion of certain minor financial holdings such as tax reserve certificates.
Source: Financial Statistics.

households alone account for over 60 per cent of total money holdings in both countries and a still higher proportion of other liquid financial assets. He concluded that 'Therefore, the basic theory of financial asset choice should place considerable emphasis on the explanation of the holdings of the household sector' (p. 45). Concentration on the saving propensities of the personal sector is therefore a legitimate basis for analyzing the growth of the NBFIs and their role in the economy.

The past two decades have witnessed a relative decline in the amount of money holdings as a source of wealth. As noted earlier, this tends to be an aspect of a high income economy. Saving is the accumulation of assets by an individual and therefore is a leakage from the circular flow of income. Assets have both convenience and income attributes and financial assets which combine these attributes are designed to satisfy the propensities to save discussed earlier.

However, as income rises the relative importance of convenience and income attributes of financial assets changes. According to Dorrance, the trade-off between the two attributes will alter in such a way that the importance of convenience declines as persons become more 'wealthy' and so can obtain credit on the basis of their existing wealth, i.e. existing wealth is used as collateral for raising convenience (transactions) finance. So Dorrance concluded

'Consequently, assets that combine convenience and income elements rise relative to money in individual portfolios. The monetary contribution to security declines as incomes rise. Therefore, the ratio of money to total assets tends to fall as total asset holdings rise'. (p. 53)

This explains why non-bank intermediaries have appeared and are so prevalent in high income economies. Initially, individuals are concerned with survival. However, once this is ensured they desire security and comfort and so seek to accumulate assets to satisfy the precautionary motive of saving which is now accorded a higher priority. Finally, they seek luxuries and require assets which generate income to satisfy this demand. The consequence of this process is a declining ratio of cash to income as incomes rise, or conversely, an increasing ratio of non-bank savings instruments to income, as Goldsmith had already discovered.

The consequence of this reasoning is that NBFIs satisfy the changing saving preferences of individuals in high income economies. The banks have been unable to satisfy this need either because of inertia on their part or, as they regularly argue, because they are effectively constrained from diversifying into other areas because of their role in the monetary process and therefore as vehicles through which monetary policy operates. Recently, however, it has been pointed out that the banks need to maintain liquidity and capital adequacy as a result of their primary role as the guardians of confidence in the financial system[10]. By keeping a large proportion of their sterling deposits in the form of short-term accounts repayable within seven days the clearing banks serve to maintain the public's confidence in the knowledge that funds can be withdrawn at any time, subject to specific account terms. Similarly, by maintaining the value of the total capital in their command the banks are effectively shielding depositors from capital losses which could occur if individuals undertook to invest on their own behalf instead of requiring the banks to act as their agents.

However, certain intermediaries, for example building societies, face the same problems. The difference between the deposit taking intermediaries and the banks in this respect is that the former rely more heavily on the personal sector. It is argued that personal sector funds are inherently stable

10 See R. Leigh-Pemberton, 'Banks, Building Societies and Personal Savings,' *National Westminster Bank Quarterly Review*, May 1979.

and this stability reduces the need for the savings institutions to maintain confidence. In other words, because they rely on the personal sector and that sector is both the major provider and user of their funds, they exist in a fairly stable situation which allows the intermediaries to concentrate attention upon diversifying their financial instruments to take advantage of the changing saving requirements of the personal sector. On the other hand, it may be argued that since the banks are a major source of finance for industry (especially small businesses), their lending activity is an inherently more risky business than, for example, providing mortgages for house purchase.

Because of this, the NBFIs have tended to concentrate in relatively risk-free activities, or at least in activities where risks are calculable. So that, while they face a stable deposit base and fully control their own lending activities, the banks enjoy neither of these advantages. It is not surprising, therefore, that in their evidence to the Wilson Committee the commercial banks requested a complete review of the regulations, controls, subsidies and incentives applied to different financial institutions. Basically, they argued that the different operating conditions imposed upon the banking and saving institutions are not efficient from the viewpoint of overall resource allocation in the financial services industry and that a policy of fiscal neutrality would encourage healthy competition for funds. This in turn would force the banks to compete more effectively and innovate more successfully.

3 Summary and conclusions

This chapter has been concerned with defining financial intermediation and identifying various features of the savings institutions which differentiate them from banks. It has been said that they tend to be a characteristic of a sophisticated financial system, which in turn is indicative of a high income economy. Furthermore, the changing reasons why people save as an economy develops have been offered as a primary reason for the growth of the NBFIs. Finally, it has been noted that the financial instruments issued by the non-banks as they go about their business are not classed as money for they are merely money substitutes i.e. alternative forms of debt.

This final contention is crucial on two counts in explaining the role of the NBFIs in the conduct of monetary policy, to be discussed in Part Two of this book. First, it implies that the banks fulfil a unique role as the only suppliers of money in the economy and accounts for the banks bearing the brunt of monetary policy. Furthermore, this belief has in the past coloured the banks' attitude to competition for personal savings with the non-banks. Secondly, the inability of the NBFIs to influence directly the supply of money implies that the regulations imposed upon the banks for the purpose of monetary control may remain in the long run. But, as we shall see, the 1980s have witnessed a shifting emphasis in the application of monetary policy, partly as a result of the increasing importance of certain financial institutions in the British financial system.

The growth of the non-bank financial intermediaries is consistent with certain features of a high income economy as follows

(i) Increasing income alters the propensity to save of those fortunate individuals who inhabit the high income economy.

(ii) A major consequence of the revision in the propensity to save is that cash receives less priority in a person's typical wealth portfolio.

(iii) As persons seek to hold assets which combine income and certainty, intermediaries will develop financial instruments which satisfy this demand. This is known as financial innovation and the proliferation of financial instruments has been identified as an indicator of the prevalence of non-banking financial intermediaries in certain economies.

In the UK the various institutions which have fulfilled the need for financial innovation created by a high income economy will be discussed in the following chapters. Evidence regarding increased saving generally and the distribution of financial assets in particular serves to reinforce the argument that the non-banking institutions have been the primary vehicles for financial change in the British economy. In turn, this has created problems for the definition of money and the conduct of monetary policy.

The Government white paper on Competition and Credit Control (CCC) presented in 1971 sought, amongst other things, to relieve the banking system of the tight controls which were considered inimical to competition and innovation in the financial system. The immediate consequence of this policy was to produce a money supply explosion, and any action undertaken by the monetary authorities to achieve fiscal neutrality, which was recommended by the Wilson Committee, must be conducted with reference to the possible implications for the financial system and the conduct of monetary policy.

There are three areas in which we can now assess and clarify the contribution of the savings institutions in the financial system. First, attention must be devoted to assessing the functions of the different types of intermediary in order to identify the transactions facilitated by each type. Secondly, due consideration should be given to the methods adopted by the various NBFIs to attract savings. Thirdly, the general structure of the financial system, existing procedures for monetary control and the relevant government policies need to be considered, for these define the environment within which the NBFIs operate. It was previously stated that the non-bank savings institutions cannot be regarded as an homogeneous group. In describing their individual functions the following chapters seek to confirm this view.

Topics

1 Discuss the factors which create an appropriate climate for the growth of non-banking institutions. Have these institutions been responsible for financial innovation in Britain?
2 Examine the theoretical distinction between banking and non-banking institutions and the practical arguments offered against a policy of fiscal neutrality.
3 Discuss the reasons why personal savings have increased in the past decade. Where has the extra saving gone?
4 Distinguish between liquid assets and others and consider the consequences for the economy of a shift in saving from one to the other.

2 Investment institutions

1 The functions of money and alternative financial assets

The original motivation for the use of metals as media of exchange lay in their attributes of divisibility and storage. The inconvenience of weighing metal bars led to the introduction of coins, again for reasons of divisibility but also, as Smith (1776) noted, because the aristocracy could monopolize and often interfere with the content of the coinage in order to economize on precious metals and effectively cheat their creditors by paying debts in the form of coins which were 'not a full shilling'.

The use of money developed primarily in response to the need to facilitate extended exchange. Once an exchange economy has been created, the income which is surplus to the everyday requirements of the population needs to be stored in some form. It is natural in such a circumstance that persons will prefer to hold wealth in the form of an asset which maintains its value. Such an asset is normally termed 'capital certain' and it is generally true that assets which provide capital certainty do not need to yield a return as high as those which are relatively 'capital uncertain'. An example of a capital certain asset is a building society deposit, whereas an ordinary share is a less capital certain asset since there is a chance of losing a proportion or, in fact, all of one's original investment.

It will become apparent that the major savings institutions under discussion in this and the following chapter differ markedly from banks in their origins. Without exception they began, at least in the UK, as specialist brokers in some financial service providing both advice and finance to individuals wishing to undertake financial transactions. This has in many cases developed into providing advice upon wealth maintenance and the issuing of liabilities to cater for the varying needs of savers. Nevertheless, although nowadays many hybrids have developed which attempt to span various areas of financial service, the non-bank financial institutions share the characteristic of beginning their development by issuing liabilities which were primarily stores of wealth. On the other hand, the banks evolved from issuing money to finance transactions and only belatedly did they begin to offer financial assets whose function is primarily a store of wealth. Hence, the banks originated as the providers of a monetary transmission service whereas the non-bank intermediaries provided specialist transactions advice with the emphasis on security.

The growth of the non-bank savings institutions can be explained by resorting briefly to the traditional theoretical approach of indifference curves. By pursuing the method adopted by Dorrance (1978) in his explanation concerning the proliferation of 'wealth assets' in individual wealth portfolios for developing countries, we can examine why certain forms of financial intermediary other than banks should develop. Figure

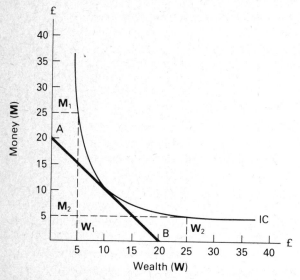

Fig. 2.1 Simple wealth portfolio

2.1 illustrates the typical portfolio of an individual which consists of money and other non-monetary forms of wealth, both expressed in pounds. The former is measured on the vertical axis (M) and the latter along the horizontal axis (W). The indifference curve (IC) illustrates the varying combinations of money and other forms of wealth which yield this individual equal satisfaction. So the individual is indifferent as to whether he should hold $M_1 W_1$ or $M_2 W_2$, since both combinations yield equal satisfaction in that they facilitate his everyday transactions and saving activity.

However, if we become more precise about the circumstances of this person, we can determine the combination of financial assets he will prefer to choose in a particular situation. In order to do this we need to introduce a budget line AB. This line indicates that this individual's total wealth is £20. If he held this total wealth in the form of cash only this would correspond to the point M = £20. If he held his wealth in the form of W only, then this would correspond to the point W = £20. Joining the two points allows us to observe all possible combinations of M and W which can conceivably exist to support his particular standard of living. Turning to Fig. 2.2, the individual will obviously seek to achieve the best combination of M and W i.e. that which yields highest satisfaction. High levels of satisfaction are indicated by higher indifference curves ranging in this case from IC_1 to IC_3. He will seek to achieve the highest of these curves subject to his limited income. Therefore, he would not be content with IC_1, on the other hand IC_3 would be unattainable given his wealth. Since IC_2 is the

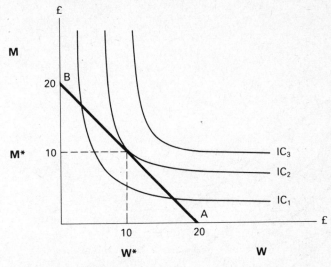

Fig. 2.2 Optimal combination of M and W

highest indifference curve he can reach i.e. the best combination of M and W subject to his total wealth, then he will choose the combination M*W* where the highest indifference curve is at a tangent to the budget line AB. This is the combination of money and other forms of wealth which best suits his individual needs. In order to maintain an adequate reserve of cash to finance his transactions without selling his other assets he keeps £10 in the form of each. In effect M*W* is the optimal combination of money and other wealth assets which suits his individual needs.

Of course, this analysis is impractical because it implies, unrealistically, perfect knowledge concerning our constantly changing individual wealth positions. Nevertheless, if we extend the argument to cover the whole of a population in a developed economy, certain additional factors become obvious. It is well known that as a person's income increases he uses proportionately less cash to transact his business, i.e. as a person's income is doubled it is unlikely that he will undertake double the number of transactions and require double the amount of cash. Proportionately less cash is required because it does not necessarily follow that the same proportion of cash will be needed to finance his extra transactions brought about by the increase in income.

The explanation for this is based on the relation between increasing wealth and the demand for money. As will be seen later in Chapter 5, understanding the demand for money is crucial in explaining the growth in savings institutions since holding wealth in the form of money is the alternative to holding wealth in the form of another asset. Indeed the

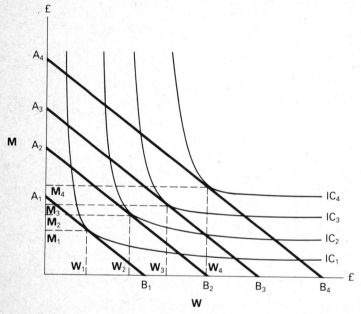

Fig. 2.3 Demand for financial assets with increasing income

provision of alternatives to money is the *raison d'ête* of the NBFIs. Thus, even if wealth per capita increases, it does not necessarily follow that people will spend proportionately more. Spending depends upon personal preferences, and wealth is often accumulated in order to afford the means to pay the price of a more expensive commodity at a later date. This implies saving, which for our purposes can be demonstrated as a declining proportion of 'money' in a person's wealth portfolio and an increasing proportion of capital certain assets, which for simplicity we can collectively term financial instruments.

In the terms of our diagram, this means that at higher levels of aggregate income the indifference curves of a nation will behave in the manner illustrated in Fig. 2.3. As the budget line AB moves outwards to reflect the successively higher levels of income achieved by the population, the combinations of M and W alter in such a way as to reflect an increasing desire to hold a greater proportion of W in the total wealth portfolio and a lesser proportion of money (M). Eventually, at the highest indifference curve IC_4, the amount of W in the total wealth portfolio actually exceeds money, which more closely approximates to the situation today in many developed countries.

The reason for this is that although the income effect implies an increase in the demand for each form of wealth holding, people are more willing to substitute capital safe assets for cash as income increases. Thus in the diagram, W_4 is greater than M_4 (at the outset M_1 equalled W_1). This demonstrated the changing character of wealth portfolios as wealth increases and has enormous implications for the growth of non-bank institutions since this provides a theoretical explanation of the demand for alternatives to money. It must be borne in mind, however, that those alternatives are not perfect substitutes for money. For example, if one holds a bond which yields regular income but matures in five years, and there is no secondary market in that bond, then it may only be realizable for cash if some loss in face value is incurred, i.e. one may have to sell it at a discount to a willing purchaser. The surrender value of a bond or some other form of financial asset, such as superannuation contributions, is therefore not necessarily a perfect substitute for cash.

There is nothing to gain at this stage by concentrating too heavily upon the theoretical issues involved in demonstrating the growth of alternatives to money. It will be more productive to examine the institutional setting which exists to provide alternatives to money in our economic system. We therefor continue with an appraisal of the history and operation of the primary non-bank financial intermediaries in the UK economy and speculate, in the light of the report of the most important committee since Radcliffe (1959), upon their expected development in the future.

It will become apparent to the reader that no clear classification system exists for the non-banks. Many of them undertake business which directly competes with the banks and often their operations overlap. The classifications adopted in this and the following chapter are for convenience only but will in general be agreeable to most practitioners in finance. The common feature shared by most of the institutions under discussion is that their liabilities are generally not included in the UK monetary definition, sterling M3. However, as we shall see later, an effort has been made since 1979 to overcome this surprising omission in the monitoring of expenditure capability in the British economic system and more recently one of them, the TSB, has been officially included in the monetary sector.

2 Superannuation funds and insurance companies

According to the Treasury (1977), these institutions accounted for 30 per cent of the total use of personal sector funds in the period 1956–1975[1]. The most significant feature of holding wealth in the form of a financial instrument issued by these institutions is that the saving is contractual. By this is meant a commitment by the saver to enter into a long-term contract whereby the funds cannot be withdrawn without some penalty being imposed, usually in the form of a reduction in the capital value of a realized asset. The two types of financial institutions share the feature of providing a financial return to specific beneficiaries out of a fund which itself is the result of contributions by future beneficiaries. These contributions are known as premiums in the case of the insurance industry and superannuation contributions in the case of the pension funds. The terms 'pension funds' and 'superannuation funds' are often used interchangeably, and will be so used throughout this chapter.

Another feature shared by these institutions is that they operate what are known as 'funding' arrangements. It is normally the case that, in the setting up of a life assurance or pension scheme, contributions exceed outgoings and this generates a 'fund' from which pensions or insurance claims are appropriated. Hence, the term 'funding' in this respect. The function of each institution is then to manage the fund in order always to finance current outgoings from that fund, whilst ensuring that the capital value of the fund is sufficient to be able to afford the outgoings expected in the future.

It was generally believed in the mid-1970s that the insurance companies and pension funds were becoming increasingly powerful in that they collectively held by far the greatest share of the total equity (ordinary shares) in the stock market. Although they are without doubt the most significant institutions in this respect, holding 36 per cent of the total equity of the stock market in 1980, a report commissioned by the Stock Exchange in 1981 contested the figure which had been quoted by the Wilson Committee[2]. The Committee had stated that the proportion of ordinary shares beneficially owned by persons fell from 66 per cent to 38 per cent over the period 1957 to 1975 and estimated this to have fallen further to 32 per cent in 1978. However, the Stock Exchange considered the Committee's data to be unreliable and believed 35 per cent to be a more realistic representation of private shareholdings in UK equities.

Nevertheless, the report demonstrated the importance of the non-banking institutions in respect of investment in the UK stock market. The leading holders of ordinary shares were the insurance companies (19 per cent) followed closely by pension funds (17 per cent) and investment and unit trusts (15 per cent) with other institutions accounting for the remain-

1 'The Financial Structure of the UK Economy', HM Treasury in *Evidence on the Financing of Industry and Trade*', Vol. 1, Wilson Committee, HMSO, London, 1977.

2 'Study of Shareholdings in British Companies', Stock Exchange, Sept 1981.

ing 14 per cent. This demonstrates the magnitude of the funds handled by the large non-bank financial institutions in the British economy and naturally prompts the question concerning the source of funds. This chapter and Chapter 3 concentrate deliberately upon how these institutions obtained their increasing slice of personal saving.

Only the life assurance component of the insurance business is considered here, as motor insurance (and other insurances) only repay on the occurrence of a chance event and constitute a relatively small part of the total insurance business. Because of the features shared by the insurance companies and pension funds they are classified under the same heading but we will consider the history and recent development of each in turn.

Superannuation funds

Superannuation or pension funds have experienced rapid changes in both the size and nature of their activities throughout the 1970s largely, as we shall see, because of the legislation enacted by successive governments. Originally pension funds were developed to relieve poverty, which had been considered a government responsibility since the Poor Laws of 1597 and 1601. As industrialization progressed the existing measures became increasingly inadequate and it was not until 1908 that a belated attempt was made to provide for those who could not generate sufficient income to maintain a subsistence standard of living. The National Insurance Act of 1911 dismissed the need for a means test for pension rights and introduced compulsory insurance. Although this was a new aspect of public policy, some private pension arrangements, usually called occupational schemes, had begun as 'friendly' or 'fraternal' societies. According to the National Association of Pension Funds the development of occupational schemes can be traced back to certain provisions under the Income Tax Act of 1918 and the Finance Act of 1921 with a marked acceleration in their growth after the Second World War[3].

It was not until then that occupational schemes were extended to manual as well as clerical workers. However, fundamental legislation which confirmed that pension schemes were 'approved' for taxation purposes was contained in the Finance Acts of 1970 and 1971. This legislation enabled contributions to be tax deductible for both the employer and employee and effectively subsidized the growth of this type of contractual saving. Indeed in 1981 total investments under the control of occupational pension funds exceeded £40 billion[4].

3 'Written evidence by the National Association of Pension Funds', *Evidence on the Financing of Industry and Trade*, Vol. 3, Wilson Committee 1978.

4 *Pension Funds and their Advisers*', A.P. Financial Register, 9 Courtleigh Gardens, London NW11, March 1980.

The present pension fund sector has evolved through a piecemeal process, consideration of which is beyond the scope of this book. The result is a system of national insurance and retirement pensions operated through the National Insurance Fund, (which is not a true 'fund' in the conventional sense), and a mixture of occupational schemes, which can be public or private depending upon the nature of the industry within which they operate.

It is the occupational schemes with which we are here concerned. Both the public and private sector schemes share the feature of divorcing insurance and retirement payments from the liabilities of the employer. The reason for this is to afford an employee added protection, for if the employer goes into liquidation a pension fund remains in existence and claimants upon the company's assets have no rights to claim compensation from it. The system therefore protects an employee's future benefits from the vagaries of the market place.

Throughout the 1970s there was a definite rift in the policy adopted by successive Conservative and Labour administrations towards the encouragement of occupational schemes. Both have attempted to revise the provision of income in old age so that it provides more than a subsistence return, whilst reducing the burden upon government financing. The debate centred upon whether such objectives are best accomplished by revising the existing system of social security or by encouraging private (occupational) schemes. Conservative Governments have favoured the latter and Labour the former. As a result, neither has been maintained consistently.

Several government white papers concerning the prospects for occupational pension arrangements have called for intelligibility. In fact the details concerning pension rights and contributions are often quite the opposite. A more important problem has arisen however, as occupational schemes have become more popular. The problem is one of constraining occupational mobility. When an individual transfers employment he is now forced to consider the valuation of his pension rights: a difficult task normally left to an actuary. The employee then has to negotiate with the new employer in order to minimize the financial loss of transferring. Of course, some industries have arrangements for such transfers but the problem would be eliminated if schemes were organized on an industry basis, as they are in France[5]. Nevertheless, the problem was considered by the Occupational Pensions Board in the summer of 1981 (cmnd 8271) and various measures to improve the protection of occupational pension rights have been proposed.

5 See T. Wilson, Chapter 6, *Pensions, Inflation and Growth*, Heinemann, London, 1974 and also 'The effect of U.K. legislation on the development of occupational pension schemes', Pensions Management Institute, 1978.

Superannuation funds: size and significance

There are various concessions applicable to pension funds granted by the Inland Revenue and this is what is meant by an 'approved' savings medium. Full tax relief is given on the contributions to a pension scheme. If one contributes to an occupational scheme, then the pension contributions are deducted from salary before tax liability is assessed. If one relies entirely on a state scheme then National Insurance contributions are adjusted accordingly and deducted from salary automatically under the Pay As You Earn system. Other advantages are that the 'fund' is exempted from tax so that none is paid on the income from investments. Additionally the lump sums often paid on retirement are tax free with the pension payments taxed as earned income. The major constraint upon pension schemes as an efficient form of saving is that the majority of the benefits are postponed to the distant future so reducing the liquidity of this savings medium. As a result of persistent inflation, some pension payments made through the state scheme are inflation proofed.

In fact the inflation proofing of certain state run schemes has created the rather iniquitous situation whereby the retirement income of most state sector employees is protected against inflation while that of most private sector employees is not. Almost all pensions are based upon salaries in the years immediately prior to retirement. From then on the pensions do not automatically rise unless there is special provision made in the trust deed of the fund. This is especially important when one considers that a relatively modest 10 per cent level of inflation halves the value of money in seven years. In 1981, 68 per cent of state sector schemes were guaranteed to keep pensions in line with inflation with a further 8 per cent raising pensions by three to four per cent a year. On the other hand in the private sector two thirds of schemes contained no inflation proofing whatsoever and only 23 per cent guaranteed increases of three to four per cent. These figures, plus the fact that 84 per cent of schemes were compulsory, created, it was argued, a system which encouraged immobility of labour and a tendency to cling to public sector jobs. Indeed the Scott Committee was set up to investigate the functioning of state sector pension schemes but the report has not yet been acted upon[6].

A corollary to the index linking of pension payments is the index linked government stock issued first in April 1981, as an efficient inflation proofed investment designed initially for pension funds. This indicated an explicit recognition of the increasing significance of the funds under management and the importance attached by the existing Government to maintaining the real value of retirement income. Indeed at the time some cynics had argued that the emphasis of government policy was misdirected, in that it sought to maintain the value of funds at a time when British

6 Scott Report: 'Inquiry into the Value of Pensions', Cmnd 8147, Feb. 1981.

industry was in a recession. This led to the extraordinary position whereby some companies had pension schemes which exceeded in value the market capitalization of the company. This was certainly true in the case of ICL which was capitalized at £50 million in 1981, and possessed a pension fund worth over £100 million. In the private sector Duport, a steelmaker, could be bought three times over by its own pension fund.

The increasing significance of the pension funds in the UK is demonstrated by reference to Table 2.1. The table shows the net assets acquired

Table 2.1 Pension funds inflows and wages and salaries

Year to 4th quarter	(£m) Net acquisition of assets	(£m) Wages and salaries	Asset %
1965	489	19,111	2.56
1966	533	20,389	2.61
1967	516	21,173	2.44
1968	575	22,566	2.61
1969	572	24,188	2.72
1970	725	26,994	2.72
1971	876	29,691	2.95
1972	1,083	33,163	3.27
1973	1,374	38,079	3.61
1974	1,663	45,900	3.62
1975	2,511	59,292	4.24
1976	2,971	66,586	4.46
1977	3,179	73,622	4.32
1978	3,705	83,587	4.44
1979	4,695	97,661	4.81
1980	5,514	115,103	4.79

Source: Financial Statistics

each year by all pension funds which exceeded £5.5 billion in 1980. This contractual saving increased to such an extent that it constituted almost five per cent of total wages and salaries earned. As far as the distribution of this saving is concerned, Table 2.2 demonstrates the impact of changing government policy. It is obvious that the public sector occupational schemes experienced the most rapid growth between 1965 and 1975 but have since been overtaken by the growth of private sector and local authority schemes. The table illustrates the three major types of pension funds: local authorities, private sector and other public sector schemes. The latter includes the schemes of the major public corporations and excludes only very few public schemes, such as the Civil Service, for whose employees the pensions are charged directly to the Exchequer and do not depend upon the management of a fund.

Without doubt, the largest pension schemes are in the public sector. In 1981 these were: the Post Office (£1.76 billion), NCB (£1.49 billion) and the British Rail Board (£1.15 billion), much bigger than the largest occupational scheme managed by BP (£717 million) and ICI (£640 million). In the same year 15 per cent of all registered schemes had funds exceeding £50 million[7].

Funding is the most important problem faced by those who manage a pension fund. This involves the maintenance of a surplus of contributions

Table 2.2 Pension funds, net acquisition of assets (£m)

	1965	1975	Growth	1980	Growth
			%		%
Local authorities	75	335	16.1	963	23.5
Other public sector	140	1,163	23.6	1,789	9.0
Private sector	274	993	13.7	2,509	20.4

Source: Financial Statistics

over outgoings in the form of assets which have the correct blend of capital certainty and income. Although no two fund managers will agree on the precise composition of that blend, the funds tend to follow similar trends over time as changing economic conditions render various assets more or less risky. Since the funding problem involves managing assets in such a way that the fund can always maintain its payment of pensions, the portfolio of investments will continually be subject to 'fine tuning'. The function of investing in a combination of assets which yields a sufficient return to meet the excess of annual pension payments over annual contributions is the responsibility of an executive staff. This may be 'internal' to the fund, with decisions on investment being vetted by an independent board of trustees. Alternatively, the funds may be managed 'externally' by professional organizations such as merchant banks, stock-brokers or by insurance companies or some combination of internal and external agents. Naturally, the size of funds tends to be associated increasingly with internal management as organisations seek to exercise more control over their own affairs. Whatever the organizational arrangements, however, pension funds always have the same objective, 'to maximize the rate of return by investments which involve an acceptable level of risk, having regard to the nature of the liabilities'. (Wilson Committee, p. 134.)

Determining the acceptable level of risk is, of course, a subjective and often difficult problem and the combination of assets acquired will be influenced by such factors as relative interest rates, the level of inflation

7 See *National Association of Pension Funds Year Book*, 1981.

and exchange rate fluctuations. Since investment in government stock is relatively risk free this tends to be the yardstick against which the pension funds compare the yield on other assets. Very often a proportion of a fund will be invested in gilt-edged stock as a stabilizing element, with ordinary shares and property used to hedge against inflation in the long run. Table 2.3 illustrates the importance of government and company securities in the

Table 2.3 Distributions of net acquisition of assets by pension funds (£m)

Year	British govt securities*	Company securities	Property	Short-term assets	Loans and mortgages	Total
1966	37	352	48	15	86	533
1967	68	302	79	−5	66	516
1968	15	347	116	19	77	575
1969	3	375	132	12	56	572
1970	−18	483	115	134	40	725
1971	296	514	129	−64	70	876
1972	15	690	175	158	75	1,083
1973	190	471	292	287	132	1,374
1974	86	209	322	781	258	1,663
1975	930	1,197	426	−307	247	2,511
1976	1,176	1,108	570	−28	145	2,971
1977	1,116	1,412	535	−67	183	3,179
1978	1,306	1,425	590	359	25	3,705
1979	1,897	1,746	499	221	−31	4,332
1980	1,710	2,772	855	−97	10	5,250

* Net of other public sector investments.
  Figures are in cash values.

Source: Financial Statistics

portfolios of the pension funds and the increasing interest in property as an investment. Nevertheless the majority of investments are held in British government and company securities. Furthermore, the similarity in the investment policies of the different types of fund is evident from Table 2.4, where the proportions of the total assets do not vary markedly between each class of fund.

The inflation-hedge problem had become particularly pronounced during the last decade. The liabilities (pension payments) of the funds are linked to earnings which are subject to inflation and, therefore, the funds must attempt to cushion their assets from the ravages of inflation in order to maintain pension payments. As part of their effort to do this, some funds have invested in assets outside the UK, encouraged by the lifting of foreign exchange controls in 1979. Indeed in the final quarter of 1980, the pension funds alone devoted 30 per cent of their net acquisition of assets to

Table 2.4 Net acquisition of assets by class of fund, 1980 (£m)

	British govt securities		Company securities		Property		Short-term assets		Loans and mortgages		Total
		%		%		%		%		%	
Local authorities	319	33	570	59	109	11	−35	−3	–	–	963
Other public sector	458	26	916	51	458	26	−48	−3	5	–	1,789
Private sector	933	37	1301	52	288	12	−19	−1	6	–	2,509

Source: Financial Statistics

overseas securities. Although this is seen by some as anti-social behavour, (because investment—the creator of employment—is effectively exported), the funds continue to seek any outlets which will allow them to pursue their avowed aim. However, the issuing of index linked gilt-edged securities goes some way towards reconciling this conflict of interest. At present there are no legal requirements obliging pension funds to account to the public, merely a requirement that new schemes be vetted by the Occupational Pensions Board. It will surely be just a matter of time before some statutory body is set up to enforce acceptable codes of conduct. The topic of regulation is considered in Chapter 8.

Insurance companies

The major function of insurance companies is to pool the resources of many people to provide for unforeseen contingencies (the risk of the occurrence of which is quantifiable), or the provision of financial assistance in the event of death. It is the assurance or long-term section of the insurance business where our particular interest lies since this has been the major growth area and is that section of the insurance business where the financial instrument issued is the most liquid. The life assurance policy is encashable, but is subject to the loss of transactions costs incurred in redeeming the policy by the insurer on behalf of the client. Nevertheless, the assurance (insurance) policy is the most liquid liability issued by the insurance companies and is thus an important consideration when examining the financial asset portfolio of persons in any developed nation.

It is not surprising that insurance companies act as the managers for some pension funds since their own asset portfolio is similarly structured, the major components being company securities, government stocks, local authority securities, land, property and loans and mortagages. Indeed, it is for this reason that the two types of non-bank intermediary are here subsumed under the same heading. Like the pension funds the assurance component of the insurance industry prefers long-term investments to match the long-term nature of their liabilities.

This is illustrated in Table 2.5, which gives a breakdown of the investment of UK insurance companies for their long-term business. Table 2.5 distinguishes between the major investments in their asset portfolio. By far the greatest component is government securities, followed by company securities. The similarity of their asset portfolio to the pension funds is obvious. Moreover, the increasing importance of the insurance companies in financing British industry is evident from the size of their investment in company securities, which exceeded £1 billion in 1980. In the UK the 'long-term' business covers life assurance and long-term sickness insurance and is distinct from the 'general' business which seeks to indemnify policy holders against incurred losses and involves motor, property and personal

Table 2.5 Insurance companies' net investments, long-term funds, 1976–1981 (£m)

	1976	1977	1978	1979	1980	1981*
British govt securities	1,511.7	1,833.4	2,425.3	2,541.4	2,222.0	784.5
Local authority securities	39.0	110.2	10.2	93.1	137.3	12.7
Total	1,550.7	1,943.6	2,435.6	2,634.5	2,359.3	797.2
Company securities:						
Ordinary	200.9	466.1	686.2	860.4	1,295.0	367.6
Preference	8.6	(2.7)	21.5	5.8	(5.6)	(41.4)
Debentures	(87.3)	(103.3)	(81.2)	(74.1)	(34.8)	22.9
Unit trusts	77.8	77.5	99.2	74.2	63.2	83.6
Total	200.1	437.6	725.8	866.3	1,317.7	432.6
Other investments	353.8	336.3	623.1	867.8	1,166.8	315.6
Cash and short-term assets	(20.6)	145.1	243.1	77.6	80.7	(82.2)
Total cash and investments	2084.0	2,862.6	4,027.6	4,450.6	4,945.8	1,449.4

* First quarter

Source: Business Monitor MQ5

accident insurance. The life business is sub-divided into individual and pensions with the long-term individual business sub-divided into industrial and ordinary sections. It is the ordinary business which most of us will experience directly, since this part of the insurance involves the payment of monthly insurance premiums with which we have become so familiar.

Indeed, the growth of the long-term section of the business was a relatively late development when compared with the general section. The latter had existed since the sixteenth century when marine insurance was provided in order to spread the risks involved in that trade. The Great Fire of London in 1666 spurred the growth of fire insurance and it was natural that insuring one's business against most eventualities would continue. Only in the eighteenth century, after Lloyd's had already set up an international centre for marine insurance in London, was long-term life insurance initiated. The shift from insuring one's business to insuring oneself had been made.

In the nineteenth century, insurance against various types of eventuality continued to spread and this century has seen the UK leading the way in insuring new forms of risk, often associated with the arrival of completely new industries such as telecommunications, atomic energy and drilling for offshore oil. As far as life assurance is concerned, the insurance companies have expanded the links with other forms of investment outlets for personal saving, through the introduction of unit-linked pensions and insurance policies, as well as extending insurance to cover certain personal financial risks such as mortgage protection policies.

As the size of the risks borne by industry increases so will the forms of insurance react in sympathy. On an international scale this development is called re-insurance and co-insurance. Although this is a complex manoeuvre on the part of the insurers, they are in fact agreeing to share between themselves the risks involved in insuring a particular client. This enables them to handle insurance business which would be beyond the capacity of any individual insurer. Indeed, it is no more than an extension of the principle by which Lloyd's has been operating since the eighteenth century. Lloyd's itself is a market consisting of under-writers and brokers who share risks through the principle of unlimited liability. Members have to undertake a means test to join the market and a complex system of rules exists in order to maintain self-regulation and ensure complete security for clients. The system is obviously efficient since Lloyd's is still regarded as unrivalled throughout the world for its financial security and integrity.

The most liquid financial instrument issued by the insurance companies, the life insurance policy, is usually offered on either a with-profits or without-profits basis. The former requires the policy-holder to pay a higher premium in order to obtain a share in the profits of the insurance company (or, more specifically, the office which is responsible for managing those funds). The difference in the premium paid for the two types of policy is known as the bonus loading and enables the insurance company to cushion the effects of fluctuations in the results obtained in the management of its asset portfolio, for like the dividends on ordinary shares, a bonus can only be paid if a profit is made. Thus, if in the extreme case the insurance company achieves zero profits, then its poor performance is cushioned by the higher income received via the bonus loadings in the with-profits policy. Conversely, if the insurance company achieves handsome profits it stands to pay out more in the form of bonuses to the with-profits policy holders. The arrangement effectively irons out the fluctuations in income to the company and stabilizes the business.

Because of the stability introduced into the long-term insurance business by such with-profits schemes it follows that those companies with a large proportion of without-profits policies in their liability portfolio must try to 'match' this with a correspondingly high proportion of fixed interest securities in their asset portfolio. On the other hand, a company which holds a large proportion of with-profits policies can, because of the stability introduced into its business, invest a greater amount of the fund in ordinary shares to try to achieve a higher return by bearing greater risks. These considerations illustrate the 'matching' problem experienced by both insurance companies and superannuation funds, i.e. the nature of the liabilities they issue determines the policy they adopt in the management of their asset portfolio. The more long-term the nature of the liabilities the more long-term, generally, will be the asset portfolio. Similarly, a liability for a constant payment is usually matched by investment in an asset which offers a constant, risk-free return, such as gilt-edged stock. The management of any fund are concerned with achieving its stated objective, which was defined above, no matter what type of institution is responsible for that fund. The matching of assets and liabilities and the spreading of investments both combine to reduce the risks of managing a fund.

The size and growth of the insurance companies as illustrated in Table 2.6. The long-term business held over £47 billion of assets in 1980. The size of their assets is not surprising when one considers that in 1976, four out of every five households in the UK had life insurance cover of some kind and the total number of life policies then, according to the Insurance Company Associations, exceeded 100 million[8].

Table 2.6 The size and growth of life insurance business

Year	Total assets £m (Long-term business)	% Growth p.a.
1969	22,361	–
1970	23,172	3.6
1971	24,125	4.1
1972	25,354	5.1
1973	26,665	5.2
1974	28,069	5.3
1975	29,789	6.1
1976	31,869	7.0
1977	34,586	8.5
1978	38,371	11.0
1979	42,733	11.4
1980	47,687	11.6

Source: Business Monitor

For their long-term business the stated aim in managing the asset portfolio is that 'investments must be chosen in order to ensure that at all times the fund can meet its liabilities to its policy-holders and also provide a safe but competitive savings medium,' (p. 96, Wilson Report). However, it should always be remembered that management of an asset portfolio is, of course, secondary in importance to the issuing of policies—after all, the provision of insurance is the industry's business.

The issuing of policies is tailored to the needs of the individual and here we return to the individual's propensity to save discussed in Chapter 1. The choice for the saver is whether to obtain a return in the form of a constant income over a period of time or whether to accept a lower initial income

8 See oral evidence given by insurance company associations on 14 November 1978, Vol. 2, the Wilson Report.

with the prospect of increasing income and the capital value of his saving in the future. The circumstances of the individual and the economic climate will be the factors which determine that choice. The role of insurance companies is twofold in this respect. First, they must issue policies in competition with other savings media in order to meet the needs of the saver and, secondly, they must then manage the fund to achieve their stated objective.

Like the pension funds, insurance companies also use gilt-edged stock as the measuring rod by which the return on other investment alternatives is assessed. Second in ranking to these are local authority bonds and bonds issued by public boards. Since the insurance companies hold much of the stored wealth of society they naturally assume a significant degree of social responsibility. However the primary legal obligation of insurance companies is to the policy-holders. Occasionally, of course, cases of mismanagement arise and the outcome is usually some form of legislation to protect further the interests of the policy-holder. This occurred after the failure of several companies in the early 1960s when the solvency margin was compulsorily doubled in 1967[9].

The long-term business of the insurance companies is controlled by the Department of Trade and to some extent by the Chief Registrar of Friendly Societies in his capacity as Industrial Assurance Commissioner. The Insurance Companies Act of 1974 sought to ensure that the companies were primarily responsible to their policy-holders whilst the Policy-holders Protection Act of 1975, in the wake of the 1974 crisis, provided that when an insurance company went into liquidation 90 per cent of its liabilities to policy-holders would be met out of a levy from other insurance companies. Legislation, such as the 1974 Act, has often merely formalized what has for years been prudent financial practice by the insurance companies. There are arguments for and against making the system of controls more rigid but the industry has rarely experienced a real crisis. Even after the 1974 economic crisis only one life insurance company actually went into liquidation.

The insurance companies and pension funds are increasingly important financial intermediaries and are vital in the re-directing of saving to investment purposes. In the paper 'Banking and Finance' (Sept 1976) the National Executive Committee of the Labour Party proposed nationaliza-

9 The 'solvency margin' is the excess of the value of assets over liabilities. There must, in law, be an excess in order to transact general insurance business. In the year 1974–5, the insurance companies' solvency margins were squeezed because of two factors. The high rate of inflation meant that their liabilities were increasing in value whilst the depressed stock market reduced the value of their assets. At worst, the companies may not be able to afford to service their liabilities and this would lead to a collapse of the system. To guard against this, the solvency margin is monitored regularly and a minimum ensured by legislation and supervised by the Department of Trade.

tion of the seven largest UK insurance companies on the grounds that funds could be more readily channelled into areas where shortages existed as a means of increasing investment in British industry. What the Committee failed to recognize was that the decision to invest is made ultimately by the investor not the financial intermediary. The institutions argued their case for independence before the Wilson Committee on the grounds that the depressed investment activity in Britain was a result of a crisis of confidence rather than a shortage or misallocation of funds.

3 Investment trusts, unit trusts and other specialist intermediaries

Investment and unit trusts are institutions to which persons have entrusted their savings in order that they may derive the benefits of a diversified wealth portfolio, economies in the purchasing and selling of financial assets and the professional advice of the trustees. The essential distinction between investment and unit trusts is that, although both are in the business of investment portfolio management, the former are 'closed end' institutions whilst unit trusts, like the other institutions discussed in this chapter, are 'open ended'. That is, unit trusts can accept funds from anyone and there is no limit to the amount they can accept. They re-invest the funds and issue 'units', i.e. their own financial instruments, to the saver. Investment trusts however, must issue capital when they are formed, like any other company, in order to raise funds which they then invest similarly to the unit trusts. The outcome is that investment trusts must rely on their professional expertise in timing their issue of new capital and in the strict legal sense they are not real 'trusts'. No such problem exists for the unit trusts which compete alongside banks and other non-banks for a slice of personal saving by offering immediately realisable financial instruments. Both institutions rely heavily upon their investment performance in enabling them to offer attractive terms to potential investors.

Investment trusts

Although some have existed for over a century, formal recognition of investment trusts did not come until the formation of the Association of Investment Trust Companies (AITC) in 1932. Members of the AITC make returns to the Bank of England which publishes this information in its quarterly bulletin. At the year-end 1980, the total assets of the Investment Trust Companies (ITC) stood at £7,270 million. They act as a means through which individuals obtain investments in both the UK and overseas at a cost less than they would incur if they acted independently.

ITCs are joint stock companies and as such they can issue both equity and prior charge capital (debenture and preference shares)[10]. The overriding advantage of investment trusts is that they offer the investor an equity share in a 'geared' fund which is spread both geographically and industrially[11]. The most predominant feature of ITCs is the geographical spread of their investment portfolio. The figures presented in Table 2.7 demonstrate this, with 39 per cent of funds invested abroad in 1980. Clearly the ITCs do invest abroad to a greater extent than any other non-bank savings institution with a large proportion (22 per cent in 1980) devoted to investment in North America alone, as Table 2.8 illustrates.

One must consider the geographical breakdown shown in Tables 2.7 and 2.8 tentatively, however, since they can vary widely during a given year depending upon several factors. First, the market prices of the investments will alter, so one would expect that when the Dow Jones Index is high in relation to the *Financial Times* Ordinary Share Index a given proportion of foreign share-holdings would accordingly rise in value, compared to the remainder of the portfolio. Secondly, variations in the sterling exchange rate will also infuence those values. This was particularly obvious in the mid-1970s when the depreciation of the exchange rate had by 1976 accounted for a 60 per cent appreciation in the value of foreign investments in sterling terms[12]. Of course, in the late 1970s, the pound began to appreciate in value causing the opposite to be the case. Of particular importance to the investment trusts was the removal of the constraint imposed upon those investing abroad by the Chancellor, Sir Geoffrey Howe, on 24 October 1979. The investment currency premium was effectively a tax on those who wished to purchase foreign currency in order to invest abroad. The abolition of this and other controls on foreign investment gave the ITCs even greater scope for geographically diversifying their investment portfolios. The result, as Table 2.7 demonstrates, was a rapid acceleration in overseas investment by ITCs.

The investor in an ITC seeks both income and capital appreciation. The objective of a trust has been stated by the Association of Investment Trust Companies (AITC) as follows, 'to provide shareholders over the medium

10 'Prior charge' capital is a financial instrument offered for sale which, in the event of future liquidation, has a prior claim upon the assets of the company. Similarly, interest on such financial instruments is paid prior to the declaration of a dividend on ordinary (equity) capital.

11 Gearing is the ratio of prior charge to equity capital in the trust capital structure. Essentially the advantage of gearing is that the trust can time its capital raising exercises to obtain funds cheaply, thereby enabling it to take advantage of a greater number of subsequent investment opportunities as they arise. Gearing exaggerates the impact on asset value per share of any given rise in the total value of assets.

12 This is because if one held an investment expressed in terms of a foreign currency, one could now purchase more pounds for a given amount of that currency. When converted this naturally inflates the value of foreign investments.

to longer term with a secure and increasing return both in income and capital terms on their investment[13].

Table 2.7 Geographical distribution of investment by ITCs

Date	Overseas (%)	UK (%)
1961	32	68
1966	36	64
1971	29	71
1972	36	64
1973	41	59
1974	50	50
1975	42	58
1976	48	52
1977	34	66
1978	35	65
1979	32	68
1980	39	61

Source: CSO Financial Statistics

In order to finance any contingency payments the ITCs will occasionally borrow directly from the banking system but this is only a short-term measure. The investor in an ITC relies upon the management's expertise in reading economic and often socio-political developments. Any new investment will only be undertaken with reference to the performance of existing holdings and expected future performance, and this implies a professional interpretation of economic events. It is unusual for the ITC to invest in small unquoted companies or provide capital for new ventures but it may do so if sufficient evidence is provided to support a sound track record. However, this is unlikely to become a prominent feature of investment trust business in the future since it is traditionally a financing function undertaken by the banking system. Nevertheless, the oil discoveries in the North Sea provided a spur to the growth of ITC investment in domestic industry. Several international oil companies needed partners situated in the UK in order to obtain drilling concessions and this need was met by some ITCs.

Operationally an investment trust cannot hold more than 15 per cent of the value of its investments in unlisted company securities and its own ordinary capital must be listed on the Stock Exchange as with any other public company. Investment in any one company is restricted to 10 per cent. The Trusts are also restricted to a retention ratio of 15 per cent of their income in any accounting period. From 6 April 1965 until 31 March

13 Written evidence by the Association of Investment Trust Companies, para. 4, in 'Evidence on the financing of industry and trade', the Wilson Committee, HMSO 1978.

1972 any capital gain earned by the trust was taxed at a rate of 30 per cent. From 1 April 1972 however, the treatment altered so that 'chargeable gains' were reduced to a portion of the total gain as certain expenses were allowed to be written off before tax liability was assessed. The argument for taxation of this smaller chargeable gain has now been removed completely. Nevertheless the income earned, as distinct from capital gained, is still taxed at the standard rate of corporation tax. From 1 April 1977 the effective rate on chargeable gains was 10 per cent and the ITC shareholders were allowed an equivalent tax credit. The reduced effective rate of tax on income can, of course, be transmitted to the investor in the form of a greater return.

The investor in an investment trust does not buy the underlying assets of the trusts as in the case of the unit trust, but holds shares in the company. Since these shares are quoted (listed) on the Stock Exchange then their market values will alter. The difference between the value of a share in a trust and its underlying value in terms of the assets acquired in the trust is known as the discount.

The growth of ITCs was stifled to a significant extent in the early and late 1970s as rapid inflation and high interest rates devalued the importance of equities. Nevertheless in 1980, 90 per cent of their total funds were invested in equities as reference to Table 2.8 will confirm. The enormous public sector borrowing requirement (which creates the need for high rates of interest in order to sell gilt-edged stock) had contributed to the situation where investment in equities yielded an insufficient return and the cost of raising new capital in the form of fixed interest debt was relatively expensive[14]. When combined with dividend restraint and the controls on foreign investment it is not surprising that ITCs failed to expand significantly throughout the 1970s and turned their attention to tax efficient investments in order to lure investors. The removal of dividend restraint and foreign currency controls coupled with the appreciation of sterling renders investment in equities at home and abroad a more viable business and we can expect the ITCs to react by increasing further the amount of equity investment they undertake in the future.

Irrespective of these factors, the ultimate criterion which ITCs take into consideration when undertaking investment is profitability as well as the track record of the management of the particular business concerned. Such

14 The Public Sector Borrowing Requirement (PSBR) is regarded as a major contributor to the growth in the money supply. However, it is the *method* of financing government expenditure which determines the impact of the PSBR upon the supply of money. The selling of gilts to the non-bank private sector may actually cause the money supply to fall in the short-term, but in order to convince persons to purchase gilts, the authorities need to offer high rates of interest. This is why a policy of high interest rates is practically consistent with controlling the growth in the money supply. This problem is discussed further in Part 2.

Table 2.8 Investment trust portfolio composition, 1980

(a) Geographical spread £m

Total	UK	%	USA	%	Canada	%	Japan	%	Australia	%	Other	%
7,270	4,465	61.4	1,601	22.0	207	2.9	370	5.1	176	2.4	451	6.2

(b) Industrial spread £m

	Total	Govt and public securities	%	Listed company securities						Unlisted comp. securities						Unit trust	%	Property	%	Other FA's	%	Other real assets	%
				Ordinary	%	Pref.	%	Loan cap.	%	Ordinary	%	Pref.	%	Loan cap.	%								
UK	4,465	234	5.2	3,758	84.2	39	0.9	30	0.7	250	5.6	23	0.5	18	0.4	10	0.2	17	0.4	78	1.7	6	0.1
Overseas	2,805	19	0.7	2,696	96.1	12	0.4	74	2.6	—		—		—		—		—		4	0.1		

Sources: Bank of England and Financial Statistics

factors as dividend policy, growth and cost consciousness will be considered by the trust managers. Without profits, a business will be unable to maintain its investment programme and will begin in effect to consume its own capital. The outcome will be further difficulty in raising finance as investors, including ITCs, analyze its record and require exceptionally high returns to invest in the failing company.

In spite of the difficulties faced by the ITCs in achieving growth comparable to say, building societies or insurance companies and the problems associated with investing in equities, particularly abroad, they are nevertheless still a crucial force in the directing of saving to investment opportunities. Indeed, this importance has been recognized by certain developing countries who have actively encouraged the spread of investment trust companies as an efficient means of providing venture capital.

Unit trusts

Unit trusts are similar to ITCs in that they raise capital in the savings market in order to invest in a portfolio of investments. There are, however, certain essential distinctions between the two institutions. First, their investment portfolios differ in that unit trusts tend to invest almost entirely in equities. This has the dual effect of rendering them essential as a vehicle for directing the funds of small savers to the home stock market whilst leaving themselves open to wide fluctuations in the value of their portfolios as conditions in the stock market vary. Secondly, as noted before, unit trusts are 'open-ended' which means that a person may invest in the trust or liquidate his holdings at will. Thirdly, unit trusts cannot issue preference or prior charge capital except for foreign currency loans[15]. The advantages of gearing in the fund are also therefore unavailable.

Unit trusts issue units to their subscribers the value of which vary according to the valuation of the asset portfolio to which the unit is linked. As a result, the equity claims they issue are very similar, in terms of liquidity, to the equity investments which constitute such a large proportion of their asset portfolio. Most unit trusts are members of the Unit Trust Association (UTA) which was originally formed in 1959 as the Association of Unit Trust Managers and the total membership of the unit trust movement was estimated by the UTA in 1978 to be 2 million. As with several other non-bank intermediaries, the attraction of investing in a unit trust derives from the pooling of risk, although the diversified portfolio in this case is frequently confined to UK stocks and shares. Through investment in the trust, a person acquires a fractional interest in a managed

15 Although these loans may not be arranged without reciprocal arrangements for their repayment.

fund and a portion of the dividends and interest which accumulates from that fund, the investments being valued daily at current market prices.

The formation of a unit trust is initiated through the drawing up of a trust deed. The two parties to the trust deed are the managers of the trust, who are charged with administration and responsibility for taking investment decisions, and a trustee, usually in the form of a clearing bank or insurance company, who holds the underlying investment. The unit trust company itself however, is constituted like any other limited company. Units of a unit trust can only be offered to the public if the trust conforms to the Prevention of Fraud (Investments) Act 1958 (Section 17) and control over the operations of the unit trusts is exercised by the Department of Trade. Although the Secretary of State for Trade and Industry does not usually intervene in the management of a trust, any transgression of the law on contemporary prudent financial practice can be met by refusing to authorize the trust in the future. As we shall see in Chapter 3, much the same type of control has recently been imposed upon the banking system by requiring the banks to become recognized banks or licensed deposit taking institutions.

Table 2.9 demonstrates the number of units held over the period 1965–1980 and the value of the total funds invested by the unit trusts. Although this information is regarded as reliable it should be borne in mind that the number of funds making returns in any year may vary. For

Table 2.9 Unit trusts. Units and funds 1965–1980

Date	No. of unit holdings (m)	*Total funds (£m)
1965	1.42	522
1966	1.64	582
1967	1.71	854
1968	2.15	1,482
1969	2.39	1,412
1970	2.40	1,397
1971	2.31	1,991
1972	2.29	2,647
1973	2.24	2,060
1974	2.20	1,310
1975	2.19	2,512
1976	2.12	2,543
1977	1.99	3,461
1978	1.95	3,873
1979	1.82	3,937
1980	1.72	4,968

*Market value plus cost of purchasing new securities plus management charges and accumulated undistributed dividends.
Sources: Bank of England and Financial Statistics

example, in 1978 and 1979 the number of trust making returns was 375 and 351 respectively. Nevertheless, the figures presented in Table 2.10 indicate that the total funds invested in 1980 exceeded £4 billion. The figures also indicate that, when the overseas and domestic investments are combined,

Table 2.10 Unit trusts; portfolio composition 1980*
(a) *Geographical spread* (£m)

Total	%	UK	%	USA and Canada	%	EEC	%	Australia and Far East	%	Other	%
4090	100	3115	76.2	480	11.7	54	1.3	377	9.2	64	1.6

(b) *Industrial spread* (£m)

	Total	%	Brit. Govt. Sec.	%	Ordinary capital	%	Pref. capital	%	Loan capital	%	Other	%
UK	3115	100	57	1.8	2977	95.6	41	1.3	15	0.5	25	0.8
Overseas	975	100	—	—	954	97.9	4	0.4	8	0.8	9	0.9

* The discrepancy between the totals in 2.10 compared with 2.9 arises from the apportionment of management charges. The portfolio composition is unaffected.
Source: Financial Statistics

97 per cent of total assets are held in the form of equities. As with the investment trusts, the most significant overseas investment is across the Atlantic.

The managers of the fund seek always to impress upon the investors the risk associated with the investment and the objective of the fund. Thus one often sees advertised the prospect of high yields, income certainty, capital certainty or growth and indeed the objective of the fund is often prominent in the title of the trust as reference to the *Financial Times* by the reader would confirm. The objective gives a clue to the type of investment appropriate to the fund. For example, property units are units which are linked to trusts where the investment depends upon the fortunes of the property market. In 1980 property units had a total market value of £1,107 million as a result of the increasing popularity of property as an inflationary hedge throughout the 1970s.

A fund which professes to be able to provide a low but regular income source to the investor will be heavily involved with investment in 'blue chip' companies[16]. The provisions incorporated in the trust deeds restrict

16 'Blue chip' companies are those whose share prices are included among the thirty used to derive the commonly quoted *Financial Times* Ordinary Share Index. They are generally regarded as the safest equity investments.

the investment in one company to 10 per cent of any one class of capital (for example, equity). Furthermore, the value of this holding cannot exceed 5 per cent (sometimes $7\frac{1}{2}$ per cent) of the fund. The trust deeds also restrict the investment in real property (unlike investment trusts) and severely restrict investment in unlisted companies (again unlike the investment trust).

Unit trusts, unlike the larger institutional investors, tend to devote a significant proportion of their investment to small and medium-sized companies where growth prospects may be encouraging but the risks are correspondingly greater. They seek to achieve their objectives of increasing the unit holders' investment and providing a steady flow of income by maintaining frequent contact with the companies in which they have invested. On the whole, they take a long-term view of a company's earning prospects and assess all the relevant factors which influence those prospects in the economic environment. It is precisely because of their ability to gauge a company's prospects that they play, along with the pension funds, such a significant part in underwriting new issues of shares and maintaining the secondary market in securities.

In the period 1973 to 1974, the unit trusts experienced a radical shock due partly to legislative measures but, more importantly, because of the rapid deterioration in the equity market at that time. However, in the 1980s they have undergone a resurgence in the wake of a reduction in the investment income surcharge paid by some unit holders, the exemption from tax of capital gains made within a trust, and the comparatively generous capital gains exemption of £5,000 for individuals. Furthermore, as a result of the increasing magnitude of public sector debt plus the capital gains advantages offered to the trusts, gilt-funds have proliferated with fifteen being set up in 1980 alone. The abolition of exchange controls encouraged the unit trusts to diversify geographically and influenced the spread of funds specializing in particular geographical areas. In 1981, the leading group in terms of performance were those trusts which invested in Far East investments. Since the performance of the trusts will in general be correlated to be general performance of the world's stock exchanges it is not surprising that, given the exceptional performance of the Tokyo and Singapore markets, the trusts which concentrated in those areas should show a greater capital appreciation than the rest.

A final consideration concerning both unit and investment trusts is the limited extent to which they have in the past invested in fixed interest securities. The reason for this is that the income earned from fixed interest securities had always been treated like any other income to a company and was liable to corporation tax.

However, if an individual invested personally in a fixed interest security he was liable only to pay the basic rate of income tax. The fiscal disadvantage of investing in bonds effectively stifled the development of 'bond funds' which are common in the USA and EEC. On the whole, the major tax advantage of investing in trusts is the treatment of capital gains. Trusts are entitled to set off management expenses against income in order to determine their tax liability and recently the capital gains made within trusts have been exempted from tax. These advantages are not open to the individual and can be translated into a more favourable income return by the investment and unit trusts. Furthermore, the economies in administration achieved by both types of trust in making investments can also reduce the total cost of investing in equities for the small investor.

Specialist intermediaries

In Chapter 1 it was described how the process of intermediation requires the constant revision of the methods of holding wealth and that the non-bank savings institutions are visible evidence of this process. It was also pointed out that, unlike the banks, the NBFIs began by providing advice on how to finance particular transactions. Later, certain institutions have developed which cater solely for capital maintenance and the provision of income such as the unit and investment trusts. Alongside these major institutions which give our financial system its present structure are many specialist institutions. Because of their very nature, in that they often arise to cater for a specific need, which may be removed by legislative or socio-political change, they are rarely permanent and on the whole in the UK have tended to develop in response to the ever more complicated tax environment. Although one should not generalize by concluding that the more complicated a tax environment becomes, the greater the development of private specialist institutions designed to exploit it, in the high income UK economy this certainly seems to be the case.

However, the tax factor is merely another aspect of the needs which the specialists cater for. On the whole, specialist intermediaries exist in the public and private sectors catering for the needs of industrial, commercial and personal borrowers and investors which are not adequately provided for by the other institutions we have discussed. For example, an institution may be set up to provide equity finance for companies which may otherwise find difficulty in raising finance via the issue of equity (ordinary shares) on the Stock Exchange. Such an institution is Equity Capital for Industry (ECI) which was set up in 1976 to fill a gap in the provision of equity finance for small and medium sized firms. In March 1979, it had investments in eight companies, which accounted for 24 per cent of its capital of £41 million. ECI was set up by the participation of a number of large financial institutions and is thereby a private sector intermediary. There are, however, several specialist public sector institutions.

Public sector

A public sector specialist institution is Finance for Industry (FFI) which is the holding company for the Industrial and Commercial Finance Corporation (ICFC) and Finance Corporation for Industry (FCI). The holding company was set up in 1973 but the two institutions which operate under the auspices of the FFI have existed since 1945. ICFC concentrates upon equity and loan financing for small and medium sized firms whilst FCI caters for the loan requirements of larger firms. Although the share capital of FFI is held by the Bank of England and the London and Scottish clearing banks, it still has sufficient independence to exercise complete discretion in the granting of finance and applies the normal commercial criteria. Being backed by huge resources allows the FFI to take risks which would be too great to bear for a single financial institution. From its formation up to 1979, FFI had committed over £650 million to industry.

In 1975, the National Enterprise Board (NEB) was set up to provide equity and loan finance to ailing firms, predominantly in manufacturing. The NEB provides advice concerning the restructuring of firms and in turn has acted as a holding company for public shareholding in private firms. The Board seeks to encourage greater efficiency and in so doing, hopes eventually to apply the conventional commercial criteria to its investments with a view to returning an investment to the private sector[17].

Beside these major institutions there are other public agencies which also seek to provide specialist financial assistance. The most notable of these are the Export Credits Guarantee Department (ECGD), the National Research Development Corporation (NRDC) and the Scottish and Welsh Development Agencies (SDA and WDA). The ECGD has since 1919 encouraged exports by insuring the credit to finance them. Effectively, it acts as a cushion against the risk of financial loss when trading in overseas markets. The NRDC is another public corporation which provides finance for the development and exploration of inventions. Of course, this is a particularly risky area for investment and is often subject to a long time-lag before an invention becomes an innovation and yields a return. Most of the NRDC's assistance is provided to small companies who of course lack the resources required to pursue an invention through to its application. Finally, the development agencies provide similar facilities to the NEB but on a local scale for the countries of Scotland and Wales. They act as vehicles through which public funds can be channelled into local industry and guarantee that local priorities are met by ensuring that investment decisions of major importance are made with reference to those most affected.

17 See M. Parr, 'The National Enterprise Board', *National Westminster Bank Review*, Feb. 1979, for further information.

Private sector

As well as the ECI already mentioned, there are other specialist private sector institutions which cater for specific financial needs. Many of them are subsidiaries of the larger financial concerns but there is an increasingly flourishing area of small individually or co-operatively motivated intermediaries. Examples of the former are leasing and factoring companies. Leasing is an activity whereby a company (the lessor) acquires ownership of an asset and rents it to another party (the lessee). Although the lessee makes a series of payments the ownership still resides with the lessor and this is what distinguishes leasing from hire purchase. The spread of leasing has been encouraged by the tax concessions which operate upon the purchasing of assets, although these concessions were previously most common in markets for industrial property and commercial premises. A leasing company can obtain the concessions by purchasing the asset outright and renting out the asset to another party who could not themselves have afforded to purchase that asset outright. Therefore, the institutions who have the facility to make such initial capital commitments can earn a rental yield whilst effectively financing investment in British industry. A measure of the importance of this activity is illustrated by the fact that members of the Equipment Leasing Association purchased £2.4 billion of assets in 1980 for subsequent leasing, constituting 12.5 per cent of the total capital investment in plant and machinery in the UK. The activity of leasing companies is, of course, entirely dependent upon the continuance of capital investment allowances.

Factoring is concerned with the selling of book debts to an institution which is usually the subsidiary of a larger financial institution. The factoring agency then becomes responsible for the collection of those debts by running the clients' sales accounting system from the invoice stage onwards. The major factoring companies in the UK are members of the Association of British Factors and in 1980, the Association was responsible for the factoring of £2 billion of sales. Members of the Association are all backed by clearing banks and other major financial institutions and offer an ever widening range of financial services to their clients.

The remaining private sector financial intermediaries again cater for specific needs. For convenience we can distinguish between two types and observe two particular illustrations. The first identifiable type is the personal financial planning service. The financial planning concept probably owes its origins to the introduction of Capital Gains Tax (CGT) in April 1965. The importance of that legislation was not the tax itself but the specific measures which could legitimately be taken to avoid it. Shortly after that date insurance companies began to issue bonds as an alternative to directly investing in stocks and shares, the profits on realization (if any) were, of course, subject to the new tax. Effectively the insurance companies were investing in stocks and shares and could pass on part of the profits to the investor as a yield on a bond. Profits realized by the holders of such bonds were not subject to the Capital Gains Tax, or any other tax, (and indeed are still not subject to any tax on realizations now, provided the bonds were acquired prior to 20 March 1968).

From 1968 onwards, various Finance Acts removed some of the initial tax advantages. In particular, the 1974 Finance Act had a severely restrictive effect upon certain types of bonds. Nevertheless, the tax efficient approach to investment was by then well established and the period had spawned hybrid financial planning institutions such as Plan Invest Group (PIG). When, in 1974, Capital Transfer Tax (CTT) replaced estate duty, the service of personal financial planning not only required a sound knowledge of taxation and the various exemptions and reliefs as well as an understanding of the mechanics of finance but also a comprehension of life assurance. This implied a widening of the brief of personal financial planners to incorporate the skills not only of tax specialists and finance experts but also of accountants, solicitors, life assurance and pension exponents. The outcome is a combination of professional expertise rarely to be found housed under the same roof and dealing with such a range of issues that the private individual (usually a high rate taxpayer) would be unable to cope with them all. It remains to be seen, however, just how far such a development proceeds as complete harmony between such diverse professions may often lead to conflict of interest and a wariness concerning the usurping of their individual importance. The development of organizations such as PIG, which handled £10 million of funds in 1980, therefore relies heavily upon the complexity of a nation's taxation and legal systems. Such financial organizations have been further encouraged by the abolition of exchange controls in October 1979, which widened further the possible range of financial assets to be held in a person's wealth portfolio.

4 Summary and conclusions

This chapter has been concerned with the primary investment vehicles in the UK. It was described at the outset how individuals would theoretically respond to a general increase in their wealth and how this creates an appropriate climate within which non-banking institutions may flourish. Within this framework the precise configuration of a financial system will be moulded by the history and tradition of the particular economy under investigation. In particular, the existence of a sophisticated banking system in the UK has served to dictate the type of non-banking organizations which have developed.

The contrived fiscal climate of the past twenty years has encouraged the spread of non-banking institutions and this chapter has assessed the size and significance of the leading non-deposit takers in the UK. The institutions which have benefited the most from increasing contractual saving are the life insurance and superannuation funds. Both share the same objectives in managing their funds and the similar content of their investment portfolios bears witness to this fact. The investment and unit trusts fulfil similar roles in that they draw upon personal saving to provide for the investment demands of industry. These institutions also share the similar objectives of providing security of income, high yields, or capital growth to investors.

Finally, the functions of certain specialist intermediaries have been assessed. The common feature shared between the institutions discussed in this chapter is that they do not rely upon the placing of deposits for their source of funds. Deposit-taking is a feature shared by the institutions which constitute the subject of the following chapter and in itself poses a new set of problems for the financial intermediary.

Topics

1 Define the following: factoring, leasing and portfolio diversification.
2 To what extent has the removal of exchange controls influenced the investment policies of certain investment institutions?
3 Assess the factors which have encouraged the growth of non-banking institutions at the expense of the banks during the past decade.
4 Discuss the relative merits of equity and gilt-edged investment.
5 Why were index-linked gilt-edged stocks issued primarily for pension funds? With which financial assets are they most likely to compete since their general availability in March 1982?

3 Deposit taking institutions

In November 1981, the Trustee Savings Banks were officially included in the banking sector for purposes of statistical definition. This was the culmination of a decade of debate about the role and functions of saving institutions, particularly the TSB and the National Savings Bank, which remains outside the banking system. Until the redefinition of the banking sector both institutions were regarded similarly as 'other' financial institutions and were not free to determine their own lending policies. Because of this traditional link, the TSB is included in this chapter for consideration. Furthermore, like the other institutions discussed in this chapter, it taps the personal sector market for funds although, as we shall see, recent developments have brought the essential distinctions between banks and non-banking institutions into sharper focus.

1 The National Savings Bank

The Post Office Saving Bank was initiated by a Gladstonian Act of Parliament in 1861, although the original idea can be traced to Samuel Whitbread in 1807[1]. However, the notion of a National Savings Bank working through the machinery of the Post Office was not effected, according to Horne (1947), until the 1860s—some fifty years later than the Trustee Savings Banks had successfully entered the field. The Post Office Savings Bank became the National Savings Bank in 1969, when the Post Office became a public corporation. It began exclusively to channel deposits from the person to the public sector and, apart from working balances, the funds are passed on to the National Debt commissioners who invest the funds in British government securities, local authority (long-term and temporary) debt and any other special public investments, e.g. the Agricultural Mortgage Coporation securities, etc.

The National Savings Bank is directly monopolized by the Government and is essentially a government-sponsored vehicle for mopping up personal savings to finance public borrowing. Many of its accounts are small and

1 Whitbread, (son of the brewer), in fact pursued the idea during his parliamentary career with the Whigs; unfortunately, his business suffered as a result of the time devoted to his career and he became bankrupt and committed suicide in 1815.

relatively inactive and cater for those who do not necessarily save in order to invest but who save in order to provide a safe place to hold transactions balances, exemplifying the Keynesian motive of 'precautionary' saving.

Nevertheless, because of the changing saving preferences of the personal sector, the NSB expanded into the 'special investment' business by separating its internal structure into ordinary and special investment departments. Thus in 1966, the NSB began to offer investment accounts offering a higher yield to investors. Table 3.1 illustrates how the NSB has

Table 3.1 Deposits of NSB 1957–1980 (£m)

	1957	1962	1967	1972	1977	1978	1979	1980
Ordinary Accounts	1,677	1,760	1,673	1,490	1,633	1,798	1,835	1,741
Investment Accounts	—	—	116	494	1,419	1,204	1,531	1,868
Total	1,677	1,760	1,789	1,984	3,052	3,002	3,362	3,609

Source: Financial Statistics

benefited from this innovation. Clearly, without the investment accounts, the total deposits held with the NSB in 1980 would have been less than those held in 1962. At the present time, the ordinary accounts permit an individual to deposit up to £10,000. Up to £100 a day may be withdrawn on demand from any of the NSB branches at 21,000 post offices but the rate of interest offered is comparatively small. However, interest received is tax free up to a limit of £70 per annum. The investment accounts, on the other hand, have a deposit limit of £200,000 and withdrawals are made at one month's notice. The rate of interest offered is normally significantly greater than on the ordinary accounts but is taxable, though it is paid without deduction of tax at source, unlike the building societies.

The ordinary funds of the NSB, unlike the TSB, are still regarded as directly financing the central government's borrowing requirement and are treated in the national financial accounts accordingly. The investment account is included in the sector described as 'other financial institutions' in the national statistics and Table 3.1 illustrates clearly how this has been the engine of NSB growth since 1967.

The Department of National Savings has been the focus of attention for increasingly ingenious devices contrived by different governments to finance their borrowing. Besides the well-known Premium Bonds, the Department is responsible for the sale of National Savings Certificates, which are sold by the Saving Certificate and Pay As You Earn office through post offices and banks. Recently the National Savings Certificates have become very competitive and are issued and withdrawn at the dictate of the Department according to prevailing interest rates in the economy.

Indeed the index-linked savings certificates, formerly 'granny bonds', sought to take advantage of inflation by offering to maintain the real value of savings over a given period of time.

The overriding advantage of Certificates is that they offer a tax-free yield to the saver which, when grossed up at an appropriate rate, invariably compares favourably with alternative investments. For example the nineteenth issue, made in February 1980, offered a tax free yeild of 10.33 per cent over a five-year period with a then maximum holding of £1,500. Over £250 million were purchased in the first month, dealing a severe blow to institutions such as the building societies. This competitive pressure was maintained in 1981 and 1982 and the Conservative Government became so confident in the attractiveness of this form of saving that the Chancellor announced a target level of £3 billion to be obtained through national savings in 1982/3, as part of the new strategy of 'diversified funding'. It is obvious that such savings media depend entirely upon the fiscal advantages conferred upon them by governments. Those institutions having to rely upon their own investment and administrative efficiency in determining the yields they offer to investors are certainly at a severe and false disadvantage. One institution beginning to experience the wind of competition is the TSB.

2 The Trustee Savings Bank

The philosophy of allowing savings banks greater independence and freedom to develop and apply their professional expertise in order to enable them to compete more effectively with other deposit taking financial intermediaries is embodied in the TSB. Although the origins and development of the savings banks are similar, the 1970s witnessed a metamorphosis of the TSB from a publicly controlled institution mobilizing personal sector funds for public use, to a semi-independent banking institution. In 1973, the Page Report had recommended that the TSB should no longer be a part of the National Savings 'movement'. Further, the Committee recommended that the savings stamp no longer had a significant part to play in National Savings and recommended its suspension[2].

The Page Report was the thin end of the wedge so far as the TSB's disassociation from the Treasury was concerned. It laid the foundation for the dismantling (in 1979) of the tax advantages of saving through the TSB, allowing it greater discretion over the disposition of funds, and enabled a complete restructuring which reduced the number of regional banks within

2 Report of the Committee to Review National Savings, chaired by Sir Harry Page, Cmnd 5273, 1973.

the group from seventy-three in 1973 to sixteen in 1981. These and other changes were initiated in the Trustee Savings Bank Act of 1976.

The earlier Trustee Savings Bank Act of 1969 defined a savings bank as 'a society formed in the United Kingdom, Isle of Man or any of the Channel Islands for the purpose of establishing and maintaining an institution in the nature of a Bank' (1.3), and required the TSB to 'encourage thrift within the financial capacity of the bank' (para. 100), *after* the consent of the National Debt Commissioners. The emphasis on thrift was, the Page Committee considered, outdated. Indeed, in their evidence to the Committee (para. 100), the Trustee Savings Bank Association said 'while not relinquishing in the least their principle objectives of encouraging thrift . . . the savings banks are now institutions which cater for many of the ever increasing personal financial requirements of their depositors'. The Committee noted that, in fact, the TSBs had interpreted their objectives more broadly than the statutory definition implied. This served to illustrate the inappropriateness of the (then) current legislation. The situation arose whereby the law relating to the activities of the TSB was frequently changed in order to legalize every new facility offered by the institution. Given these considerations and in particular the fact that, in the Committee's opinion, the TSBs no longer had a role to play in the National Savings movement, a radical change in the status of the TSB was recommended.

Such a change in status has taken time to reach fruition. Five years later, a 1978 report on bank charges[3] recommended yet another review of the constitutional arrangements for the TSB by the Treasury in spite of the intervening Act in 1976 which had attempted to release the TSBs from Treasury control, established the Trustee Savings Banks Central Board and introduced a federal structure. The TSB still relies largely on private individuals for funds and is rapidly approaching full independence from the state (at least as full as the other listed banks), but for the time being the TSBs are still required to hold deposits with the National Debt Commissioners which amounted to £1.1 billion in 1980. The tax concessions and government guarantees afforded to the TSB were the price the Government paid for control of TSB funds. The suspension of these advantages has brought about a gradual dismantling of government control, which has taken the form of the Treasury effectively giving back the funds to the TSB to be invested according to its own priorities. The funds are being returned in seven tranches up to 1985 and are subject to the Government being convinced that the TSB has sufficient reserves[4], a viable lending program-

3 'Banks: charges for money transmission services', the Prices Commission, House of Commons, Paper HCP 337, April 1978.

4 At present the TSB is required to achieve an excess of 7 per cent of assets over liabilities. At the end of 1980 the TSB conformed to this reserve ratio as a group.

me and the professional expertise to operate in a prudent financial manner. In fact, lending facilities had been in existence since the TSB Act of 1976 and bridging loans and credit cards (Trustcard) came into operation a year later.

Previously, the ordinary accounts of the TSB offered a yield, a proportion of which, (£70), was tax-free and this obviously afforded these savings institutions a competitive advantage vis-a-vis the commercial banks. In the light of the rapid growth of the TSB and its expansion into new areas of activity the commercial banks began, after the Page Report, to question the validity of retaining this competitive imperfection in favour of the TSB. In November 1979 the right to tax-free interest of TSB ordinary accounts was removed as part of the price paid for full independence from the state. At the same time the Ordinary Department was closed and four types of account are now offered by the TSB. These are: savings accounts, investment accounts, term deposits and cheque accounts. Savings accounts offer a certain but low rate of interest with no limit and withdrawal on demand. Investment accounts offer a higher rate of interest but require between seven and twenty days' notice of withdrawal. Term deposits effectively lock money away for longer terms than a year and therefore pay the highest rate of interest with a minimum deposit of £1,000. Finally, cheque accounts offer a full range of money transmission services in much the same way as the clearing banks. Overdrafts are also now available.

Before these changes the Ordinary Department of the TSB was considered part of the central Government's financing, with the remainder

Table 3.2 Deposits of TSBs 1957–1980 (£m)

	1957	1962	1967	1972	1977	1978	1979	1980
Sight deposits								
Savings A/Cs	807	917	1,051	1,245	1,665	1,710	1,525	1,372
Current A/Cs	—	—	5	32	260	382	507	635
Time deposits	319	613	1,216	1,878	2,610	2,908	3,290	3,778
Total	1,126	1,530	2,272	3,155	4,535	5,000	5,322	5,785

Source: Financial Statistics

subsumed under the other financial institutions sector in the published financial accounts in precisely the same way as the NSB. Of necessity this has now changed, as the TSB has become a recognized bank and is accordingly defined as a bank, constituting part of the total monetary sector. Table 3.2 demonstrates clearly the increasing significance of the TSB since the 1950s and the relative importance of the different accounts can be assessed from Table 3.3. Time (term) deposits were clearly the

Table 3.3 TSB Balance Sheet 1981 (first quarter) £m

Liabilities		*Assets*	
Sight deposits		Cash and balances at CTSB	1,123
Current A/Cs	635	and UK banks	
Savings A/Cs	1,372	Other current assets	16
Time deposits	3,778	Balances with National Debt Office	1,116
Accrued interest and		British govt securities	1,947
deposits	147		
Credit items (transmission)	14	Local authority debt	1,292
Reserves etc.	509	Agricultural Mortgage Corp.	
		securities	91
		Other long-term securities	37
		Advances (house purchase etc.)	427
		Other assets	436
	£6,455		£6,455

Figures rounded
Source: Financial Statistics

major source of finance in 1981, constituting 59 per cent of liabilities in that year.

It is undeniable that the TSB has undergone a radical transformation from a conventional savings bank to a fully fledged commercial bank. In 1981 the TSB possessed a consumer loan book exceeding £300 million, a Trustcard system and a computerized clearing facility. In February 1981 the TSB acquired United Dominions Trust (UDT) for £110 million and therefore obtained £600 million worth of hire purchase business (for UDT is a finance house). The continuing expansion of the TSB throughout the 1980s will have the effect of replacing the public sector debt held in its asset portfolio with loans to the private sector. With 1,648 branches in 1981 the TSB is poised to become a major competitor to the commercial banks.

3 Building societies

The building societies have been the focus of much attention and debate throughout the past decade. They have experienced the most rapid growth of all the financial institutions discussed in this book, while at the same time their deposits have demonstrated an increasingly liquid character—to such an extent that they are now generally regarded as 'money substitutes'. More will be said about the latter topic in Chapter 5. For the moment, we need to concentrate on their present size and recent growth and consider the implications this has had for the financial system in general.

The societies, which advanced £10 billion in 1980, are by far the largest providers of mortgage finance in the UK and depend almost completely on the personal sector for their supply of funds. A good account of their historical development can be found in Cleary's (1965) work concerning the building society movement. However, a more precise economic definition of their functions and role in the mortgage market can be found in more recent research by O'Herlihy and Spencer (1972) and Ghosh (1974). The researchers have sought to determine specific relationships in the liability and asset portfolios of these institutions. Indeed, such efforts provide a useful insight into how the societies react to changes in both deposit inflows and the prevailing interest rates in the economy but are limited in the extent to which they set these institutions in the context of the overall financial system.

Sayers (1967) has defined the societies as

'. . . non-profit making associations, whose primary objects are to encourage both thrift and home-ownership by marrying the accumulation of small savings with the needs of house-purchasers for loans that can be steadily repaid out of income'. (p. 157)

This definition is still appropriate today, although at the time of writing anticipated legislation could change this dramatically.

The societies are often referred to as the 'movement'. This is an inherited term reflecting the social reasons behind their beginnings in the last quarter of the eighteenth century. The 'movement' sprang from the requirements of a new industrialized working population, spawned by the industrial revolution. Twenty-three societies existed in 1800 but the first society is believed to have been set up in Birmingham in 1775. By the end of the nineteenth century there were over 1,500 societies and they continued to proliferate up until the First World War. From 1945 to 1972 the total assets of the societies increased fifteen-fold.

Before looking more closely at their operations, we need to examine their recent growth. This growth has brought about the situation whereby the societies now account for a greater proportion of total liquid assets of the personal sector than the banks, as we saw in Chapter 1. A corollary of this growth has been a decline in the number of societies as merger activity has increased. The position is now such that the larger societies count their assets in terms of billions of pounds. In 1980 total building society assets exceeded £53 billion, of which £42 billion were in the form of mortgages. Table 3.4, illustrates the significance of the building societies and the massive proportion of their assets which is held in the form of mortgages. It is an increasing share of the personal sector deposit market, as we noted in Chapter 1, which has enabled them to achieve this accumulation of assets and maintain their position as by far the largest providers of housing

Table 3.4 Building societies assets (£m)

Year	*Total Assets	Mortgages	Cash and investments	Other
1973	17,709	14,624	2,863	222
1974	20,289	16,114	3,893	283
1975	24,364	18,882	5,161	321
1976	28,131	22,500	5,159	472
1977	34,680	26,600	7,477	603
1978	39,723	31,715	7,385	723
1979	46,126	36,986	8,280	860
1980	53,797	42,404	10,350	1,043

*= Book values

Source: BSA Bulletin, April 1981 and Financial Statistics

Table 3.5 Building society advances

Year	Advances (£m)	Number of loans	Average advance £
1973	3,540	551,000	*N/A
1974	2,950	438,000	N/A
1975	4,965	652,000	7,479
1976	6,117	717,000	8,394
1977	7,524	788,000	9,548
1978	8,710	784,000	11,109
1979	9,119	705,000	12,935
1980	10,014	695,000	14,409

*N/A = Not available. Before 1975, the data is less reliable.

Source: BSA Bulletin and Financial Statistics

Note: The discrepancies between the tables are due to restatements and variations in the numbers reporting.

finance. Also, since the early 1970s advances for house purchase have increased rapidly, as Table 3.5 demonstrates.

The importance of the societies in the financial system cannot, therefore, be denied. The means by which they have achieved such rapid growth are through catering for the potential house purchaser and small saver, offering attractive rates of interest (which benefit from a tax concession), opening for longer and more convenient hours than the banks and combining to achieve economies in the transmission of savings to the purpose of house purchase. More recently the societies have also demonstrated an increasing versatility in the financial instruments they are prepared to offer savers.

The increasing concentration of the building societies has been investigated by Hill and Gough (1979) who demonstrated that the five largest

Table 3.6 Building societies and mortgage assets

Year	No.	Mortgage assets (£m)
1900	2,286	46
1910	1,723	60
1920	1,271	69
1930	1,026	316
1940	952	678
1950	819	1,060
1960	726	2,467
1970	481	8,752
1976	364	22,529
1977	339	26,426
1978	316	31,599
1979	287	36,629
1980	273	42,404

Source: Registrar General's Reports and *Building Society Affairs*

Table 3.7 Merger activity of building societies by asset range

Year	0–£1m	£1m–£10m	£10m+
1968	20	6	1
1969	15	4	0
1970	16	0	1
1971	11	3	1
1972	8	5	0
1973	7	0	2
1974	13	11	6
1975	19	7	5
1976	6	5	2
1977	8	7	2
1978	7	13	3
1979	8	18	3
1980	4	10	0

Source: Registrar General's Reports

building societies accounted for over 50 per cent of the movement's total assets. Table 3.6 illustrates how the number of societies has fallen drastically since the turn of the century, while the assets held in the form of mortgages have grown enormously. Similarly, Table 3.7 demonstrates the number of societies which engaged in merger activity between 1968 and 1980. Although the rate of activity exhibited a slow down from 1975, the Registrar General of Friendly Societies (Registrar General's Report 1976) stated that it '. . . is not thought to reflect any considered view that the process of rationalisation by merger will soon have run its natural course'. (p. 4)

So we can expect the merger activity to continue in the future, though obviously it is likely to be at a declining rate because of the decreasing number of societies that remain. It should be noted that the merger activity does not reflect greed for power on the part of the large societies, nor does it reflect the achievement of monopoly profits, for as we shall see later, the societies are disallowed by law to make profits. More likely, the merger activity is a natural response to the increasing severity of competition for a share of personal sector saving plus the need to remove the anachronism of tiny uneconomic concerns inherited from the heyday of building society proliferation. Indeed, in the early 1970s, there were societies in existence with assets of less than £100!

Table 3.7 confirms this viewpoint, since the vast majority of mergers have taken place in the asset range from zero to £1 million. Not only does this reflect a striving for efficiency within the movement, but also an increasing professionalism in the societies' approach to the fiercely competitive environment of personal sector saving.

Originally, the movement had sought to attract the small saver who was interested in house purchase at some future date. However, as Newbould and Doyle (1974) discovered, this situation had changed with several distinct classes of saver coming into being

'The "investors" class of investor, while numerically small, can represent a significant proportion of funds to some building societies. This is the interest-elastic segment of the market and it is clear that they should be offered rates competitive with those elsewhere in the market'. (p. 12)

The term 'interest-elastic' implies that, when interest rates change, certain savers switch funds from one savings institution to another to obtain a more favourable return. We shall see later that in the 1970s the interest-elastic class of personal sector saver became more active in the switching of funds from the banking to non-banking intermediaries. As a result, the call for greater harmony in the rules governing the competitive situation between the banks and non-banks reached a crescendo by the end of the 1970s and culminated, *inter alia*, in the specific recommendations of the Wilson Committee (1980). Since several of the Committee's recommendations relate to the operations of the societies, we turn to this issue next.

Building society operations

All building societies are required to prepare a set of rules which state how the society is to be governed and the general conditions for the raising and lending of funds. The rules have evolved from the various acts of Parliament relating to friendly and building societies of 1874, 1894, 1939 and 1960, the provisions of which were consolidated under the Building Societies Act of 1962.

There are in fact two types of society allowed under the legislation—permanent and terminating societies. The latter are societies whose rules provide for the termination of business on the achievement of some specified goal (usually financing the building of one or a number of houses). However, the vast majority of societies are permanent and some retain this adjective in their title.

There are two categories of building society members: investors and borrowers. The former invest money in or subscribe for the shares of a society while the latter are the recipients of an advance or loan. The two are, of course, not mutually exclusive. It is quite normal for a person to be a 'mortgagor' while at the same time saving with the society for reasons other than future house ownership. The provision of a mortgage allows the society to hold the deeds to a property while the mortgagor repays a combination of capital and interest over a number of years. On termination of the mortgage the seal of the society is affixed to the mortgage deed which is returned to the owner of the property. There are many variants on this theme tailored to meet the needs and capabilities of the individual borrower.

Similarly, there are also many variations of the two basic means by which the societies raise funds. The societies raise funds by issuing two basic financial instruments: shares and deposits. The difference between the two lies in their legal status and the interest they pay. Shareholders (who greatly outnumber depositors), have a participating interest in the society. The depositor is merely a lender to the society. In certain circumstances the depositor is entitled to priority payment compared with the shareholder, e.g. in the event of liquidation. Because of the additional security enjoyed by the depositor the interest return is generally lower than the share rate. At the same time the shareholder has a voting right in the affairs of the society, although in practice this is rarely exercised. The closest parallel to this situation in the corporate world is the relationship between shareholder and debenture (loan stock) holders. The latter lend money to companies for a fixed interest payment while the former share in the profits of the company and enjoy a dividend if profits materialize.

Of course, shares and deposits are the liabilities of the societies and at the same time the assets in the wealth portfolios of those individuals who constitute the personal sector. We have seen how the majority of the assets held by societies are in the form of mortgages. However, they also hold a small proportion of public securities and balances with the banking intermediaries. The balance of the assets held in the form of completely liquid (cash at bank) or near liquid (government and local authority securities) assets is usually referred to as the 'liquidity ratio'. The liquidity ratio is designed to cushion the societies from the adverse effects of heavy withdrawals or other contingent liabilities. Because of the safety-first policy which has tended to be pursued by the societies they are often accused of holding excessive liquidity. The accusation arises particularly when there is a severe shortage of mortgage funds. Obviously, the greater liquid assets are as a proportion of total assets the less must be accounted for by mortgages. Often the reduction of the liquidity ratio by one per cent would release millions to be used for mortgage finance. In spite of this, the societies have resolutely maintained that they are the most knowledgeable concerning the prudent level of liquidity which must be maintained in order to hold the confidence of investors.

Besides the argument concerning excessive liquidity, the societies have also been accused of excessive high street branch proliferation. It is not uncommon in the UK for a high street to be dominated by a mixture of building society and clearing bank branches yet it seems to the bewildered investor that they each fulfil a similar function. By far the greatest accusation levelled at the societies is, however, that the protection of their position in the financial sytem through the fiscal advantages detailed below has brought about an endemic inefficiency in the provision of housing finance. Since 1939 the Building Societies Association has recommended the rates at which members should lend to home buyers and borrow from depositors and shareholders. However, the supply of funds for the housing market has often been regulated by factors other than price, usually at the connivance of government and as a result of efforts by the Association to maintain a weakening cartel arrangement.

Successive governments have maintained the fiscal advantages of saving with and borrowing from building societies and have frequently intervened to keep the politically sensitive mortgage rate below the general level of interest rates. At the same time the cartel system operated by the BSA has frequently prevented the mortgage rate falling as fast as it might have done in a free market, since adjustments were influenced by a self imposed time-lag dictated by the arrangement of BSA meetings. The consequence is that the housing market has been alternatively swamped with and starved of funds, destabilizing house prices and driving housebuilders into excessive caution or even liquidation. The protection of house buyers from market forces was based on the assumption that protection would secure a steady and cheaper supply of mortgage funds whereas the market can often operate to do precisely the same at less public cost.

A question mark now hangs over whether the business of the building societies will continue to be mutual or become rather more commercial in nature. The market for personal saving has become more competitive as through the 1970s the societies, albeit with the help of government induced competitive advantages, diverted savings away from the banking system.

The competitive advantages afforded the societies result directly from several factors. First, the societies pay interest net of tax and the tax paid on their interest is negotiated annually with the Inland Revenue. This is known as the 'composite' rate of tax which is calculated by the Inland

Revenue and depends upon the prevailing level of taxation and allowances, with reference to the proportionate amounts invested in building
societies by those who are and are not liable to tax. The societies
effectively receive a reduction in the tax rate according to the number of
non-taxpayers who are estimated to save with them. This facility is not
available to other financial institutions which compete for personal sector
funds. The result is that the grossed-up rates offered by the societies may
often be more favourable than comparable rates obtained elsewhere. A
second advantage which exists is the 'cartel' arrangement by which
societies agree to offer broadly similar rates on their deposits and shares.
Although the advantage may not be obvious, it implies that the 'movement' reacts uniformly to changing economic circumstance and does not
suffer from the disadvantage which results from cut-throat competition.

It was this uniformity of action, coupled with the tax advantage
described above, which supposedly enabled the societies to maintain low
interest mortgages compared with other intermediaries. The reasons for
this are quite simple. The benefit from the tax advantage allows the
societies to offer lower rates to investors than they would otherwise have to
offer if their rates were not effectively subsidized by the tax arrangement.
In turn, the payment of low interest rates to investors allowed the societies
to offer mortgages at lower rates than other financial institutions would
have to charge in order to cover the cost of those funds. The public
therefore benefits from the tax advantage since this concession is passed on
in the form of low cost mortgage finance. Any weakening of this situation
by the removal of the tax concession or the abandonment of the cartel
arrangement would lead to an increase in the cost of mortgage finance
from the building societies. In fact what has happened is that the banks
have begun to compete more fiercely with the societies for lending
opportunities while the BSA cartel has disintegrated, ushering in a new era
of severe competition in the mortgage market in the 1980s.

Whatever changes the future may hold, there is no doubt that the
increasing volatility of interest rates throughout the 1970s contributed to
the closer scrutiny of the societies' ability to respond in a turbulent
economic environment. The probable outcome will be a mis-match of
interest rates, affecting cash flows. The former will be adjusted automatically by the societies while the latter will contrive to be adjusted after a lag.
The problem they face in this respect is that attempting to become more
competitive with other savings institutions in the investment rates they
offer may conflict with the traditional policy of containing mortgage costs.
However, since double digit mortgage costs are already a feature of the
1980s this problem will become less of a constraint.

Another problem the societies face is that they have attracted such a
large proportion of personal sector saving that expanding their share still
further may prove to be difficult. The idea has been mooted that they will

strengthen their ties with pension funds and insurance companies in order to tap other intermediaries which, after all, provide limited mortgage finance themselves. On the other hand, some commentators argue that since only 50 per cent of the adult population hold building society accounts, then this leaves half of the personal sector available to tap as a source of liquid funds. It is likely, for the time being, that the societies will offer an increasing range of savings media, such as marketable term shares, in order to continue to cater for the small saver and to tap the wholesale (corporate) market. Indeed, in 1980, the Alliance was the first society to issue fixed-rate marketable yearling bonds. These effectively compete with certificates of deposit circulated by the banking system.

There are a multitude of special schemes which now exist and through which the societies obtain funds. Besides the traditional share and deposit accounts, term shares became popular in the 1970s but have since given way to convertible term shares, which guarantee a premium over the rate paid on ordinary shares in exchange for the investor sacrificing his liquidity. Certain accounts also offer more than the standard rate of interest because they impose a minimum investment level as well as penalties for withdrawals. Besides these, there are planned savings schemes available, which are quasi-contractual, save as you earn schemes and even a building society equivalent to the 'granny bond' with a guaranteed premium for investors over a certain age. So the innovation displayed by the societies has been impressive and very recently they have sought to raise funds from sources other than the personal sector directly by negotiating syndicated credits from the banking system. Like the TSB, the societies are stepping beyond their traditional role and are awaiting legislation which will enable their move into money transmission services.

In the immediate future, the most likely change in building society operations could be the bringing of investment rates into line with competitive rates. The effect of this action may be twofold; the suspension of the tax advantage they enjoy and a greater severity of competition with the banks in offering mortgages (the rates on which would also rise as explained before). The outcome would mean a weakened competitive position *vis-à-vis* the banks since the latter generally offer larger mortgages to provide for the second mortgage purchaser on which margins are the most remunerative. In the past, the banks have tapped this market because the societies have traditionally operated a maximum imposed by statute on the mortgage finance they would provide. The banks had responded by catering for this market segment even though the rates they charged were considered likely to be excessive in comparison. In fact, because the banks charge a flat percentage over their base rates and smaller variances in the rates on larger loans compared with the societies, this has meant that a bank mortgage has in many cases worked out cheaper to the borrower. The upshot has been that the banks lent £450 million for mortgages in 1980 and were expanding rapidly in 1981 as the average size of mortgages demanded went beyond the average advances offered by the societies.

A major factor which impairs the societies' ability to maintain their relative attraction as savings institutions is concerned with the practical operation of building society accounts by investors. In the economic environment of high interest rates and inflation of the 1970s, individuals became increasingly aware of the declining value of cash and the economics of comparing interest offered on competing financial instruments. One of the responses by individuals was to hold a society account and operate it as if it were a bank current account. Obviously this meant that cash which was operated as a liquid fund for transactions purposes still earned interest. Although this situation favoured the societies in so far as they enjoyed a switching of funds away from the banks in their favour, it was inevitable that eventually they would recognize that the cost of this development was the increased administrative burden involved in catering for regular small withdrawals and deposits. In April 1980 the Bradford and Bingley was the first to take overt action to discourage the use of accounts in this way by penalizing those who use the accounts too regularly. The penalty was operated in the form of a lower interest rate offered on accounts used beyond a specified limit.

To conclude this section we need to consider the most important question concerning the increasingly commercial nature of the societies' operations and whether they should be brought under the umbrella of monetary control operated by the Bank of England on behalf of the Treasury. The question arises as a consequence of the increasing size of the movement and the questions that have arisen concerning the 'moneyness' of their financial instruments, a topic we will turn to in Chapter 5. There is little doubt that the friction between the banking system and the societies has heightened in the 'eighties. With the banking system's lending for house purchase sometimes exceeding 30 per cent of total new lending the traditional distinction between the societies and the banks for the purposes of monetary control has been questioned. For example, from May 1979 to May 1980, lending by the London clearing banks rose 32.7 per cent, while lending by the total banking system for house purchase rose 34 per cent over the same period. This reflected the inability of the societies to quench mortgage demand and individuals opting to obtain larger, and in many cases, cheaper bank mortgages. More important however, may be the implication for the money supply. Bank lending, as we shall see later, contributes to the money supply and controlling the money supply became a primary government policy objective at the end of the 1970s. The increasing provision of home loans by the banks was recognized as adding to the money supply and was therefore inflationary. However, lending by the building societies is not similarly regarded due to the technicalities of the money supply definition. Careful consideration of the growth of building societies is therefore of great importance and may necessitate the application of banking-type controls to these non-bank intermediaries in the future. This topic will be discussed further in Chapter 6.

4 Credit unions

In the UK, credit unions, sometimes known as savings and loans co-operatives, began their existence in Northern Ireland, where ninety-four were in operation in 1980. However, in the same year, there were over fifty credit unions operating on the mainland. The largest CU in Britain in 1980 was the Credit Union of Derry, which began operations in 1959 with five members and now has over 10,000 members.

Because of the highly developed financial system in the UK, CUs have been fairly slow to evolve. Their spread to the British mainland is largely the result of the influence of Irish and West Indian immigrants who had often benefited previously from such a union in their home countries.

The concept of the credit union is not new. They exist in both developed and developing nations from the Cameroons, Taiwan, Korea and Brazil to Canada (where 38 per cent of the population are members of CUs) and the USA where there were over 23,000 in existence in 1980. Their outstanding feature is that they provide both a community and financial service and provide credit at rates much cheaper and with less severe conditions than the larger financial institutions.

A credit union is usually formed by several persons in the same locality, ethnic group or even in the same firm. Persons make small regular contributions to the CU and may at the same time take out a small loan from the union. The granting of a loan is determined by a committee which is elected by the members of the CU. As a result, all depositors are shareholders of the Union and thereby have the right to vote. The loans are usually provided for the purchase of household goods or a car or to finance a rare expenditure, such as a wedding. The repayments are small and usually at very low interest. Occasionally, the repayments can be interrupted or temporarily suspended if the committee gives permission. The concept of the credit union, the spread of which is encouraged by the Credit Union League of Great Britain, is to enable people to create their own surpluses and to co-operatively share in those surpluses by providing small loans.

Of course, as the operations of a particular type of intermediary becomes increasingly significant in the workings of the financial system, certain legislative measure have to be undertaken to protect depositors and make those responsible for the CUs accountable in law for their actions. The Industrial and Provident Societies Act of 1969 does precisely this for Northern Ireland, while the Credit Union Act of August 1979 provides the same for the rest of the UK. The latter Act developed a legal framework within which CUs could operate. They are debarred from investing in property, except where offices are required, though most tend to operate from church halls and the like. The funds are held at banks and 98 per cent of them are available for lending. Each CU must submit accounts to the Registrar of Friendly Societies and must take out insurance. This latter requirement is particularly important, for if a member dies there can be difficulties encountered by the bereaved spouse if an outstanding loan is still to be repaid. The insurance provision ensures that in such an eventuality the loan is repaid by the insurance company and the amount of saving accumulated within the CU is immediately doubled and paid to the dependants.

One problem experienced by the CUs in Great Britain is that as they increase in size their funds will begin to accumulate interest upon which tax would have to be paid, effectively reducing the total surpluses accumulated. The 1979 Act therefore allowed the CUs six years' grace before tax would have to be paid on the interest earned. However, it simultaneously imposed a maximum saving of £2,000 per person to discourage the abuse of this advantage. Although the interest received from saving with a CU is very low, this only serves to illustrate the fact that persons become members for reasons other than wealth maintenance. They are essentially based on trust and provide loans on conditions which would be uneconomic for the larger concerns which were set up for entirely different reasons and therefore adopt completely different criteria in the determination of their lending policies.

5 Summary and conclusions

This chapter has concentrated upon the primary deposit takers which compete with the established banks in the UK financial system. The degree of success achieved by these institutions relies upon the degree of innovative zeal applied to tailoring the liabilities they issue to the changing pattern of saving propensities displayed by the personal sector. Undoubtedly, the fiscal advantages enjoyed by the non-banking institutions creates a prolonged imperfection in the financial system and is likely to be removed only by complete fiscal neutrality. The likelihood of such a policy ever being invoked is in itself a function of the size of the public sector borrowing requirement.

It could be argued that the prolonged fiscal advantages enjoyed by certain institutions may damage their capacity for financial innovation. Furthermore, the continuing problem of financing public expenditure has provoked the public authorities into deliberately manipulating the financial markets in order to finance public expenditure. The public financing problem has been heightened by the TSB seeking independence from the state, with the result that increasingly generous National Savings schemes have been required to compensate. The effect has been to further destabilize the competitive ability of institutions such as the building societies, which must soon be relieved from their present operating constraints in order to re-assert their position as the major repositories for personal sector saving.

Finally, the growth of credit unions in the UK serves to remind us that financial innovation is not entirely dependent upon the fiscal treatment of financial institutions. The interplay of tradition, culture and need have created the climate within which such specialist intermediaries can flourish. The following chapter, in contrast, considers the plight of the traditional banking institutions over the past decade.

Topics

1 Describe the role and assess the significance of the following:
  (a) Building societies
  (b) Trustee Savings Banks
  (IOB Part II, Monetary Theory and Practice, April 1979).
2 Discuss the changing role of the TSBs in the British financial system.
3 Why have credit unions suddenly begun to develop in the UK? How can they operate economically under conditions of such small loan repayments and charging such low rates of interest in comparison with those prevailing through-out the rest of the financial system?
4 Evaluate the impact of the Government's decision, in March 1982, to finance an increasing proportion of the public deficit through National Savings.

4 Banking intermediaries in the UK

1 Introduction

In Chapter 1 it was explained that the banks developed rather differently from the NBFIs in the UK financial system. The essential distinguishing feature is that the banks developed by issuing money first and offered services other than the transmission of money secondarily. On the other hand, the NBFIs began by offering other non-monetary services and only lately, particularly evident in the case of the TSB, have they began to encroach into the field of money transmission. Whether the distinction between money and credit is notional or real and whether the distinction can be ascertained theoretically or empirically is not at issue in this chapter. A grasp of the fundamental components of the financial system is required first and foremost before we broach the theoretical problems associated with the growth of the non-bank institutions in Part 2 of this book.

Accordingly, a brief overview of the primary banking institutions, their role and functions is undertaken in this chapter. The reason for brevity is that the banking system has received so much attention elsewhere. The reason for undertaking a critical examination of the banks is that traditionally they have been the vehicle through which monetary policy has operated. Furthermore, one can only begin to comprehend the true function of the banking intermediaries with reference to the changing methods of monetary control in the UK. The 1970s saw a particularly profound influence upon the structure of the UK financial system and the savings market in general, through the introduction of the policy on competition and credit control in 1971. As a result of this policy and others, plus a combination of inflation and a system of floating exchange rates, a turbulent period of excessive monetary growth appeared in the UK throughout the 1970s. The new liberalism in the conduct of monetary policy did not, however, last very long. The incoming Conservative administration of 1979 imposed strict monetary controls and, in 1980, issued new guidelines for the control of liquidity.

As the discussion of the changing conduct of monetary policy unfolds the reader should be aware of the underlying thread that the policies, however disparate, are always aimed at the banking system and the links in the chain of monetary effect rely upon the relationships between the institutions we shall now discuss. Where the chain of influence is uncertain or proved to be mistaken the authorities have rapidly redefined the sphere of influence in the pursuit of greater monetary control. This has taken place in the guise of redefining the money supply and, indeed, redefining the banking system itself.

Listed banks

The Banking Act of 1979 initiated a system of legal definitions for banks and other Licensed Deposit Taking institutions (LDTs). Before that year only banks which were 'listed', i.e. those submitting returns to the Bank of England, were recognized as having banking status. However, it was often the case that certain institutions which called themselves banks in fact operated outside the direct sphere of influence of the Bank of England. Some banks will have previously been issued with certificates by the Department of Trade under Section 123 of the Companies Act 1967, which certified that they conformed to the Moneylenders Acts. By virtue of this fact they were entitled to call themselves banks. In order to overcome this problem the Banking Act required deposit-taking institutions to apply to the Bank of England to become a recognized bank.

Essentially the Act sought to bring the UK into line with the European Community's directive on credit institutions. The criteria which the Bank of England adopts to determine a recognized bank are determined by Schedule 2 of the Act.

The following factors are taken into account

  (i) A good reputation must exist for the deposit taking institution.

 (ii) A wide range of banking services, specialist or otherwise, must be provided such as

    (a) current and deposit account facilities or accepting funds in the wholesale money market.

    (b) Provision of loans and overdrafts or lending in the wholesale money markets.

    (c) Foreign exchange services.

    (d) The handling of bills of exchange and promissory notes, including financing foreign trade.

    (e) Financial advice and the provision of facilities for the purchase and sale of investments.

Wholesale, as distinct from retail banking, is determined by the size of the deposits accepted by the banks and the negotiability of the rates on those deposits. Retail deposits are the well known current, deposit and savings accounts which are repayable at short notice and upon which there is a stable rate of interest i.e. it does not vary from one individual/organization to the next. Wholesale deposits are the larger deposits, usually exceeding £50,000, where the rate of interest is negotiated and the disposition of funds between banks is sensitive to variations in the rate of interest. As we shall see later the policy of Competition and Credit Control (CCC) encouraged the commercial banks to enter more vigorously the field of wholesale banking.

The classification of banks by the Bank of England was an exercise strongly influenced by the desire to increase efficiency in the collection of banking statistics. However, not only does the revision of the legal definition of a bank cause a re-classification to take place but occasionally amendments to the definition of the supply of money can have the same effect. This occurred in May 1975 when the banks which operate in the UK were classified according to whether they were

  (i) UK banks
 (ii) Overseas banks, or
(iii) Consortium banks

At that time there occurred a break in the money supply series because of the amended collection of bank statistics. The Bank of England (*Quarterly Bulletin* 1975, p. 162) considered this amendment necessary and stated 'There have been serious inconsistencies—in both the concept and coverage—in the information provided by the banks for internal banking statistics and for external statistics.' It was expected that new reporting systems would improve the quality of the banking statistics provided by the Bank of England.

A more recent classification of banks in this country has been provided by the Wilson Committee Report and is consistent with the classification of 1975[1]. Tables 4.1 and 4.2 below provide evidence concerning the size of these banks and their balance sheets. It is apparent that in 1981 the London clearing banks were the largest domestic banks in terms of assets and Table 4.1 clearly illustrates the relative importance of the discount houses and the Banking Department of the Bank of England.

The clearers are retail banks (six in all) which have expanded into wholesale and international banking throughout the 1970s. Although Table 4.1 demonstrates the increasing importance of overseas banks in the UK, their individual sizes are small compared with the major domestic banks. So although the assets of the 'other' overseas banks exceeded those of the clearers this total was shared among over two hundred individual banks in 1981. Table 4.2 gives a selection of balance sheet items for the same banks. Clearly the vast majority of sterling deposit liabilities are held with the clearers while the foreign banks are primarily responsible for

[1] Committee to Review the Functioning of Financial Institutions, Cmnd 7937, HMSO 1980.

Table 4.1 UK Banking sector: Balance sheet totals, June 1981

	Total assets/liabilities *£m*
London clearing banks	70,303
Scottish clearing banks	8,404
Northern Ireland banks	1,598
Accepting houses	15,689
Other British banks	51,311
American banks	76,087
Japanese banks	57,661
Other overseas banks	76,005
Consortium banks	15,228
All UK banks—total	372,286
Listed discount market institutions	5,083
Bank of England Banking Department	2,093
Total	379,462

Source: Bank of England Quarterly Bulletin

foreign currency deposits. More importantly the total for sterling advances indicates that nearly 53 per cent of domestic borrowing in the form of advances was provided by the clearers in 1981.

Before discussing briefly the functions of the different types of banks we need to investigate the banking function itself and compare this with the function of the non-banking intermediary discussed in the previous chapters.

2 The banking business

The distinction between retail and wholesale banking has already been made. As a corollary to the growth in wholesale banking the sterling Certificate of Deposit (CD) was inaugurated in October 1968. The CD is a document which confirms that a wholesale deposit has been made with a bank. When the certificate matures the deposit is repayable in full. However, the holder of the CD may require liquidity before the certificate matures. If this is the case, he can sell the bill at a discount in order to obtain the necessary liquidity and the new holder knows that the full value will be paid on maturity. In times of severe liquidity shortage the CD has proved a useful negotiable instrument in the banking sector where an efficient market in the financial instrument exists. However, CDs are only one example of the financial instruments issued by the banks. Probably the

Table 4.2 UK banks: Selected balance sheet items, June 1981

	Sterling deposit liabilities		Other currency		Sterling advances		Total assets/ liabilities	
	£m	%	£m	%	£m	%	£m	%
London clearing banks	44,137	46.1	15,880	6.2	29,748	52.8	70,303	18.9
Scottish clearing banks	5,075	5.3	1,772	0.7	3,780	6.7	8,404	2.3
Northern Ireland banks	1,299	1.4	12	—	892	1.6	1,598	0.4
Accepting houses	5,566	5.8	8,326	3.3	2,303	4.1	15,689	4.2
Other British banks	18,023	18.8	28,507	11.2	8,418	14.9	51,311	13.8
American banks	9,009	9.4	66,887	26.2	5,763	10.2	76,087	20.4
Japanese banks	1,501	1.6	56,112	22.0	805	1.4	57,661	15.5
Other overseas banks	9,809	10.2	65,180	25.5	4,012	7.1	76,005	20.4
Consortium banks	1,404	1.5	12,786	5.0	651	1.2	15,228	4.1
All banks in the UK	95,823	100	255,462	100	56,372	100	372,286	100

Source: Bank of England Quarterly Bulletin

best method of understanding true nature of the banking business is to investigate in more detail the asset and liability portfolios of the banking sector.

Table 4.3, adapted from the Wilson Report (1980), presents the balance sheet of the banking sector for the period 1957 to 1979. It is apparent that holding of CDs and balances with other banks has been the fastest growing component of banking assets. This reflects the increasingly vigorous competition which exists in the banking sector and between that sector and the non-banks encouraged initially by the 1971 CCC policy and the increased marketability of CDs as financial instruments. It is further noticeable that this growth did not 'take off' until after 1968.

Taking each component of the balance sheet in turn, the increase in the amounts of notes outstanding (in Scotland and Northern Ireland only) has risen by 7.6 per cent compound over the period. Note issue was the original *raison d'être* for the banking system but the very small proportion of the total accounted for by notes illustrates how the original function has diminished in importance. Notes are nevertheless a liability since the banks promise to pay the bearer on demand. Similarly deposits are also liabilities since they correspond to the financial assets held by individuals and organizations with the banks and are therefore funds owed to those two parties by the banks. Over a third of sterling deposits are 'sight deposits', a definition which stems from May 1975 when current accounts needed to be amended to measure more precisely those deposits which were repayable on demand. Thus sight deposits include current accounts and those interest bearing accounts which are immediately repayable e.g. wholesale deposits which are callable. On the other hand 'time deposits', as their name implies, are only repaid after a specified period has elapsed. The total of sight deposits, time deposits plus capital and minor items constitutes the total identified liabilities of the banking system. It may seem surprising to the reader to learn that in June 1981 only one third of total deposits were denominated in sterling, the rest were foreign currency liabilities. This serves to remind us that the UK banking system is influenced greatly by foreign deposits and how dependent the system is becoming upon those deposits. In 1981 deposits constituted 92 per cent of total banking liabilities.

On the asset side of the balance sheet the first item is notes and coins plus deposits with the Bank of England. These are the most liquid assets held by the banks and are held at the 'banker's bank' i.e. the Bank of England. Just as an ordinary bank can influence a person's expenditure by requiring a certain minimum to be kept in a private bank account, so the Bank of England may impose limitations upon the bank's lending activities by requiring more or less to be held in its own vaults. If the Bank insists that more be deposited in the form of this item in the asset portfolio then less is available for the banks to lend, this would then be a restrictive

Table 4.3 Balance sheet of banks in the UK, 1957-79

	At end or mid-December: £billion							% Growth compound
	1957	1962	1967	1972	1977	1978	1979	
Liabilities								
Notes outstanding	0.1	0.1	0.1	0.2	0.4	0.5	0.5	7.6
Deposits	8.7	11.9	21.2	65.4	178.1	203.9	246.4	16.4
Other liabilities	—	—	—	—	13.1	14.5	16.9	—
Total identified liabilities	8.8	12.1	21.3	65.6	191.6	218.9	263.8	16.7
Assets								
Notes and coin and balances with Bank of England	0.7	0.8	1.0	1.2	1.8	1.8	1.9	4.6
Balances with other banks and holdings of CDs (1)	0.2	0.7	2.3	17.1	40.3	45.5	60.4	29.6
Money at call and short notice	0.8	1.2	1.7	2.3	2.8	3.2	3.6	7.1
Bills discounted	1.8	1.5	1.4	1.6	3.6	2.6	3.1	2.5
Special and supplementary deposits	—	—	0.2	0.1	1.2	1.1	0.8	—
British government securities	2.7	1.9	2.1	1.9	2.8	3.0	2.7	—
Loans and advances	2.3	5.9	11.9	42.8	129.0	150.0	177.5	21.8
Other investments and assets	0.1	0.2	0.7	0.9	10.2	11.7	13.8	25.1
Total identified assets	8.6	12.2	21.3	67.9	191.6	218.9	263.8	16.8

(1) For the period 1957-67, the figures exclude balances with, or loans and advances to, deposit banks, which accounts for the discrepancies between assets and liabilities.

Source: Bank of England Statistical Abstracts and Bank of England Quarterly Bulletin

action. On the other hand, if the Bank were to give back some of these balances this would act to free funds and allow further loans to be provided. This item has traditionally been used by the Bank as a tool of monetary policy but, as will be seen later, the methods adopted have altered significantly since the 1960s.

Turning to the second item in the asset portfolio, it was previously explained that the CD is a negotiable instrument and can be bought and sold not only by individuals and institutions in the wholesale deposit market but also by the banks themselves. The UK banks' holdings of CDs are therefore merged with other liquid holdings such as balances with other banks. These assets combine to provide supplementary liquidity which may be called upon to finance exceptional withdrawals or overnight shortages of cash. The compound growth rate of 29.5 per cent over the period illustrates the role the banks have played in creating a viable market in this financial instrument. The role of the next item in the asset portfolio is similar. Money at call and short notice is so called because the money, which is lent to the discount houses, can be recalled very quickly. The funds are lent to the discount houses who deal in commercial bills as well as almost all those issued by the Treasury to finance the Government's short-term expenditures. The banks, of course, earn a return on these funds which are secured by the assets of the discount houses and the knowledge that the Bank of England is always prepared to act as the 'lender of last resort'[2]. Nevertheless, the primary function of this asset is to provide liquidity on demand to the banking system.

Of course the banks themselves hold some commercial bills. A commercial bill is in fact an IOU from one person/organization to another which promises to pay a specific amount by a specific date. However, if one requires cash immediately then as with the Certificate of Deposit the bill will have to be sold at a discount i.e. less than face value, in order to obtain the liquidity required immediately. Obviously the banks do not engage in this activity to a great extent, for although the bills provide a yield on maturity they do not provide capital certainty since in order to obtain cash quickly one must usually sell them at a further discount.

The next item in the asset portfolio is special and supplementary deposits. Special deposits are essentially a means by which the authorities may mop up excess liquidity in the banking system. They are deposits which are required to be kept at the Bank of England, and effectively restrict banking intermediation because they cannot be recalled on demand. The first call for special deposits was made by the Bank of England in April 1960 when 1 per cent of the gross deposits of the clearing banks ($\frac{1}{2}$ per cent for Scottish banks) was required to be placed with the Bank. This component of the asset portfolio is strictly adopted as a direct means of

2 See discount houses later in this chapter.

control over bank lending. Furthermore, on occasion the interest rate paid by the Bank on these deposits has been used to penalize the banks if they have not conformed to previously issued directives. This happened in May 1969 when the rate was halved because the banks had not complied with a previously imposed ceiling on advances. Supplementary special deposits had a similar role to play in the asset portfolio. However, whereas special deposits are levied as a proportion of total assets, supplementary special deposits have been related to the *growth* of total deposits (sometimes called eligible liabilities because they are eligible in considering lending policy). Thus the latter effectively taxed the growth of bank lending in order to influence the supply of money but was abolished in 1980 in preparation for the operation of a new monetary regime.

In discussing the non-banking institutions in Chapter 2 it was apparent that they were increasingly responsible for purchasing government securities. The banks have had a less important role to play compared with the non-banks in this respect and this is evident when one considers the item concerned with British government securities in Table 4.3. Indeed, quite fortuitously, the banks held precisely the same amount of government securities in 1979 as they had in 1957. Since the total asset portfolio had grown by 17 per cent compound over the period, we can conclude that government securities are playing a less significant role than before as a stabilizing element in the asset portfolio. Also, since 1971, the authorities have not made a market in gilts, so they have become increasingly 'capital uncertain' as a result. The reason for this declining role attached to gilt-edged securities is that the controls imposed upon the banks to ensure stability of their asset portfolios is such that they do not need to resort to the usual measures to stabilize them i.e. to hold as much government stock as do the other, relatively uncontrolled, institutions.

Undoubtedly the largest component of the banking sector's asset portfolio is the provision of loans and advances. This element of the asset portfolio accounted for 67 per cent of total assets at the end of 1979. However, although it is the clearing banks and others who predominantly deal in retail banking which are the main providers of loans and overdrafts, much of their new business is increasingly concerned with wholesale deposits and the provision of specialist advice and services to organizations who wish to raise finance or provide for contingencies. Of course, the provision of advice has traditionally been the function of the merchant banks, to be discussed later.

The final component of the asset portfolio listed in Table 4.3 is the 'other' category. Although constituting only 5 per cent of total assets, the high compound growth rate of 25 per cent over the period reflects the increasing diversification of banking activities, especially during the 1970s and expenditure upon premises, computerization and investment in subsidiaries.

In general the banks' choice of assets is influenced predominantly by liquidity and solvency considerations. This stems out of their reliance on short term funds i.e. funds which can be withdrawn quickly. It is natural and indeed evident that by seeking to adjust their liability portfolio to become more long-term in nature (via the attraction of wholesale deposits), this will enable the banks to diversify into new business ventures; for example the provision of mortgages or expanding the services for providing small business finance as the likelihood of insolvency and illiquidity diminish. When the insurance companies were considered earlier in Chapter 2 it was evident that the more long-term the liability portfolio operated by a financial institution the more long-term assets can be acquired. The banks are merely applying the same logic to their own sphere of business, the problem being that banking policy is often obstructed by regulations imposed by the monetary authorities.

As a consequence of their concern for guaranteeing their solvency and maintaining their liquidity, the banks hold a significant proportion of their assets in the form of securities with minimum default risk. Furthermore, when lending, the banks have strict guidelines which are imposed in the determination and granting of a loan or overdraft, again with the emphasis on security. Finally, like so many of the non-bank intermediaries previously observed, they too seek to diversify their asset base geographically and industrially to reduce their dependence upon the fortunes of any particular area or industry. Of course, if the banks could match precisely the maturity of loans and deposits the problem of illiquidity would never arise because every time a deposit needed to be repaid an asset would be liquidated to provide the precise amount of funds required. In practice, however, this is an impossibility and banks perform their intermediary function by lending on a much longer average maturity than they borrow. Confidence in their ability to repay a deposit is maintained by carrying liquid funds plus the knowledge that any temporary deficiency in liquidity can be overcome by borrowing overnight in the money market. In practice, a bank's assets will exceed its liabilities to depositors by the amount of its capital and reserves, both of which are monitored by the Bank of England.

The nature of the banking function in the UK has been briefly described and the reader should now be aware of the basic structure of the banking balance sheet. In order to ascertain the distinction between the non-banks and the banks a comparison between the asset portfolio of selected institutions is recommended. In the meantime it should be noted that as certain non-banks specialize in one particular type of finance so the banks have their own, albeit loosely defined, territories. The main categories of bank are now considered in turn.

3 The London clearing banks

As well as being the dominant force in retail banking, it is the clearing banks that have diversified into wholesale business in the past decade and are continuing to expand their international activities. The clearers are also responsible for most of the country's cash distribution and money transmission facilities. The term 'clearing' refers to the fact that the Banker's Clearing House or Banker's Automated Clearing Services, both of which are owned by the clearers, set off the debits and credits between the different banks and, having undertaken this netting out process, settle the balances automatically. The clearers also collect the notes from the Bank of England and distribute them to branches through 100 cash distribution centres.

In 1959 there were eleven London clearing banks in existence. However, through a series of mergers during the 1960s the number has been reduced to six. The major clearers, i.e. National Westminster, Lloyds, Midland and Barclays, are commonly referred to as 'the big four', with Coutts and Williams & Glyn's making up the six. The two latter banks are usually excluded in common reference to the 'big four' because Coutts is a wholly-owned subsidiary of National Westminster and Williams & Glyn's is a subsidiary of the Royal Bank of Scotland Group, itself 16 per cent owned by Lloyds. In size the National Westminster and Barclays separately account for approximately 30 per cent of total clearing bank liabilities, the Midland and Lloyds almost 40 per cent, with Williams & Glyn's responsible for less than 3 per cent. All of the banks have merchant and wholesale banking subsidiaries, engage in international activities, participate in syndicated credits and are involved with the hire purchase and leasing businesses.

It is natural that in an economy like the UK's, with no restrictions upon branch banking such as in the USA, the banking industry will tend towards concentration, as the economies of scale inherent in any business activity which is standardized encourages combination. This is particularly so in the case of the clearing banks. The clearing system is both complicated and expensive. Further expansion by a bank, i.e. encouraging more deposits, is accompanied by a less than proportionate increase in the costs of clearing, since the burden of paying for the clearing facility is shared among a greater number of account holders. Concentration is also consistent with the banks' objective of maintaining confidence by ensuring security. A large bank is much more likely to withstand adverse financial conditions than is a small bank since the reliance of a large bank upon one or a small group of depositors is removed. As the risk of fluctuations in income is reduced by diversifying an asset portfolio, so the risk of insolvency is reduced by attracting as wide a variety and as large a number of depositors as possible.

The clearing banks are the most publicized due to their numerous branches and the severe competition to encourage new depositors, which manifests itself in marketing methods aimed towards the individual. They often receive a great deal of publicity when profits are declared, which is likely to be adverse in periods of high interest rates. The reason for this is that because the administrative charges of operating certain accounts do not vary with the rate of interest, (such as current accounts which yield no explicit interest), then an increase in market interest rates usually implies a greater return for the banks, while the costs of operating interest free accounts remains the same. This has been termed the endowment effect. Rather than pay a rate of interest on current accounts, the banks set off the value of the balance held in the account against charges which would otherwise be levied on that account. The yield on the account to the individual is not so much a rate of interest but a reduction in bank charges which would otherwise have to be paid for operating the payments into and out of the account. This is termed a 'notional rebate' and, as the rebate does not automatically react to an increase in market rates of interest, the banks may occasionally experience a 'windfall' of profits. Of course the opposite is also true, in the case of a general reduction in market rates the banks may suffer a compounded loss.

In 1980 there were three Scottish clearing banks, again as a result of merger activity during the 1950s and 1960s. Each has its own link with the London clearing banks. Besides the already mentioned Royal Bank for example, the Clydesdale bank is a wholly-owned subsidiary of Midland and the Bank of Scotland 35 per cent owned by Barclays. During 1981, the Royal Bank of Scotland was the subject of two abortive rival take-over bids worth over £500m from Standard Chartered Bank and the Hong Kong and Shanghai Banking Corporation. The extremely delicate situation was the subject of a Monopolies Commission report because it posed political as well as investment questions. The Royal Bank, which remains independent, was the largest Scottish clearer at the time of the bids, with 44 per cent of the market.

It is likely that the 1980s will continue to witness the growth of 'universal banking' in the UK as a corollary to the increasing competition in the financial system. The term 'universal banking' is applied to a financial institution with banking status which seeks to cater for every financial intermediary function for a community. The clearers have, in recent years, extended their activities through subsidiaries into the field of investment (merchant) banking which has traditionally been the reserve of the accepting houses (see below). This implies an intensely competitive stance for the clearers who compete with all the other financial institutions, bank and non-bank, in the various markets. The most severe competition exists however in the field of retail banking where the greatest competitors are the TSB, building societies, National Girobank and the Co-operative

Bank. More recently however, some major North American institutions have made great efforts to encroach upon the UK retail banking business, though not all are subsidiaries of American banks. This, however, is not unusual, for in so far as wholesale banking is concerned foreign banks have displayed a significant presence in the UK for decades. Indeed around 30 per cent of lending to British manufacturing industry was provided by foreign banks in 1980, mainly those with head offices in the USA, West Germany and Japan.

4 Merchant banks

The term merchant banking derives from the early years of banking when only merchants required the facilities for the financing of extended exchange. The term has been retained because it reflects the nature of those banks which provide different kinds of financial services to the business community. As a result these institutions rely on specialist skills and provide advice over a wide range of financial services, from the analysis of investment projects to the issuing of shares and derive much of their income from corporate fees. They necessarily concentrate upon the wholesale market and hence bear the brunt of increased competition brought about by the diversification of the clearers into wholesale banking.

By far the oldest and most important type of merchant bank are the accepting houses. The six largest accepting houses in 1980 were Kleinwort Benson, Schroder Wagg, Hambros, Hill Samuel, Samuel Montagu (now part of the Midland Bank Group), and Morgan Grenfell. There are seventeen such houses in the City, all being members of the Accepting Houses Committee. The balance sheet totals are provided in Table 4.4.

The term 'accepting' developed in the mid-nineteenth century and derives from the fact that the houses accept bills of exchange, although the Accepting Houses Committee was not formed until 5 August 1914. Members of the AHC hold bills, accepting the responsibility for repayment, for which they charge a commission[3]. The bills are generally sold on the discount market with the price varying according to the discount offered. The greater the discount on a bill the lower the price it will command and the higher the rate of return it will yield. However, as well as being discountable within the discount market the bills are also discountable at the Bank of England so ensuring security. The security element is a two way affair however since the Bank and the discount market rely upon

3 The original motivation for the AHC arose from the special circumstances which existed before the First World War. Before the War, there had been a substantial amount of trade between Britain and Germany which meant that many bills of exchange, or acceptances, were unlikely to be met. The AHC rallied the merchant banks which provided mutual support and obtained assistance from the Bank of England.

Table 4.4 Balance sheet totals of AHC members, 1980

Members	£m
Kleinwort Benson	2,388
Schroders	1,817
Hambros	1,669
Hill Samuel	1,542
Samuel Montague	1,380
Morgan Grenfell	1,069
Mercury Securities	919
Lazard Securities	729
N. M. Rothschild	527
Barings	474
Guiness Mahon	303
Brown Shipley	240
Singer & Friedlander	317
Robert Fleming	223*
Arbuthnot Latham	129
Charterhouse Japhet	204
Rea Brothers	111

*There were seventeen members until April 1980 when Antony Gibbs was excluded after a takeover bid from Hong Kong. The AHC requires that the parent company be a full member of the British Bankers Association. However, in November the number reverted to seventeen with Robert Fleming joining the AHC.

Source: Financial Weekly and *The Financial Times*

the accepting houses' reputation as a measure of the acceptability or worthiness of a bill.

The accepting houses constitute approximately 4 per cent of the banking system's total assets. As merchant banks their operations concentrate largely on the corporate sector. Table 4.5 illustrates that the largest proportion of the total assets of the accepting houses in 1980 was held in the form of loans and bills with the majority being provided in the form of other currencies. So far as liabilities are concerned, it is apparent that the accepting houses rely on deposits in the same way as any other bank except that nearly 80 per cent of their deposits are time deposits or CDs, reflecting the wholesale aspect of their business. This is reinforced by the evidence that they lend more to the financial sector than other banks and lend less to the non-manufacturing production industries than retail banks. They also maintain a higher degree of liquidity than the retail banks.

All the accepting houses are members of the Issuing Houses Association which is an organization consisting of 50 banks and firms responsible for the floating of shares subsequently traded on the Stock Exchange. This not only involves advising a company upon the correct mix of financial instruments to be issued but also the drawing up of a prospectus (the

Table 4.5 Balance sheet of the accepting houses 1981

	£m	%
Liabilities		
Sterling deposits	5,566	35.5
Other currency deposits	8,326	53.1
Other liabilities	1,796	11.4
Total liabilities	15,688	100.0
Assets		
Sterling:		
Notes and reserve assets	436	2.8
Market loans and bills	1,596	10.2
Advances and investments	2,777	17.7
Total sterling assets	4,809	30.7
Other currencies:		
Market loans	5,028	32.0
Advances, bills and investments	2,585	16.5
Total other currencies	7,613	48.5
Miscellaneous assets and acceptances	3,266	20.8
Total assets	15,688	100.0

Source: Financial Statistics

detailed track record of the company), underwriting the issues and acting as registrars both of the shareholding and debenture arrangements. They also fulfil a major role as managers of the investment portfolios of some pension funds, insurance companies, investment and unit trusts and various charities. This serves to illustrate the distinction between the merchant banks and the retail institutions. The latter more closely parallel the operations of the non-bank savings institutions we have observed and tap the same market for funds. The former operate primarily in the wholesale sector and therefore tap a different market than the retailers. Furthermore, merchant banks cater for the specific needs of corporate clients and those institutions who manage increasingly sizeable investment portfolios but do not possess the management expertise to do so independently.

A recent development in which the members of the AHC have been instrumental is the provision of 'syndicated credits'. This is a method by which companies can obtain funds to finance a specific operation, say the financing of the tapping of oil in a particular 'bloc' of the North Sea. The oil industry typically experiences lengthy delays between the initiation of a project and yielding a return on investment. The provision of a reliable credit source is therefore crucial to such investment. An accepting house can assist either by providing credit directly for the project or organizing a syndicate of financial sources to fulfil the same function. Again, it is the reputation of the institution which is important in the arranging of a syndicate and it is not unusual for the same organizations to reciprocate in terms of their individual contributions to different syndicates. The total amount of syndicated credits provided and arranged by members of the AHC now exceeds £10 billion per annum.

Those merchant banks outside the AHC include well-known and respected institutions such as County Bank and Keyser Ullman which are subsidiaries of National Westminster and Charterhouse respectively. The world of merchant banking is witnessing severe competition as international banks increasingly locate in the City. According to the Wilson Committee the number of banks in London more than tripled between 1958 and 1978, reflecting the development of Euromarkets.

'Euromarkets' is a term which relates to markets for currencies located outside the territory in which any particular currency is the domestic currency—e.g. the Euro-dollar markets in London, the Cayman Islands and the Far East, the Euro-sterling market in Paris and so on. An excess of a particular currency may sometimes bring the development of a secondary market in that currency, as in the case of Euro-dollars, where the supply of the currency is not directly influenced by the monetary authorities which were responsible for issuing that currency originally. The Euro-currency markets received considerable stimulus from the balance of payments surpluses and deficits of major countries which occurred as a direct result of oil price increases in the 1970s.

As a result, it is possible that in the future we may see a dwindling in the importance of the merchant banks. If the tendency towards conglomeration in industry continues, it is likely to reduce the demand for the traditional services of the merchant banks, as the number of clients dwindles and large firms develop their own in-house financial capability. In response to this, the merchant banks have already moved into 'fund management', i.e. the management of an investment portfolio for both corporate and private clients. The major competitors in this area of their activity are, of course, the insurance companies followed by stock brokers and specialist financial agencies. The future growth achieved by the merchant banks may lie in this area, but is more likely to lie in the development of new methods of raising finance for companies and public corporations utilizing surplus funds, such as oil revenues, which occasionally appear in certain sectors.

5 Finance houses

The finance houses are normally treated as banks for the purpose of credit control. Furthermore, since many are subsidiaries of banks their liabilities are included in the money supply definition, which serves to distinguish them from the non-bank intermediaries. Though most of them tend to be owned or controlled by clearing banks there are notable exceptions such as the United Dominions Trust, itself a listed bank, which was acquired by the TSB in 1981 as part of the latter's quest for independent banking status.

Historically, the finance houses have been closely associated with hire purchase. However, like most of the institutions so far discussed, the finance houses have diversified their range of activities from personal loans and contract hire to leasing transactions, though the crux of their business is still the provision of medium-term credit facilities to business organizations and consumers. Like the commercial banks, some finance houses accept deposits from the public and indeed some are themselves listed banks. The Wilson Committee (1980) noted that the latter account for approximately one quarter of all the sterling deposits of the remaining British banks after accounting for the two categories so far discussed. Furthermore, the report noted that those finance houses which are listed engage significantly in the business of lending and leasing to industrial and commercial companies with factoring becoming increasingly important. At the same time a diminishing proportion of their business is being devoted to lending for property acquisition and development.

The structure and method of organization adopted by the finance houses is a distinguishing feature of their operations. Although generally organized through a branch network their facilities are offered at the point of sale in the now familiar fashion. This method of finance is used by the retailer as a sales promotion technique and the retailer provides the contact point between the provision of finance and the purchase of real goods and services. This enables the retailer to obtain finance to suit the customers' requirements and in turn he operates as an agent for the finance house.

The size of the business undertaken by finance houses merits their being licensed by the Office of Fair Trading in order to ensure conformity with the consumer credit legislation, tightened up in the Consumer Credit Act of 1974. The size distribution is illustrated in Table 4.6. Almost 66 per cent of the total assets were concentrated into the hands of the largest sixteen houses in 1976, including such names as Hodge, Citibank Trust, First National Securities, Mercantile Credit and Lombard North Central. The data is based on the 1976 bench-mark survey because the reporting of statistics is not so carefully organized for these institutions except where they are listed banks.

Table 4.7 presents the balance sheet for the finance houses and other

Table 4.6 Size distribution of finance houses and other consumer credit companies* at end of 1976

Size of total assets (book values)	Number of businesses	Total assets	
£m		£m	%
50 and over	16	1,904	65.9
10–50	26	568	19.6
5–10	26	200	6.9
1–5	66	143	4.9
½–1	40	28	1.0
¼–½	56	20	0.7
Under ¼	266	28	1.0
Total	496	2,891	100.0

*Consumer credit granting companies whose main business was lending to customers or a combination of lending and leasing to customers.

Source: Business Monitor M13; Consumer Credit Grantors. The data for net acquisitions of assets cannot be used to extrapolate into current figures due to the different numbers of finance houses reporting in different quarters

Table 4.7 Balance sheet of finance houses and other consumer credit companies* at end of 1976

(a) Assets

	Amounts outstanding at book values	
Assets	£m	%
Cash in hand and deposits with UK banking sector	137 ⎫	
Other current assets in the UK	73 ⎭	7.2
Loans and advances to UK residents:		
Direct agreements	1,769 ⎫	
Agreements block discounted by UK financial institutions and retailers	22 ⎬	77.0
Other loans and advances	436 ⎭	
Company securities	66 ⎫	
Public sector securities and other financial assets	132 ⎭	6.9
Real assets in the UK for leasing, hiring or renting to customers	216 ⎫	
Real assets in the UK for own use	40 ⎭	8.9
Total assets	2,891	100.0

(b) Liabilities

	Amounts out-standing at book values	
	£m	%
Liabilities		
Deposits by:		
Banking sector	313 ⎫	
Other financial institutions	68 ⎪	
Industrial and commercial companies	250 ⎬	28.2
Other UK residents	132 ⎪	
Overseas residents	52 ⎭	
Instalment credit agreements discounted with UK banking sector and other financial institutions	13 ⎫	
Commercial bills	167 ⎪	
Other borrowing from UK banking sector	435 ⎪	
Other short term borrowing	177 ⎬	52.2
Other medium and long-term borrowing	280 ⎪	
Unearned credit charges	266 ⎪	
Other credit liabilities in the UK	170 ⎭	
Issued capital	189 ⎫	
Reserves and provisions and other liabilities	⎬	19.6
overseas	379 ⎭	
Total liabilities	2,891	100.0

*Consumer credit granting companies whose main business was lending to customers or a combination of lending and leasing to customers.
Source: Business Monitor M13; Consumer Credit Grantors

consumer credit companies from the 1976 survey. The table relates to a total of 496 companies in existence at the end of 1976. Loans and advances to UK residents is by far the largest asset item, accounting for 77 per cent of total assets. The source of funds is illustrated by reference to the liabilities section of the balance sheet which indicates that 28 per cent of total liabilities were held in the form of deposits, with the banks and business contributing most. However, deposits are decreasing in importance as a source of funds as the finance houses borrow from the banks and other sources and continue to plough back profits into their business.

The representative body for these institutions is the Finance Houses Association (FHA) which was set up in 1945 and had a membership of forty in 1980. As well as ensuring a code of prudent financial behaviour, the FHA collects statistics and in recent years has begun to calculate on the last day of each month a finance houses base rate, which is the average of the three month sterling inter-bank rate over the preceding eight weeks. The three month rate is chosen because the majority of finance house deposits are of a similar duration. The object of this exercise is to provide a bench-mark for the calculation of charges to customers on variable rate agreements.

The finance houses are not governed by any special legislation and do not benefit from any special tax arrangements, unlike some of the non-bank institutions discussed in Chapter 2. Nevertheless, most are required to become licensed deposit takers under the 1979 Banking Act. Furthermore those which are listed banks were required to maintain the 12½ per cent reserve asset ratio and were subject to other controls such as the supplementary special deposits scheme. Besides the listed houses there are eight others which had agreed to maintain 10 per cent reserve ratios and were also subject to the supplementary special deposits scheme until its suspension in June 1980. It is anticipated that the finance houses will be influenced by the Bank of England's intended guidelines on capital adequacy and liquidity in the near future.

One particular problem faced by the finance houses is the squeeze imposed by the period of high and volatile interest rates which began in 1979. The fixed-rate business written by finance houses before this period in many cases proved to be unprofitable. Subsequent business has, where possible, built the high level of money costs into the interest charges applied for particular lines of credit. This has been achieved by indexing interest charges to the finance houses base rate in order to maintain profit margins. Some 30 per cent of their total business was linked in this way in 1981. Another important problem they face is the impact of government policy upon the nature of their operations. In particular the statutory maximum repayment period for most instalment credit had stood at twenty-four months for a substantial period. This serves to constrain the business of finance houses as inflationary product prices require heavier deposits from persons who operate a self imposed credit limit according to their income. It is particulary important in times of recession that governments should be aware of the impact of credit repayment limits upon the demand for credit finance from both consumers and industry.

Many finance houses provide a wide range of auxiliary banking services but fail to become 'recognized' banks under the 1979 Act due to their limited foreign currency dealings. The houses are therefore classified as licensed deposit takers and this serves to be the essential distinction between themselves and the banks. Nevertheless they introduced leasing and factoring in the UK and are well established as major sources of funds to commerce and industry.

6 Discount houses

The discount houses play a more specialized role in the financial system compared with the banks although they are all recognized banks under the

1979 Act. Essentially they are financial institutions which operate only in the City to provide secondary markets in particular liquid financial instruments. Since the First World War, they have tended to concentrate heavily on the market for Treasury bills. These are issued weekly by the Treasury in order to finance the deficiencies in the Government's expenditure programme. As the bills are utilized as a stop gap between the making of expenditures and the receipt of income they are short-term, with the Treasury promising to pay the holder the full value in ninety-one days.

The discount houses began by discounting bills in the early nineteenth century when most lending took the form of discounting bills. At that time they were merely brokers in commercial bills for the banks. So for example if a bank had lent to its full capacity, then rather than turn a customer away they would pass the bill on to the discount market where the brokers would find a willing lender. The role of the houses was to find institutions with surplus cash and to pass on the commercial bills to be purchased at a discount, taking a small return for conducting this intermediary function.

The discount market can properly be regarded as the eleven members of the London Discount Market Association (LDMA) and two discount brokers, though some discounting is also undertaken by banks in London through their money trading departments. Collectively this is known as the 'money market' because it is the most liquid market in the City, dealing mainly with cash which is exchanged for discounted bills or lent overnight between banks in the inter-bank market, or between banks and other members of the market. The existence of the discount market complicates the operation of the British financial system but is deliberately maintained by the monetary authorities because it provides a ready source of liquidity to financial institutions holding bills and also because it is administratively easier for the Bank of England to influence conditions in the money market via these few institutions than trying to influence directly every bank in the country.

An understanding of the operation of the discount market is critical to grasping the way in which monetary policies operate in this country. However, this is one case where a snapshot of the balance sheet of the institution may not be as revealing as one would like. The reason is that as economic conditions change the asset portfolio of the discount houses can alter radically. Furthermore, as one of their principal functions is to make markets in a variety of financial instruments the content of the portfolio is rarely consistent for more than a few years. Nevertheless, it is generally the case that about 75 per cent of their assets are held as different forms of bills. These range from UK and Northern Ireland Treasury bills to local authority and commercial bills. The remaining assets are composed of short dated stocks and occasional short-term loans.

The liability side of the discount houses balance sheet is more revealing. Approximately 70 per cent of their sterling liabilities are held in the form of money 'at call' from the banks. This is money which is borrowed from the banks to purchase bills and should the banks require cash they merely call the appropriate amount from the discount houses. Money at call is therefore a valuable reserve asset to the banks because it yields a return while providing an assured fund of liquidity. However, the question immediately arises as to what would happen if the discount houses did not have the cash when it was called. The outcome would be that they would sell some of their bills at a further discount to obtain the cash required by the banking system.

It is in this context that the Bank of England's role as lender of last resort comes into focus. For the Bank regularly re-discounts bills for the discount houses. Until August 1981, when the Minimum Lending Rate (MLR) ceased to be posted regularly by the Bank, MLR was the rediscount rate. Thus, not only did the Bank maintain or deny liquidity to the commercial banks via its operations through the discount market, but it also influenced the rates of interest in the money market by varying the rate at which it chose to discount first class bills of exchange (MLR).

Obviously, the rate at which the Bank discounted bills for the discount houses would in turn influence the terms on call money from the banks so that a mechanism existed for the transmission of interest rate changes. Since 1981 the number of institutions eligible for discounting bills with the Bank has been widened substantially, in line with the new policy of conducting open market operations to influence the pattern and direction of interest rates. As a result, financial observers have shifted their focus of attention away from MLR towards the clearing banks' base rates in much the same way as 'prime' lending rates are closely observed in the USA.

In return for acting as lender of last resort the Bank traditionally required the members of the LDMA to underwrite the weekly issue of Treasury bills. Presently, they agree to cover the tender. This means that they agree to take up the excess Treasury bills on offer each week, a method of guaranteeing the funding of short-term Government deficits. After the policy of Competition and Credit Control in 1971 the MLR was determined directly by the terms of the bid made by the discount houses in the weekly tender. Since the re-discount rate was determined naturally by reference to the original rate at which the bills were tendered then the weekly bid would influence the MLR. In practice however, although the MLR was thought by many to be market determined the Treasury could still determine MLR by varying conditions in the market for Treasury bills. This the monetary authorities did by bringing pressure on the houses to bid one way or the other and by varying the supply of bills.

The bill tender no longer determined MLR from 1972 to 1978 but the authorities maintained control over this rate and occasionally imposed restrictions on outsiders bidding for Treasury bills. The Bank also deliberately created shortages of cash in the money market when it thought fit. By issuing an excess of Treasury bills, the Bank effectively squeezed the market of cash, since the houses must borrow more call money from the banks to purchase the bills. This effectively put pressure on interest rates to rise. However in this context the houses also provide a useful function for the banking system since they are, as we shall see, the only institutions able to create reserve assets for the banking system. Their liabilities are the reserve assets of the banking system, so that by increasing their borrowing from the banks they will automatically create extra reserve assets. Since lending by the banks is linked to reserve assets by a ratio, then bank lending may increase as a result. Conversely, if cash were in plentiful supply (i.e. the supply of cash exceeded the demand for Treasury bills) then the discount houses need to borrow less from the banks who then sustain a fall in reserve assets.

These must either then be replaced with a substitute reserve asset or lending must contract to maintain the correct ratio. It was not uncommon in the 1970s for the authorities to maintain a particular MLR consistent with a policy of squeeze or injection only to see money market conditions react differently as funds were shunted between the different institutions in response to outside influences and opportunities. Indeed, in early 1980, with MLR at 17 per cent, money market rates were occasionally well below this level, which indicated that cash was not in short supply and confirmed that MLR was not market determined at that time. The reason for this disparity in interest rates was that the monetary squeeze relied upon a general unwillingness to borrow at high rates of interest (which was in fact the objective of government policy in order to reduce the supply of money).

It is obvious from the foregoing that the discount houses play an important and complex role in the conduct of monetary policy in the UK. They have also been crucial to the development in the market for certain liquid financial instruments. The best example is the market in sterling Certificates of Deposit (CDs) which the houses successfully helped to inaugurate in October, 1968. Accordingly, the discount houses hold a certain amount of CDs in their asset portfolio in order to trade in those financial assets. Other elements of their asset portfolio are short-dated government stocks (between one and five years' maturity) and local authority bonds. Although these financial instruments would not count as reserve assets to the banks, the cash borrowed by the discount houses to purchase these instruments (call money) is a reserve asset. It was in response to the ability of the discount houses to create them, *inter alia*, that a general disenchantment with the system of reserve assets developed throughout the previous decade and led to a new initiative in monetary control, described later.

The holding of longer-dated assets such as government stocks of five years' maturity poses a particular problem to the houses. Because of the increasing volatility of interest rates throughout the 1970s it became imperative that the discount houses anticipate future interest rate movements. If government stock is issued at a particular premium and interest rates rise immediately after, then the price of those stocks will fall and the fall in price will manifest itself in the form of a capital loss to the holder. As a result the houses may occasionally sustain losses. This occurred in November 1979 when the houses expected a reduction in interest rates only to find MLR raised from 14 per cent to 17 per cent! The effect was heavy losses sustained by the discount houses.

Of course, the sustaining of a loss is important to any institution but may be particularly harsh for a discount house. The size of the houses' capital base (i.e. capital plus reserves) determines the size of the portfolio they may hold. In their case the Bank of England regards the ratio of 30:1 of total borrowing to capital and reserves as the maximum acceptable. So any reduction in the capital base has a thirty times greater impact on total activity. Furthermore, the houses are only allowed a ratio of 20:1 of private sector assets to capital and reserves. The latter discourages private sector business replacing public sector business, even though the former may at times be more profitable, so reinforcing the houses' primary role as the financers of the Government's weekly expenditures. These considerations illustrate the magnified importance of a loss upon the total activity of the discount houses. The only respite from this effect is for them to raise new equity, but this will depend upon the state of the stock market at the time, as the discount house Smith St. Aubyn discovered in 1982.

Because of the obvious drawbacks inherent in adopting their somewhat restricted role the discount houses have attempted to extend their activities. They have done this by creating markets in new financial instruments with the Eurodollar Certificate of Deposit and the inter-bank market being recent examples. Some of the houses have also extended their activity into fund management, though as we have seen there is fierce competition in that field. However, there may be a temporary reprieve brought about by the inauguration of variable rate government stocks. This financial instrument offers a rate which is linked to the yield on Treasury bills so reducing the likelihood of sustaining capital losses on government stocks and this may serve to remove a particular thorn in the side of the discount houses.

On the whole, the discount houses still play an important part in the UK's financial system, facilitating the transmission of liquid financial instruments in the City. The following chapter will occasionally refer to the issue of Treasury bills and the creation of reserve assets as monetary policy is conducted. From the foregoing, it is obvious that the system of monetary control will naturally impinge upon the operations of the discount market. An appraisal of the policies and procedures adopted by respective governments throughout the 1970s in the following chapter will serve to illustrate how the financial system has responded to the different economic philosophies concerning the role of the money supply and the conduct of monetary policy. Whatever philosophy is upheld, the repercussions fall heavily upon the discount houses. The most interesting and recent development of re-asserting open market operations as the conventional tool of monetary policy and the restoration of the lender of last resort facility as a true measure of last resort have not diminished the importance of the houses, as we shall see.

Summary and conclusions

In this chapter we have distinguished between the different types of bank which exist in the UK and certain other important financial institutions which specialize in lines of credit (finance houses) and those crucial to the efficient operation of the money markets (discount houses). The feature shared by all of these financial institutions is that their liabilities are considered to be the most liquid in the range of financial instruments and thereby comprise the several operational definitions of money adopted for the purposes of monetary and financial policy. It is undoubtedly true that changing government policy has had a profound impact upon their operation and it has been argued, most forcefully by the banks themselves, that this has constrained their ability to compete for funds with other financial intermediaries.

The last decade, in particular, has witnessed a shifting emphasis in the conduct of monetary policy, from interest rates to the money supply. This process has not been smooth and the effect has been to create an increasingly volatile financial climate. The new monetary regime, inaugurated in August 1981, was the result of a decade of rapid inflation and a change in the focus of economic policies to this major problem. The economic philosophy of monetarism had a crucial role to play in the application of monetary policy after 1979. The concept of monetarism is dealt with in Part Two; in the meantime the following chapter considers the practical changes which took place in the 1970s and assesses their consequences upon the banking and non-banking intermediaries.

Topics

1 What is meant by liquidity and why does a commercial bank need it? How and to what extent does a commercial bank provide for liquidity in the use it makes of the deposits lodged with it? (IOB Monetary Theory and Practice. September 1979.)
2 Discuss the operation of the market for Treasury bills. What does a decline in the discount rate on these and commercial bills signify?

3 Examine the impact upon finance houses of a simultaneous increase in the size of deposit necessary to obtain hire purchase and a rise in the sterling inter-bank rate.

4 Describe the differences between commercial and merchant banks and between retail and wholesale deposits.

5 Discuss the term 'capital adequacy' and explain its importance in maintaining confidence in banking.

5 Monetary policy and control of the money supply

1 Monetary policy in the 1970s: Introduction

The past decade has seen a succession of different approaches to the conduct of monetary policy. Although later chapters will examine the theoretical bases of the different policy approaches, it is preferable at this stage to consider the ramifications of the different methods upon the financial system and examine their success.

Our starting point is 1971 when the policy of Competition and Credit Control (CCC) was introduced by the Heath Administration. Before that date there had existed a combination of hire purchase controls (which had officially existed since January 1952), other direct controls upon the credit extended by banking and non-banking institutions, and variations in interest rates. The latter operated through the Bank Rate which preceded MLR. The obvious problem associated with the conduct of what Gowland (1978) has properly called 'financial' rather than monetary policy was that the transmission of credit was not fully explored and, as the Radcliffe Committee (1959) pointed out, certainly not fully understood. Furthermore, the increasing problems resulting from the use of sterling as an international reserve currency implied a dependence of interest rates on international pressures sufficient to occasionally disrupt interest rate policy.

Before 1971, the conduct of 'financial' policy was not directed specifically towards monetary targets. Such a policy was the outcome of several factors during the 1970s which convinced a later Conservative Government that the money supply was a deterministic variable rather than a mere indicator. The actual tools of financial policy prior to CCC were fairly simple. Often the authorities would issue directives to the banking system to tighten credit or to extend lending to particular quarters. Thus the actual lending policy of the banks was influenced by the Bank of England whereas, during the 1970s, the emphasis was placed upon creating the conditions to make certain decisions uneconomic as an indirect form of control. The ultimate sanctions were, and still are, the Bank's control over interest rates (directly or again indirectly), the definition of assets which constitute liquidity, and bankers' deposits with the Bank of England. These sanctions have of course been reinforced by the recent legislation which affords the authorities the discretion not to recognize a bank or disallow the discounting of bills if necessary.

It was the conduct of 'financial' policy which caused a credit squeeze between 1956 and 1958. The unpopularity of this squeeze, plus the unanticipated ramifications in many sectors, led to the setting up of the Radcliffe Committee. Partly as a result of the Committee's findings, monetary policy was extended to non-clearing banks and finance houses in order to spread the burden of the policy more evenly. So the major distinction between monetary policy in the 1960s compared to the 1950s was the base upon which it was constructed. The methods of interest rate variations, (which effectively began in 1951 when the Bank Rate was raised for the first time since 1932), and a combination of direct controls were common to both decades but in the 1960s the targets to which the policy was applied were refined. This laid the foundation for the preoccupation with monetary control *in toto* which became fashionable with economists in the late sixties and politicians a decade later. A battery of ceilings on bank lending and requests by the Bank of England existed in the late 1960s, so also did an ambitious monetary indicator, Domestic Credit Expansion (DCE) which was introduced more or less forcibly into the UK monetary vocabulary by a 'letter of intent' given to the International Monetary Fund in 1968[1].

There had existed for some time constraints upon bank lending which were similar to those adopted in the 1971 policy when the now abandoned reserve assets system of monetary control was introduced. These were called the 'cash ratio' and 'liquidity ratio' which could be varied by the Bank of England. They acted as constraints upon lending by the clearing banks by requiring them to maintain 8 per cent of their assets in the form of cash and balances at the Bank of England and 30 per cent in the form of specified liquid assets, though the latter was lowered to 28 per cent in 1963. Since a loan is an asset to a bank (and a liability to the borrower) then any measures which insist that a certain proportion of assets must be held in specified form act as a constraint upon bank lending since they restrict the proportion of assets which may be held in the form of loans.

Throughout the 1970s monetary policy had been implemented primarily through the 'reserve asset' system which operated upon the supply of bank credit by influencing the banks' ability to lend. During the decade, interest rate variations had also been used to influence the demand for credit and the marginal return from holding particular assets by the banks. Consequently, policy had a supply side bias with occasional (and sometimes

---

1 DCE is the public sector borrowing requirement plus the change in bank lending to the private sector minus changes in private sector lending to the Government. Effectively it is a method of measuring most of the increase in the money supply after adjustments for inflows and outflows on the current account of the balance of payments. A limit upon DCE was the price the UK had to pay for loans from the IMF.

inconsistent) demand side manipulation. This delicate tuning operation was carried out to achieve a rate of credit expansion consistent with government objectives. In the late-1970s, the process continued and the money supply became the primary objective of monetary/financial policy, for reasons to be discussed later. In March 1980, the Bank of England issued a discussion document which sought to refine the measurement of liquidity in the UK in response to the apparent failure of existing monetary controls and in anticipation of the future difficulty of controlling the supply of money as banks and other financial institutions began increasingly to internationalize their operations[2]. An important aspect of the paper was that the reserve asset ratio was to be removed as the central weapon in the armoury of monetary controls. Before reviewing the implications of the paper and the resultant methods of monetary policy in the 1980s it is necessary to spell out the earlier measures introduced in 1971 and experience during the decade 1970–1980.

2 Competition and Credit Control

In 1971 the CCC policy attempted to encourage a more competitive situation in the financial sector. The philosophy was that by encouraging freer competition the authorities could influence the monetary aggregates through manipulating interest rates. This was stated by the Bank in 1978[3]. The money supply was adopted as an indicator of the effectiveness of monetary policy but did not assume a central role until December 1976 when the IMF made the introduction of limits on DCE (which is a major factor in determining changes in the money supply) a precondition for a loan of $3.9 billion. Lewis (1980) has called the 1971 policy the second rediscovery of interest rates (the first was in 1951).

However the CCC policy went further than re-asserting interest rates as the fulcrum of monetary policy by defining reserve assets and applying them to non-clearing banks and finance houses. Special deposits were also extended to these institutions. It drew upon the same basic techniques but extended the means of monetary action to other financial institutions (but not all). Nevertheless, the main problem with the application of monetary policy during the 1970s was still the difficulty in drawing the line when

---

2 In fact three papers were presented that year, one of which was the Green Paper, 'The Measurement of Liquidity', Bank of England, March 1980. It was the Radcliffe Committee which first introduced the concept of liquidity into the language of monetary policy. D. Gowland has defined liquidity as 'a weighted average of all assets in the economy with weights declining as assets become less liquid', *Monetary Policy and Credit Control*, p. 5, Croome Helm, London, 1978.

3 'Reflections on the Conduct of Monetary Policy', Mais Lecture, *Bank of England Quarterly Bulletin*, March 1978.

measuring money, a problem to be discussed in Chapter 7 and which assumed major importance as a direct result of the growth of the non-banking intermediaries.

According to Lewis, 'Because of its position, about halfway along the liquidity scale, sterling M3 is supposed to indicate how well the system as a whole is responding to the monetary controls'. (p. 45) Obviously the definition of the broadly defined money supply (M3) is crucial in the monitoring of the impact of monetary policy. If the measures are ineffective then the money supply will not react. If the money supply is inappropriately defined the whole basis of policy disintegrates. This is why so much attention is devoted to the definition of money in Chapter 6.

The arguments in favour of strengthening competition in financial markets were strong. The Governor of the Bank of England pointed out in 1971 that the battery of lending ceilings and other forms of direct control often led to a misallocation of resources[4]. Furthermore the authorities were not convinced that the existing methods could control credit in a financial system experiencing a metamorphosis. The Radcliffe Committee had presented the 'balloon' argument as the reasoning behind its call for control over a wider spectrum of liquidity. The argument follows the reasoning that if the authorities impose controls to restrict some areas of banking activity then other areas will expand to compensate. The argument was later extended to mean also that if the banks *in toto* were restrained in their lending activity then the non-banks would merely expand and frustrate government policy.

If a bank or other financial institution takes measures to evade the restrictions imposed by the authorities the effect is known as 'disintermediation'. That is, if a particular aspect of intermediation, say to finance house purchase, is taxed by the authorities, then to avoid the tax the banks will merely divert resources away from this area of activity to another. Similarly 'parallel, markets imply the same intermediary function being fulfilled by a different middleman. This occurs when a particular type of intermediary function is squeezed by action undertaken by the authorities in their pursuit of the objectives of monetary policy.

For example, if bank lending is squeezed and company liquidity is high then companies may lend direct to each other. This is called the inter-corporate money market and is a prime example of 'disintermediation', where the middleman is missed out. So far as 'parallel markets' are concerned it is quite possible that by restricting lending for certain purposes, say to property companies, that other non-controlled institutions may undertake the function instead. Indeed this occurred when insurance companies became willing to invest in property companies when the banks' lending to such companies was discouraged in August 1972.

---

4 'Key Issues in Monetary and Credit Policy', Governor's Address, the International Banking Conference, Munich, May 1971.

The existence of 'disintermediation' and 'parallel markets' was proof of the Radcliffe balloon argument. It was also proof, as far as the authorities were concerned, of the inability of the 1960s regime of credit control to fulfil its function. Since selective credit controls were considered to be at best ineffective and at worst impediments to an effective monetary policy, the philosophy of *laissez-faire* seemed most appropriate at the time. The authorities could influence credit by operating on its price (the rate of interest) in order to make it uneconomic for bank and non-bank intermediaries to undertake action contrary to that which was consistent with stated monetary policy. The monetary measures which operated in the early 1970s as indicators of the effectiveness of policy were not extended to include the funds of the non-bank intermediaries. It was assumed that market forces would operate upon their lending if policy were applied in a non-discriminatory fashion.

The traditional tools of bank rate (MLR) and the supply of Treasury bills were the focus of policy throughout the 1970s as a result of the introduction of the policy of CCC. The importance of the Treasury bill tender was ensured by the introduction of specific reserve asset ratios in the CCC policy. For example, all banks were required to adhere to a 12½ per cent minimum reserve asset ratio[5].

At the same time discount houses were required to conform to a 50 per cent public sector lending ratio. The reason for these measures was to strengthen the authorities' control over interest rates and asset movements in order to influence the flow of money and credit. Special deposits also played an important part in the new approach to monetary policy. The clearing banks alone were required to maintain an average balance of 1½ per cent of eligible liabilities with the Bank of England, which qualified as reserve assets but bore no interest. In effect this was part of their 'till money'. However the banks were also liable to calls for special deposits by the Bank of England which were excluded from reserve assets. Such calls were usually expressed as a percentage of 'eligible liabilities'. These were deposits made by a bank with the Bank of England and influenced reserve assets because a call for a certain increase in special deposits would replace the same amount of reserve assets. Since special deposits were not classified as reserve assets, bank lending would be restricted, (or more correctly the asset portfolio of the banks would more appropriately reflect the position consistent with the interest rates the authorities were seeking to achieve). Unlike bankers' balances at the Bank of England, special deposits yielded a rate of interest equal to that prevailing on Treasury bills.

Eligible liabilities were also the yard-stick by which the 12½ per cent reserve asset ratio was to be measured. Strictly, 'eligible liabilities' are those sterling deposits of less than two years maturity less interbank

5 This was reduced to 10 per cent in January 1981.

lending and non-callable loans to discount houses plus the excess of sterling CDs issued over those held. Foreign currency deposits only come into play if they are converted into sterling. Of course certain amendments were made to the basic ingredients of the CCC policy in the light of experience throughout the last decade. For example, in August 1972 lending priorities were again subject to official guidance. Between September 1973 and February 1975 banks were required to pay an interest rate of no more than 9½ per cent on deposits exceeding £10,000 which was the British equivalent to the American regulation 'Q'. Also, in 1973, the definition of reserve assets was marginally altered. Modifications were made to the discount house ratio after the authorities discovered that the banks and the discount houses were exchanging Treasury bills and CDs for call money just before the banking Wednesday when the minima had to be observed. If, on the day before the banking Wednesday, both the banks and the discount houses held reserve asset and public sector lending ratios below the required minima of 12½ and 50 per cent respectively, then by exchanging reserve assets for call money the banks and discount houses could ensure that they conformed to the reserve requirements. They could return to their previous trading positions immediately after the authorities have made their check. This exercise was called 'window dressing' by some observers; in fact it was quite a legitimate transaction between the banks and the discount houses. The 1973 amendments removed the single ratio to be maintained by the discount houses but brought in the 20 times multiple. Nevertheless, this did not stem the ability of the banks to create reserve assets at will since the banks could still swop CD's for call money and increase their reserve assets. In fact various permutations of swop arrangements were possible by which the banks could create reserve assets with no penalizing effect on discount house operations.

The policy of CCC also ushered in a new formal relationship between the London discount market and the Bank of England and a disbanding of the clearing bank cartel arrangements on interest rates. The latter arrangement had existed since the 1930s and was an agreement between the banks to charge equivalent rates of interest to customers (base lending rates) and pay equivalent rates to depositors. It was consistent with the spirit of the new policy that such monopolistic arrangements should be dismantled. Accordingly since 1971, instead of uniformly declared base lending and deposit rates, the banks altered their rates independently after MLR varied. At the same time the members of the LDMA agreed to 'cover' the full tender of Treasury bills each Friday.

Although the discount market was still the vehicle for providing government finance and therefore providing the means through which open market operations could be conducted, the role of the inter-bank overnight market was boosted by the 1971 policy. The function of this market is to provide funds to the banks who may experience temporary short-falls in their day-to-day operations. The supply of funds to the overnight market depends upon the corporate sector and the monetary authorities. Sometimes the placing of funds in the overnight market can earn a seemingly ridiculous yield. For example in November 1967, after the devaluation, the rate on over-night money reached 1,256 per cent per annum! Although this was an unique occasion, a rate approaching 200 per cent per annum was not unusual in the overnight inter-bank market. The supply of funds will be increased if a company has accumulated liquidity on a temporary basis and expects to have to pay the money out to creditors in the near future when it may place the funds on overnight deposit. Obviously when the corporate sector is short of liquidity the supply of funds will be scarce. Similarly, the monetary authorities may experience a temporary glut of funds, for example when tax payments have recently been made and certain expenditures are about to be made in the near future.

Because of the uncertainty attached to the supply of funds in this extremely short-term market, the range of interest rates is quite wide. Consequently the market attracts speculators, especially in foreign exchange, when converting from one currency to another and then back again may provide a large yield if the initial currency depreciates in the interim. From the viewpoint of monetary control, the overnight inter-bank market provides a useful mechanism by which the authorities may penalize the banks who run short of cash. By imposing a stiffer penalty the authorities encourage the banks to hold more reserves. The stiffer penalty is expressed in the form of a high interest rate in the market which the authorities can create by depriving the market of funds. The market also influences the value of sterling and the authorities can also affect this, again by varying the supply of funds. However, the conduct of international monetary policy is beyond the scope of the present discussion.

Experience since 1971

The period 1971–1973 saw the testing of the new policy and its final abandonment in the face of an explosion in the money supply. An excessive Public Sector Borrowing Requirement (PSBR) and falling interest rates combined, *inter alia*, to create an inflationary climate which was compatible with the Government's objective of reducing unemployment by stimulating demand at the time. The Barber Budget of 1972 was important in that it represented the authorities' reaction to the increasing money supply. Gowland (1978) has emphasized this point

'The authorities' reaction to this development [*the accelerating money supply*] would obviously be crucial. It is difficult not to believe that this was the period when the authorities lost control of the situation. The authorities were so worried about unemployment that they decided not to act, in fact to encourage the trend'. (p. 48)

The cost of borrowing and taxation were cut in the budget with the PSBR expected to increase by 200 per cent over the next year. The result was an increase in borrowing by the private sector, particularly by property and financial concerns. The inflationary budget deficit was not offset by the purchases of gilt-edged stock by the non-bank private sector. In effect the Government was injecting funds into the economy (and the financial system) and reducing the means by which it would normally 'mop up' the excess funds of the private sector. Money and credit were thus in plentiful supply, their price was low and a demand explosion was triggered. The failure of the policy was not only its unwarranted extremity but also the naivety with which the authorities assumed that funds would be diverted to those areas were employment would be created. In fact this was not the case and it was recognized by the Governor of the Bank who circulated a letter throughout the banking system outlining lending priorities and asking that credit extended to property companies be curtailed. However, funds were merely diverted into lending to other financial companies who then 'on lent' to the property sector. The expansionist policy also sucked extra imports into the country, creating balance of payments problems and weakening the currency. The floating of the exchange rate in June 1972 allowed the value of the currency to reflect the economic situation. The result was an effective devaluation of sterling by over 6 per cent in one month. The impact of such a devaluation is of course to increase the cost of imported raw materials, thus stoking inflation. No effort was made in the early stages by the authorities to use interest rates to control the flow of credit.

Nevertheless, the authorities' commitment to the philosophy of market-determined interest rates was confirmed in October 1972 when Minimum Lending Rate officially replaced Bank Rate. The MLR was determined by a formula, i.e. the average rate of discount on Treasury bills plus $\frac{1}{2}$ per cent rounded up to the nearest $\frac{1}{4}$ per cent. The discount house tender would influence the average and the $\frac{1}{2}$ per cent was the penalty element determining the rate at which the bank would 're-discount' the bills. In practice, however, although seemingly market-determined, the authorities still influenced the rate by signalling to the discount market and always reserved the right to override the formula in any case.

During the early 1970s in the increasingly uncertain economic climate, there was much uncertainty and often frenzied debate concerning the meaning of monetary aggregates. As we shall see later, the money supply can be measured in various ways according to one's view of the role of money and the measurement of credit. Just as disintermediation occurs when depositors and borrowers begin to do business with one another, then the reversal of this process may be called reintermediation. At that time the new order meant that much of the activity which had taken place outside the banking system had re-entered the system with the removal of ceiling controls. The result was a worrying distortion of monetary aggregates, a factor which was to recur in the late summer of 1980 and again in 1981, creating a painful setback to government policy.

Towards the end of 1972, interest rates began to rise steadily as the Government sought to control the money supply, though in this case one of the main effects was to inflate the wider definition of money (M3) compared with its narrowly defined counterpart (M1)[6]. A contributing factor was that the higher interest rates encouraged persons to switch their funds out of the non-interest bearing current accounts into the interest bearing deposit accounts. Because the latter are not included in the narrow definition (M1) the two measures departed from each other. In fact M3 had increased by 21.8 per cent in 1972 and 27.1 per cent in 1973. The outcome was a succession of steep increases in MLR to 13 per cent in November 1973 and an abandonment of part of the CCC policy in December. It was replaced by the Supplementary Special Scheme (sometimes called the 'corset'). The outstanding feature of this new approach to controlling money and credit is that it operated a ceiling on bank liabilities (IBELs), whereas before 1971 *lending* ceilings operated on assets. This was the first evidence of an inclination by the authorities to control the supply of rather than the demand for money.

The 'corset' was a restriction placed upon expansion in the interest bearing component of eligible liabilities, (IBELs). The authorities would determine an average level of IBELs covering the make-up days for the preceding six months and impose a growth limit for those bank liabilities in percentage terms (initially 8 per cent in 1974)[7]. If that growth limit were exceeded then the banks were to be penalized in the form of having to deposit a variable percentage of the excess with the Bank of England, interest-free. As the excess increased so would the amount to be deposited with the Bank, rather like taxation scales. In fact this is how the scheme operated, it was a tax upon banking. The scheme was operated initially until February 1975, then re-introduced from November 1976 to August 1977, and introduced for the third time in June 1978 until August 1980. One of the intended effects of the corset was to lower the rate on 'wholesale' deposits because the listed banks would be unwilling to bid for further deposits once they had reached their growth limit.

The imposition of the corset encouraged disintermediation. For example if the banks are unwilling to bid for wholesale deposits then other borrowers, say local authorities, may borrow more cheaply direct from corporate depositors than if they had to borrow from the banks. Government policy is seen to be effective whereas the lending to and spending by local authorities still takes place. In this case the corset exercise is merely

6 See Stevenson and Trevithick (1977) and also K. W. Wilson (1977).
7 Make-up days refer to the third Wednesday in every month (excluding December), when banking statistics are collected.

cosmetic. The only restrictive effect of causing this disintermediation will be if local authorities' deposits lack some multiplier quality which can only be attributed to bank deposits.

The failure of CCC cannot be attributed solely to the inappropriateness of applying a competitive philosophy to an imperfectly competitive financial system. It was the unwillingness of the monetary authorities to witness the repercussions of the proper conduct of the policy that proved its downfall. The CCC policy implied greater variations in interest rates in the economy with occasional sharp rises to influence the level of intermediary activity (bank and non-banking). The authorities were unwilling to let this happen at that time because of the economic uncertainty and social discontent it would create, plus the attendant problems of financing government borrowing under such circumstances. One of the most important offsets to increased bank lending to the private sector (which adds to the money supply) is the sale of gilt-edged stock by the Government to that sector. However, in an environment of uncertain interest rates the sale of fixed interest securities is always more difficult. Moreover, if interest rates are expected to rise then the problem is compounded, for the sale of fixed interest stocks is always problematic when the prospective purchaser expects interest rates to rise in the near future. The answer to these problems was either largely to abandon the policy of CCC, which was chosen, or to consider alternative means of financing government expenditure. The Wilson Committee (1980) recognized this

'. . . the present system for issuing gilt-edged securities is widely regarded as unsatisfactory, and the innovations of recent years have not gone far enough towards easing the problems of selling large amounts of government debt against a background of continual uncertainty'. (p. 183)

It can be argued that until the authorities develop a system of funding public sector deficits in such a way that it will not frustrate the conduct of monetary policy, no effective system of monetary control can be maintained in the long run. The Wilson Committee recommended that consideration ought to be given to developing an efficient market for the sale of government stocks as a precursor to a new system of monetary control.

3 Monetary targets and monetary control

The practice of announcing targets for the money supply began in December 1976, although the bank had adopted the money supply as an indicator of the efficiency of monetary policy throughout the 1970s. This nevertheless demonstrated a shift in the focus of policy. The Radcliffe Committee had emphasized the importance of interest rates in influencing the demand for liquidity and subsequent expenditure. Almost twenty years later the emphasis had shifted to the control of monetary aggregates.

The monetary aggregates chosen and declared publicly as targets are usually M1 (notes and coin in circulation with the public, plus private sector sterling sight deposits with banks), and sterling M3 (M1 plus other sterling deposits of UK residents with the banks). It is possible however, to include an indefinite number of financial instruments and widen the definition accordingly. Indeed, an addendum to the Wilson Committee Report insisted that this was the greatest weakness of the policy of monetary targets

'The fundamental problem with monetary targets from which most of the other difficulties stem is that there is no general agreement on what money is. Indeed two features of the financial system which were stressed in evidence to us were first that different financial assets are viewed as close substitutes for one another [for example, building society deposits and bank deposits, or Treasury bills and certificates of deposit], and secondly that the financial institutions are constantly changing and adapting their behaviour and creating new forms of financial asset'. (para. 1417, p. 375)

Clearly, some members of the Committee held reservations concerning the applicability of a rigid monetary policy to a metamorphic financial system.

Indeed, in deference to this viewpoint, the Bank of England has provided information concerning the components of private sector liquidity since September 1979 and an explanatory article appears in that month's issue of the *Quarterly Bulletin*. The information, which is designed to supplement the money stock measures, shows two measures of private sector liquidity, PSL1 and PSL2. The former includes the private sector component of sterling M3 plus other market instruments and certificates of tax deposit. The second measure, PSL2, is a wider measure incorporating PSL1 and building society shares and deposits and other liquid financial instruments. The Bank has estimated the quarterly data going as far back as 1963. Although this goes some way towards identifying the changes in total liquidity which take place within the economy, no effort to date has been made to elevate the liquidity measures to policy targets.

Setting a target for the money supply involves the publicizing of concomitant public expenditure targets. As will be seen by reference to the exposition of the mechanics of the money supply in Part Two, the Public Sector Borrowing Requirement (PSBR) is an important determinant of the supply of money. Indeed it is true that PSBR targets preceded money supply targets, which were initially forecasted as an expected growth rate in percentage terms, consequent upon reductions in the PSBR.

However there is no doubt that in the early 1980s the money supply was the prime target variable.

The target is usually stated as a range, reflecting the responsiveness of the money supply to factors which are outside the control of the authorities plus the uncertainty concerning the magnitude of the impact of certain policy instruments. The wider definition of money, £M3, is usually the target variable stated publicly by the Chancellor. The authorities soon abandoned the procedure of maintaining a publicly declared target for a year when in 1977/78 the growth in £M3 was 16½ per cent while the target range was 9–13 per cent. Accordingly, from April 1978 the target was revised at six-monthly intervals.

The actual procedure adopted by the Bank to control the money supply since 1976 is in itself a subject of some dispute. Parkin (1978) believes that the money supply is controlled by 'manipulating the interest rate thereby sliding up and down the demand function for money'. Others, such as Savage (1979) and Lewis (1980), believe that the policy operates on the supply side. The latter contend that the authorities begin with a forecast of the supply side system i.e. the authorities anticipate the movements in each of the factors which determine the supply of money. This allows them to consider what the future rate of increase will be, given existing policies. The authorities then employ simultaneously a number of policy instruments which directly affect the components of the money supply so that they are in turn consistent with the stated range for £M3. The focus of debate has tended to concentrate upon the role of interest rates in this explanation, i.e. whether it is to influence the demand for money by individuals or whether it has a more instrumental role in that it either entices or discourages persons or institutions from purchasing gilts, which is a major determinant of the supply of money in circulation.

Fuller theoretical consideration of this topic is postponed until later when the discussion can be placed in its proper context. For the moment it is pertinent to assess the arguments the Wilson Committee considered were relevant concerning the conduct of monetary policy through declared monetary targets. Opinion is divided as to the effect the publicizing of monetary targets has upon confidence and therefore the relationship between the money supply and real income. In other words, very often the publicizing of intent can lead to a change in the habits of the individuals who constitute the economy. In changing those habits they may in fact frustrate policy which is enacted on the assumption that relationships remain constant. The unstable relationship between the money supply and real expenditure as well as the changing nature of the financial system are seen as the greater arguments against the publicizing of monetary targets, which may lull people into a false sense of security. The dissenters' addendum to the Wilson Committee Report contended that the consequences of monetary targetry were unduly high interest rates, reduced output, squeezed profits and a high exchange rate. These, they continued, were the consequences of the unblinkered pursuit of a target irrespective of the consequences and were naturally inclined to be extreme since the public had often already discounted minor policy initiatives once the target was announced.

One of the unfortunate effects of targeting is the reaction to the published money supply figures every month. From February 1980 to April 1981 the target for £M3 was 7–11 per cent. Each time the rate of monetary growth is publicized and the target is overshot this has a depressing effect upon the Stock Market, the exchange rate and the market for government stocks. The latter results from the belief that investors may be unwilling to buy stocks in anticipation of some future rise in rates of interest. This has the dual effect of boosting the money supply because sales of gilts to the private sector are sluggish while adding pressure for the raising of interest rates, (or at least the maintenance of high interest rates), since the Government is forced to do so in order to sell more gilts.

Another related problem in this context is that the requirement for the authorities to sell increasing amounts of gilt-edged stock leads to accusations of 'crowding out'. This is a situation where the financial assets of the private sector cannot compete with the high yields offered on gilts and are forced out of financial portfolios. The effect is to deprive the private sector of funds, reduce investment and create unemployment, all as a direct result of frantic efforts to control the supply of money by selling public debt to the non-bank private sector.

Another drawback to targeting is the method of presentation. Since the target is set according to a range which relates to the end of a six month period it allows little scope for large variations early on in the target period. Thus a 3 per cent overshoot in early months is naturally compounded by commentators who declare that if that rate were maintained the target would be overshot by x per cent. The result is that wide variations in money supply early in the period have a disproportionate effect on confidence. The Wilson Committee recommended that a constant variation band be presented so that erratic fluctuations in monetary growth would not cause adverse market reactions.

Prior to 1971, the quantiative controls upon bank lending were seen to impede effective competition between the banks and other financial institutions. It is ironic that one of the greatest setbacks to the policy of monetary targets should be the provision of alternatives to money by non-banking institutions, as well as an ever-changing financial system, since they are both the by-products of an increasingly competitive financial environment. In the refining of policy towards focusing upon monetary aggregates the system of reserve assets came under great pressure. This is partly a result of the many loopholes which existed in the reserve asset system but mostly the result of a belated discovery that the major instruments of monetary policy were very often ineffective. Indeed Lewis (1980) discovered that changes in the yield on Treasury bills and MLR could only explain, at best, 40 per cent of the movements in bank liabilities. Since the reserve asset scheme was based upon the philosophy that the authorities could operate a shortage of cash which they would subsequently provide on their own terms, it came as somewhat of a shock to discover that those terms had little effect on the variable which was the centre of attention i.e. bank liabilities or the money supply.

In response, the authorities presented three papers in 1980, one of which sought to introduce a new system of liquidity controls[8]. This implied the redefining and re-casting of the reserve asset ratio although in fact the Green Paper 'Monetary Control' touched upon a number of related topics. The most interesting points the paper noted can be summarized as follows

1 That the institutions competing for funds with the banks need to be treated equally for purposes of credit control. For example, the building societies did not have to be registered as licensed deposit takers under the 1979 Banking Act and were therefore exempted from certain regulations. The Green Paper proposed applying prudential liquidity requirements to the licensed deposit takers.

2 Consistent with the above, the paper displayed the philosophy that specific control upon banking intermediation should be removed rather than imposed upon the non-banks.

3 That the supply side interpretation of monetary control which provided the conceptual framework for targeting is not defective *per se*. It is the amount of banking intermediation and its responsiveness to interest rates which needs further investigation. The paper recognized no essential distinction between the intermediation of banks and non-banks and between financial and non-financial concerns. Indeed Lewis (1980) argued that the philosophy underlying the Green Paper was no different than that which prevailed in 1971 and is based on Tobin's (1963) view of financial intermediation.

4 The supplementary special deposits scheme was to be abandoned and reserve assets redefined. The latter topic was discussed in a separate paper on liquidity.

5 That the focus of debate should shift from concern with the precision of monetary targetry to ensuring a smoother downward trend in the growth of the money supply.

6 The paper asserted the authorities' belief that some form of monetary base control similar to that adopted in the USA may be appropriate to the UK. At the same time, however, the paper concluded that control

---

8 These were the Green Papers: 'Monetary Control'; 'The Measurement of Liquidity' and 'Foreign Currency Exposure', all presented for discussion by the Bank of England.

of the monetary base would be difficult and welcomed views on this matter.

Clearly then, the focus of policy seemed to be shifting from control over the actual magnitude of eligible liabilities (the corset) towards control of the seed of that growth (the monetary base). It is therefore necessary to define what is meant by controlling the monetary base before proceeding further.

The essential distinction between a reserve asset system and monetary base control is concerned with the mechanics of monetary policy. The basis of the reserve asset system was that the authorities could create shortages of reserve assets and, via the mechanism of interest rates, influence banking intermediation by making it unprofitable for the banks to expand their balance sheets.

In the Tobin model (1963) of the financial system all intermediation is determined by the portfolio stance of the intermediator. This stance in turn influences the taking of lending opportunities. By influencing the portfolio of the banks via varying the *price* at which they are willing to supply reserves the authorities bear directly upon the marginal cost of acquiring funds and the marginal returns from lending opportunities. This is essentially a *dirigiste* or directional policy.

On the other hand, monetary base control relies upon *quantitative restrictions* being placed upon the supply of reserve assets. Thus an upper limit would be set upon the growth in bank deposits by requiring banks to hold a certain minimum proportion of their deposits in the form of reserve assets. The retention of reserve assets would be guaranteed, the essential factor being that their supply would be strictly controlled by the authorities. Given that the biggest drawback to monetary control in the 1970s was the ability of the banks to create reserve assets freely then the recommendations of the Green Paper are unsurprising.

The most essential factor in any monetary base system is therefore that the authorities need absolute control over bank reserves. This would be extremely difficult if the definition of reserve assets were to remain unchanged. Consequently, advocates of monetary base control support the use of bankers' balances at the Bank of England plus bank notes as the most likely candidates for the central role as the base. This is often referred to in the literature as the *cash base* and the general consensus in 1980 was that the reserve asset system was inappropriate if any sort of monetary base system were to be introduced.

The method of monetary base control is seen to be consistent with monetary targeting because the target can be translated into a daily target for bank reserves. Some authors however, such as Coghlan and Sykes (1980) are sceptical of the degree of control and accuracy required being achieved by the authorities. Furthermore, they contend that a monetary base system will still require interest rate variations to control the money supply and, although the authorities would be knowledgeable concerning the central bank's liabilities, they would again have difficulty determining the appropriate base level to facilitate effectively the business of banking in the UK. This is compounded by the problem of choosing the precise funding arrangements for the Public Sector Borrowing Requirement appropriate to that desired reserve base[9].

Clearly, any system of monetary base control presents three basic problems for the UK. First, the reserves need to be defined so as to ensure complete control by the authorities, while providing a degree of certainty in predicting the effects upon the money supply. Secondly, financing the Government's borrowing requirement has to be done in such a way so as not to interfere with the stability and predictability of the base. Finally, interest rate policy is not an alternative to monetary base control but must be constructed to facilitate the effectiveness of such rigid controls.

The last point needs a little elaboration. Many believe that one can *either* control the supply or price of a commodity but not both. This is certainly the case for a monopolist. What is at dispute is whether the authorities have the degree of control over the money supply in order to be regarded as the equivalent of a monopolist. The answer depends upon whether one believes the money supply to be exogenously or endogenously determined, at topic to be considered in Part Two. For the moment, the problem can be expressed as whether or not the authorities have the power to create a change in the supply of money or whether it is the result of economic development, in which case the authorities have only an indirect role to play in its determination.

As a consequence of the monopolistic reasoning some writers believe that one can control the supply of money or its price (interest rates), but never both. The upshot is that a monetary base system must leave interest rates to be determined by the market which leads many to conclude that interest rate policy is an alternative not a corollary to money supply management. Of course, the UK is notorious for its sensitivity to international factors, especially flows of 'hot money' and its ever changing balance of payments situation. Interest rate policy has therefore often been designed in response to international rather than intra-national events. The adoption of a policy which would allow interest rates to be determined by market forces would require a radical change in the attitude of the British monetary authorities. This, plus the fact that the PSBR would be subject to occasional marked reductions, (and hence create a great deal of social discontent), are used as the major arguments against the introduction of a strict monetary base system in the fashion adopted by the USA. More

9 Indeed, Coghlan and Sykes predicted enormous difficulties in anticipating the seasonal variations in banking activity and translating this into a precise base level without seriously disrupting the efficiency of banking in the UK.

likely a quasi monetary base system would seem to be appropriate, which effectively reinforces the measures already adopted to control the supply of money. Lewis (1980, p. 57) has argued this point quite forcibly and believes that interest rate policy is the only remaining option for the authorities

> 'The banks are not to blame for this situation. They can only respond to stimuli with which they are confronted. If bank customers are not daunted by high interest rates, banks see no alternative but to bid for deposits and reserves to sustain their intermediation. In the 1950s and 1960s they were prevented from doing so by interest rate ceilings. In the 1970s, the process was made more costly by the corset. Both "solutions" are now unpalatable to the authorities, but the only alternative seems to be interest rates, used more frequently, more quickly and more vigorously'.

Indeed, the only real alternative to monetary base control considered in the Green Paper was an *indicator system*, whereby automatic adjustments to MLR would take place depending upon the discrepancy between intended and actual sterling M3. If the money supply were overshot then the lending rate would be increased. The result would be that persons would opt to hold interest-earning financial assets rather than cash and the money supply would contract, the reverse would be the case if the £M3 target were not achieved. The Green Paper in fact rejected the monetary base system for the indicator system when it seemed, at least to the editor of the *Midland Bank Review*, that much the same controls and policies would need to be adopted to make either work[10]. As a result it was considered that no immediate advantage existed for monetary base control over the indicator system.

Notwithstanding the difficulties of introducing a monetary base system, the Bank introduced new arrangements for monetary control in August 1981. Since November 1980, the Bank had been increasingly engaged in money market operations i.e. smoothing out the daily shortages of surpluses of cash in the money markets by buying and selling bills to and from recognized institutions whose bills were eligible for discount with the Bank. This was in marked contrast to the previous system, whereby the Bank lent directly to the discount market on its own terms in order to influence interest rates. Instead, the Bank bought bills outright or sold them according to whether the market was short of funds or not. In quenching the money market's demand for funds the Bank was steering interest rates within an unpublished band.

The mechanism by which interest rate would change was made abundantly clear. By operating at the very short end of the money market the

10 'Monetary Control', *Midland Bank Review*, p. 22, Summer 1980. See also T. Congdon 'Should Britain adopt monetary base control?', *The Banker*, Feb. 1980.

Bank would influence prevailing rates of interest, (but those rates were nevertheless to be market-determined rather than imposed). The operations of banks in the money markets implied that if they were required to bid higher in the light of a shortage of funds then eventually, if the situation persisted, they would be forced to adjust the other rates of interest which they in turn operated. This implied more uncertainty in interest rate policy and certainly a greater degree of volatility. The Minimum Lending Rate, while it still existed, was by-passed and reverted back to its traditional role as the penal rate for the lender of last resort.

In 1981, the Bank began to provide all market operators with rapid access to information relating to its dealings in the money market and its daily forecasts of shortages and surpluses. While the authorities were still constrained by the inflow and outflow of tax revenues and the redemption of government debt, the new approach offered a versatility in the Bank's monetary armoury. It necessarily implied the lapsing of the reserve asset system since its function of providing call money to the discount houses was unnecessary. Instead, the banks whose bills are eligible for discount with the Bank were forced to give undertakings to provide the discount houses and other market makers with funds. The difference, from the point of view of the discount houses, was that the size and costs of such funds were more influenced by market forces. Nevertheless, as recognized banks they were still free to function as before.

The disbanding of the reserve asset system could have been destabilizing were it not for the fact that the 1980 paper issued by the Bank had allowed an acceptable system of liquidity arrangements to be developed as a replacement. The determination of interest rates by the short-term money markets implied a more active policy of day-to-day money management, particularly by the clearers. The monetary authorities would act to forestall any shortages of liquidity as needs arose and without necessarily forcing through interest rate changes; that would depend upon the supply and demand of liquid funds in the money markets. As a corollary to the operation of the new system, the following measures were introduced by the Bank in August 1981[11].

> (i) Although the strict 1½ per cent of eligible liabilities maintained by the clearing banks with the Bank was removed, broadly the same amount of non-interest bearing funds previously provided by the clearers alone were to be retained voluntarily with the Bank. All banks and licensed deposit takers were required to hold non-operational, non-interest bearing deposits with the Bank and these would remain the fulcrum of money market management.

11 The details are reproduced in 'Monetary control: the next stages' and 'Monetary control: provisions', *Bank of England Quarterly Bulletin*, March and Sept. 1981.

(ii) The non-operational requirement was to be ½ per cent of an institution's eligible liabilities.

(iii) Those institutions which expected to face transitional problems due to the ½ per cent cash ratio would be allowed special concessions.

(iv) Eligible liabilities were redefined to exclude lending between those institutions in the newly defined monetary sector and certain outside agencies with money at call.

(v) Eligible liabilities were to be calculated uniformly except in the special cases of members of the LDMA and the money-trading departments of certain banks.

(vi) Spot checks were to be undertaken by the Bank in order to avoid the problem of window-dressing.

(vii) The special deposits scheme was extended to all institutions with eligible liabilities exceeding £10 million.

(viii) Eligible banks were strictly defined and were required to make the following undertakings:

  (a) Each must maintain secured money with the LDMA at market rates.

  (b) The funds in (a) should normally average 6 per cent of an institution's eligible liabilities.

  (c) The funds in (a) should not normally fall below 4 per cent of eligible liabilities.

  (d) Each should provide returns of its daily figures for monitoring and control purposes.

(ix) The banking sector definition was considered no longer appropriate since it excluded some recognized banks, licensed deposit takers and also the Trustee Savings Banks. The latter were to become subject to the cash ratio and special deposit requirements when they become authorised under the Banking Act. The new monetary sector was therefore defined as:

  (a) All recognized banks and LDTs.

  (b) National Girobank.

  (c) Certain banks in the Channel Islands and Isle of Man which opt to join the cash ratio scheme.

  (d) The TSBs.

  (e) The Banking Department of the Bank.

There is little doubt that no clear-cut solution to monetary control exists nor is one likely to exist in the future. The UK has one of the most complex financial systems in the world which provides a bewildering variety of financial instruments to cater for domestic and international financial needs. This implies extreme difficulty in applying any uniform system of control to the financial markets. The 1971 policy encouraged competition between banks and the non-banks but the past decade saw the introduction of other forms of control upon the banking system which have, indirectly, encouraged the growth of the non-banks. The onset of monetary targetry has not reversed this process and indeed created anomalies which the proposals of 1981 sought to remedy.

Irrespective of the reason for the dramatic policy changes of 1981, there is no doubt that the non-banking institutions provide a further destabilizing threat to the conduct of monetary policy and, in particular, the control of the money supply. In a nutshell, the problem revolves around the substitutability of non-bank financial instruments for those issued by the banking sector. If the two are perfect substitutes then the effective control of banking liabilities (the money supply) may be frustrated because persons will merely substitute non-bank financial assets in their portfolios which carry the same return and liquidity whilst guaranteeing capital certainty. Any squeeze on the banking system's asset portfolio may therefore be frustrated as persons obtain other forms of finance to undertake expeditures. As the monetary sector is squeezed, disintermediation occurs and lending opportunities present themselves to the non-bank (and in some cases non-financial) institutions which could lead to an accumulation of funds in the non-bank sector at the expense of the banks. This typifies the balloon argument presented by the Radcliffe Committee and we must consider whether the argument is still appropriate, particularly in the light of the 1981 reforms.

As we shall see in Part Two, the theoretical constructs underlying his reasoning are many and complex, yet they can be simply presented and need to be resolved before one can fully comprehend the implications of our changing financial system. This explains why so much attention is devoted to the demand for money and money substitutes in the following chapters. This will allow the student to recognize why non-banks are now so important whilst identifying those institutions which may be responsible for the complications inherent in controlling the supply of money and which may be included in an extended definition of money in the future.

4 Summary and conclusions

In the assessment of monetary policy as it has been conducted in the UK, it became obvious that the efforts to control the total of available liquidity in the economy have followed an uncertain path. The increasingly complex arrangements by which the monetary authorities have sought to influence the price and flows of money and credit have been met by increasingly ingenious methods devised by financial institutions to fulfil their true function of financial intermediation. The persistent problem faced by the monetary authorities in this respect is to effectively control the growth of money and the provision of credit, whilst in no way stifling the innovatory capacity of the banking system.

The new definition of the monetary sector set out in 1981 and the increasing emphasis on open market operations as the methodology of monetary policy created a new spirit of fairness in the treatment of banking institutions for the purposes of monetary control. However, before this egalitarian policy can be fully effective it must surely be extended to the non-bank financial institutions in the form of fiscal neutrality. Such equal treatment of financial institutions is in keeping with the spirit of the Wilson Committee Report, which revealed how distortions in the efficient flow of funds often resulted from the iniquitous fiscal treatment of financial institutions. Whilst the monetary authorities have made heroic efforts to remove the distortions from within the money markets, and especially in those areas which directly impinge upon the operational definition of money, it is to be hoped that the energetic introduction of fiscal neutrality between banking and non-banking institutions will remove the distortions which exist in the savings market. Such a policy can only simplify the link by which monetary change is transmitted to the real sector of the economy.

Topics

1 Account for the large fluctuations in interest rates which have occurred in Britain in the 1970s. (IOB Monetary Theory and Practice, September 1979).

2 Examine the contention that 'disintermediation' and 'parallel markets' brought about the introduction of the 'corset' in the UK. Define each aspect precisely, giving examples and dates where possible.

3 Compare and contrast monetary policy before and after the reserve asset system was introduced. In particular, what anomalies were evident when the system was in operation?

4 Compare the arguments for and against the following:
   (a) A monetary base system
   (b) Extending the definition of money to include building society shares and deposits
   (c) Supply side controls upon banking activity.

5 Why are the non-interest bearing funds held by recognized banks and LDTs at the Bank of England the fulcrum for money market management? How are the Bank's open market operations influential in determining the money supply?

6 Distinguish between capital and reserve requirements and describe the different functions they fulfil in controlling banking operations.

7 Consider the proposition that the universal adoption of monetary targeting is misconceived and will only intensify periods of recession.

Part Two The theoretical and practical implications of non-bank intermediaries

Introduction

This section is devoted to the clarification of the intermediary function and an examination of the consequences of the recent growth of non-bank institutions, with particular reference to the UK. Chapter 6 asserts the basic constructs involved in the study of financial intermediation as an aspect of monetary economics and introduces the reader to the problems created by the rapid growth of the non-banking institutions in recent years. In the light of the framework presented earlier, Chapter 6 continues to set the problems posed by the growth of the non-banks in the context of the debate between monetarism and Keynesianism.

Chapter 6 is therefore directed specifically towards comprehending the technicalities of monetary economics which are relevant to the study of financial institutions. Chapter 7 continues to analyze the investigative work undertaken in order to answer some of the questions posed in the earlier chapter and attempts to present the state of the art at the time of writing. Having provided an appraisal of the most up-to-date information available, the final chapter deliberates upon the future development of the British financial system, with particular emphasis upon the relationship between the banks and non-banking institutions, drawing upon the analysis contained in Part Two in the light of the descriptive appreciation undertaken in Part One.

6 Financial intermediation in the context of monetary economics

It was explained in Chapter 1 how the growth of financial institutions results from an economic disturbance created by the ever changing composition of the asset portfolios of individuals. Sayers (1967) had already pointed this out

> 'Economic units are in fact continually disturbing their ownership of financial claims because they are continually saving, continually taking decisions about the advantage of spending on capital goods, and continually changing their views about the composition of their portfolios of financial assets (including money) and financial liabilities'. (p. 225)

In Chapter 2 it was contended that wealthy economies, where saving was prevalent, would exhibit a greater tendency to switch between different types of savings media, resulting in the growth of those institutions whose function is to cater for precisely that need. However, if we freeze this proposition, certain basic fundamentals are evident. Among those factors which influence the decisions of wealth holders to hold one asset (financial or real) or another are the fundamental characteristics of an asset, which need to be defined precisely. Since we are concerned with financial institutions, the following discussion concentrates naturally upon financial assets.

1 Financial assets and choice

Those aspects of a financial asset which determine whether a person opts to hold it or otherwise, are its basic characteristics. The characteristics of liquidity, capital certainty and yield are the most important features of a financial asset. The similarity with the definition of money is obvious, because money is by definition the most liquid financial asset since it is exchangeable for anything. Of course, as pointed out earlier, exchange is not the only reason for accumulating a wealth portfolio and the propensities to save illustrated this proposition. Otherwise, all wealth portfolios would consist of one asset only, that being money. It is when persons have stated their exchange requirements in any period that the problem of choice between forms of holding wealth is evident. This, again, is why the growth of private non-bank intermediaries is a characteristic of high income economies.

The essential distinction, as Farr (1971) has pointed out, between money and other stores of wealth is that the latter are held in anticipation of some transaction at a known or unknown future date. Thus, although the latter require some degree of liquidity, their prime function is as a store of wealth *rather than* a medium of exchange. The distinction is crucial in the analysis of the demand for money and other financial assets. As we shall see, in the specification of a demand function for each, the role of the rate of interest is reversed, since the demand for financial assets is positively and the demand for money negatively related to rates of interest. Liquidity retains the medium of exchange function of a financial asset while capital certainty is its wealth storage attribute.

When immediate exchange requirements have been satisfied, then the problem of choice between alternative financial assets occurs. Of course, the objective of the individual in maintaining wealth and therefore his propensity to save will influence that choice. A unique combination of liquidity, capital certainty and a premium for risk will exist for each individual and will determine that choice. However, such is the nature of markets that there will exist groups of individuals who share certain features in their demand for financial assets. The competence of a non-bank financial intermediary is measured by its ability to recognize and identify these markets and exploit them to the full by providing the mix of financial assets which meets the requirements of savers. The reason why the banks have not dealt with this problem as adequately as their competitors is, according to Goodhart (1975), that the required diversification would have rendered them too unwieldy. If this contention is correct, then this mistaken belief by the British banking institutions and their limited knowledge of organizational structures could have contributed to their losing ground to the major non-bank savings institutions throughout the 1970s.

Revell (1973) has pointed out that, in the flow of income, saving and expenditure the financial system has served to separate surplus and deficit units even more. The outcome is a greater sophistication on the part of those who intermediate in order to identify the two groups and fulfil their function. Furthermore, the identification of market 'segments' allows the intermediary to tailor its organization in order to achieve the economies of scale which can ultimately be transmitted to the financial asset in the form of an enhanced or more secure return, so improving its chances of being chosen as a savings medium. However, herein lies the most contentious issue concerning the growth of non-banking intermediaries. Intermediation allows indirect finance of business investment by savers i.e. finance which by-passes the banking system. Since the control of money is a tool by which aggregate spending (which includes business investment) may be influenced, then the exclusion of this indirect financing from monetary control may render monetary policy less effective as a means of influencing aggregate spending. The theoretical route by which this problem may be examined is through the demand function for financial assets.

Liquidity and the demand for financial assets

Since the greatest shift in the preference patterns of savers has been confined to the personal sector, we will concentrate upon this group. In fact, since the personal sector accounts for the vast majority of surplus funds one can legitimately generalize from this basis. The demand for financial assets other than money will depend primarily upon two factors. Firstly, anticipated transactions will require cash, which may necessitate the conversion of wealth into cash at a certain point in time. Of importance here are both the timing and cost of the conversion process, which can be summarized conveniently under the heading of 'liquidity'. Secondly, the yield on a financial asset, possibly containing elements of both income and capital appreciation, will also be instrumental in determining choice. Of course, these two aspects correspond to the propensities for saving presented in Chapter 1. This is why Arrow (1971) labelled the former the *precautionary* approach to asset demand and the latter (which focuses upon the relative yields of a given portfolio, later adjusted as choice is made), the *speculative* approach.

Given the lack of any universally accepted theory concerning asset portfolios and consumer choice under conditions of varying states from certainty to uncertainty, many of the early studies of saving and the corresponding issuing of liabilities by saving institutions were purely descriptive. The econometric analyses which became popular in the late 1960s and continued throughout the 70s were mainly concerned with the liquidity attributes attached to the financial liabilities of non-banks and the non-cash liabilities of the banking system itself. The reason for focusing upon liquidity was that it determined, given an equivalent yield, the substitutability of other financial assets for bank financial assets. Since the money supply in various countries is defined as the liabilities of the banking system, which in turn are the assets of economic agents, then what we are really discussing is the substitutability of non-bank financial assets for money. The importance of the conclusions reached by such studies has been heightened by the general resort to monetary control witnessed in the late 1970s and early 80s.

Before continuing to discuss the substitutability debate and the demand for financial assets, it is necessary to define precisely the concept of liquidity. Probably the most vivid explanation has been presented by Hicks (1967). Liquidity is that characteristic of a financial asset which allows immediate realization at face value. Hence, cash is seen as the extreme liquidity position since it is a (non-interest bearing) financial asset which is immediately exchangeable for any other asset, financial or otherwise. However, asset choice is not just the straight one between the liquidity of cash and the illiquidity of bonds, which Keynes adopted to illustrate the mechanics of his theory of liquidity preference. The choice is in fact between a range of financial assets varying in liquidity and yield which was accepted by Keynes in his *Treatise on Money* and reiterated by Hicks (1962 and 1967). The trade-off can be described as a straight exchange of premium for the risk of holding particular financial assets.

Since the issuing agency for the financial assets held by the personal sector is competing with other agents in the same market, the liabilities of financial institutions will be similarly structured. Any new type of financial instrument issued by a financial intermediary may give that agent a temporary advantage in terms of market share, which will eventually be diminished as competitors develop substitutes. This process can be likened to the impact of a technological breakthrough in manufacturing industry. It is generally true that, unless a financial asset possesses some consistently unique characteristic, the changing spectrum of financial assets presents a range of trade-offs between liquidity and yield to the investor. An asset which is relatively illiquid will yield more than a more liquid asset in order to compensate the saver for the loss in liquidity. So far as the saver is concerned, his propensity to save will determine whether he prefers a high yield with minimum liquidity or whether he prefers a lower yielding financial asset which possesses a greater degree of liquidity. Thus, the interaction of the propensities to save for any individual will determine his choice of financial asset by requiring a particular yield and liquidity position.

Of course, the preferred liquidity position of an individual will in turn influence his choice of financial assets. However, this position will alter as conditions in the economy vary, impinging directly upon his transactions and expectations. For example, a bout of inflation may force the individual to liquidate some of his more liquid assets in order to maintain his transactions. Furthermore, because inflation is a measure of the depreciation in the value of cash, he may wish to hold a lesser proportion of very liquid assets in his total wealth portfolio. The outcome will be a new portfolio position which now meets his revised preferences. From the point of view of the financial intermediary, it must adjust its own product (liability) and asset portfolios to meet this new situation. Indeed, in the Tobinesque view of the world, this is precisely the mechanism by which monetary influence is transmitted through an economy[1]. The conclusion he reached was that in order to understand the chain of monetary influence

1 See J. Tobin (1965).

one must consider the aggregate asset portfolios of individuals and other agents within an economy.

The demand equation

Drawing upon these arguments, we can state the simple financial asset demand equation briefly and succinctly.

$$D = f(C, R, W)$$

Where D is the vector (combination) of assets chosen which will satisfy the three parameters of: C, the cash required for transactions purposes; R, the rate of interest on a financial asset and W, the total wealth of the individual. This equation states that the assets demanded will depend upon a combination of the three variables within the brackets.

Of course the actual make-up of the portfolio selected by the saver will depend upon his own preferences or, as we saw earlier, whether he is a precautionary or speculative saver. The importance of this distinction is now evident in that a different weighting will be attached to C, R and W in the equation, so requiring different asset portfolios according to the type of saver. These savers are the surplus economic units defined in Chapter 1 and provide the funds to acquire the financial instruments issued by intermediaries. Only if the intermediary recognizes and identifies the type of saver it hopes to cater for will it correctly tailor its liabilities to the needs of the market.

The asset demand equation has developed from the so-called Cambridge view concerning the role of money, originally propounded by Pigou (1917). Later work by Cambridge economists emphasized the rate of interest and expectations on variables significantly influencing the demand for money. This presented a departure from the classical view of money as a constant fraction of income required to finance transactions. Subsequent refinements of the demand equations for money and other financial assets are basically variations upon the original Cambridge theme.

Testing the equation

Various refinements can be made to the basic asset demand function in order to test it empirically. This has been accomplished by many authors with varying degrees of success. One notable effort has been made by Barrett et al (1972) in that they recognized that the actual make-up of an individual's portfolio of financial assets will depend upon the yield of an asset, competing yields on other assets, the upper limit on the probability distribution of cash requirements and wealth *per se*. Their work was particularly important because it demonstrated other complications which may arise to influence portfolio selection.

For example, there is a significant influence exerted by the particular circumstances of an individual. Barrett *et al* found that surtax payers may want to hold Premium Savings Bonds or National Savings Certificates because they are more concerned than others with reducing their tax liability. Different rates of tax at different levels of income will therefore influence the portfolio decision and could be incorporated into the wealth variable in an empirical investigation. Furthermore, in the ranking of assets for portfolio selection, not only must the yield be considered but also the costs involved in liquidating some assets would influence choice. Finally, they pointed out that persons would adjust with different speeds to the factors which influence portfolio selection. They accounted for this by assuming that in any given period, say a month or quarter, a proportion of individuals will have adjusted their portfolios while others will not. Eventually all will adjust, but it is important in studying money transmission mechanisms to know how many people react immediately and the timing of later adjustments to personal portfolios. Obviously, if there is a lag in the transmission of monetary influence, the monetary authorities could easily over-estimate the impact of monetary policy by assuming all portfolios within an economy to react immediately to economic stimuli.

Earlier, it was stated that there are two approaches to asset demand. The study by Barrett considered the precautionary approach to be more appropriate in explaining the portfolio selection behaviour of individuals and this was confirmed by their results. Nevertheless, the speculative approach deals with the same factors but merely accords them different degrees of importance in the demand specification. So, in the case of individuals who may be motivated primarily by caution then the contingency of cash requirements (for transactions) will be most influential, as it was in the study undertaken by Barrett. On the other hand the speculative approach, which is normally applied to the study of the portfolio behaviour of *institutions*, lays great emphasis upon the relative yields of the assets in the selection process. This must be so since the common objective is to maximize profit or income where they depend upon the average yield from a combination of assets and the risk attached to holding them.

There is a positive association between risk and yield in the issuing of liabilities by any individual or organization. Thus, as the risk of capital loss increases so the issuer of a financial liability must compensate the prospective investor in the form of a greater return in order to entice persons to hold the debt. Obviously, those who are willing to sacrifice their capital in order to maximize the yield obtained are risk takers and will be attracted by high risk with high yield liabilities. By their nature, these persons are speculative investors. When persons combine to provide a sound financial base capable of bearing risk, the speculative approach to asset demand becomes the appropriate form of investigation: though there has been some debate concerning the futility of trying to classify institutions into homogenous groups for this purpose[2].

The speculative method of investigation into portfolio selection is based on the work of Markowitz (1952). The method adopts the mean return from a portfolio of assets as the profitability of that portfolio and the variance of profit around that mean as a proxy variable for risk. This parallels closely the specified objectives of the financial institutions which were discussed in more detail in Chapter 2, since the common association between the different institutions was that they sought to maximize profits (or the income of their members) subject to the constraint imposed by security. Such an objective implies that there is a trade-off between those assets which provide a high yield (and therefore are high risk with associated high variances around the mean) and those which are used to stabilize the portfolio by guaranteeing capital certainty but which can only be held with some sacrifice in terms of their own yield.

The trading off of uncertainty with yield is therefore the major problem for the speculative investor. Consequently, because of the earlier work by Markowitz, later refined by Tobin (1958), many researchers have found this method of analysis successful, including Farrar (1961), Parkin (1969), Goldfield (1966), Pierce (1967) and others. Occasionally, however, the objective function has to be adjusted to comply with the practical objective of the institution under investigation. This can be witnessed in the efforts of Ghosh and Parkin (1972) in their study of building society behaviour and Ryan (1973), who dealt with the life funds section of the insurance business.

2 Substitutability and the demand for money

Since money is merely another financial asset, albeit the most liquid, one would expect it to be demanded in accordance with the principles discussed in the previous section. Cash represents the extreme liquidity position and is demanded for that reason i.e. it guarantees exchange. Cash does not yield a rate of interest but when held by an individual is certainly not costless. The concept of opportunity cost in economics allows us to identify the true cost of holding cash as the income forgone by not holding the next best alternative. In other words, a person must sacrifice the yield on some other asset or combination of assets in order to hold a fund of liquidity, this sacrifice is the cost of cash. The higher the yields on alternative assets, the greater the cost of holding cash. By this reasoning we can conclude that the demand for money is inversely (negatively) related to the rate of interest.

2 See in this respect the debate between J. C. Dodds and T. M. Ryan in *The Oxford Bulletin of Economics and Statistics*, from 1973 to 1975.

Of course there is no *one* rate of interest, as Keynes often depicted for the sake of simplicity. The appropriate rate of interest to consider is the rate offered upon the next best asset to cash in the liquidity spectrum. As the rate of interest on the asset at the margin varies so will an individual's demand for cash.

Of course, whether or not a person is willing to switch into and out of cash in his asset portfolio will depend upon the availability of close substitutes for money i.e. assets which have almost as good liquidity characteristics as money but which also provide a yield. This is why the topic of the substitutability of financial assets between each other and for those defined as money is so important. On the one hand, switching may destabilize the financial system and impede the channels of monetary influence and on the other the definition of money *per se* is called into question if the personal sector can compensate for a squeeze upon the money supply by calling upon their reserves of money substitutes in order to maintain expenditure. It is therefore of paramount importance that the topics of the demand for money and substitutability be fully understood before the consequences of recent developments in the financial system can be fully appreciated.

Since the demand for money is a function of its cost, an individual's requirements, and his wealth, we are still operating within the realm of the demand equation. It is important also at this juncture that the role of substitutability in influencing the demand for any asset be appreciated. In a perfect market, no two products which are perfect substitutes may sell at different prices. Any deviation in price would be pounced upon by consumers, driving the prices of the products back into equality according to the laws of supply and demand. Similarly, in the case of financial assets which are perfect substitutes any variation in their rates of interest or, more correctly, the differential in their rates of interest, may create a shift by asset holders out of one and into the other. Of course this is difficult to detect because the financial system is an imperfect market. Nevertheless, many studies have concerned themselves with the switching into and out of money and money substitutes in response to variations in relative interest rates in the search for degrees of substitutability or the nearness of 'near-money'.

The importance of money substitutes is that they are said to weaken the central role of money in determining the supply and distribution of credit provided by the financial system. If the financial liabilities of the non-banking institutions, which are excluded from the money supply definition, are substitutable for money, then the supposed impact of variations in the money supply may be misleading since the personal sector may adjust its portfolio of financial assets in such a way as to frustrate the intended effects of monetary policy. Johnson (1972) has pointed to this problem 'The question is whether the interrelationships in the financial sector are stable enough to permit changes in the monetary base . . . to be used to analyse and predict changes in the real sector'. (p. 41)

It has been contended by many researchers since the early 1960s that the rapid growth of the non-bank financial intermediaries has had a destabilizing effect upon certain financial relationships, such as the demand for money. Indeed, the contention has led certain authors to request a redefinition of the money supply or at least a reappraisal and refinement of that definition. However, as we shall see in the following chapter, there are as many detractors as proponents of this view. The common methodology adopted by researchers is the analysis of the trade-off between various liquid assets and money. This is achieved by defining a demand function, either for money itself or a portfolio of financial assets (including money), and examining the cross-elasticity between those financial assets. Thus, variations in the demand for money may be caused by changes in the interest rate offered on other assets or variations in the money supply may be related in some other way to the total personal sector demand for financial assets. These questions cannot be solved theoretically because of the many routes which exist as candidates for the channels of monetary influence. The solutions, if they exist, can be determined only empirically and several notable efforts which attempt to do so are discussed in the following chapter.

Summary

Before moving the present discussion to the macro-economic plane, it is necessary to summarize what has been said so far. The demand for any financial asset behaves like any other demand function where the variables which determine that demand (independent variables) are normally consistent i.e. wealth, the rate of interest and liquidity requirements. Any demand function for a financial asset will normally contain these basic elements though the degree of econometric sophistication which is applied in the analysis may often disguise this fact. The demand for money behaves in exactly the same manner but the role of the rate of interest in the demand function is reversed. The increasing liquidity of those liabilities issued by the deposit-taking non-bank institutions have called into question both the stability of the demand function for money, the effectiveness of monetary policy and the definition of money itself.

Feige and Pearce (1977) have studied the topic of substitutability and admirably present a synthesis of the efforts to solve the problems posed by the topic. Their conclusion, in view of the evidence (some of which is reviewed later), is that no definite answer is possible. Of course, since the solution requires the existence of near perfect markets, rational savers and no external impediments to arbitrage, then the absence of a final answer is not surprising. Nevertheless, they do provide a lot of questions which the analysis of substitutability may answer:

(i) The appropriate definition of money.
(ii) The impact of the growth of financial intermediaries in the effectiveness of monetary policy.
(iii) The effectiveness of interest rate competition on the profitability and net worth of financial intermediaries.
(iv) The effects of interest rate ceilings and prohibitions on the portfolio positions of financial intermediaries.
(v) Regulatory policies concerning proposed mergers of financial institutions that are regarded as being in particular lines of commerce.
(vi) The impact and wisdom of extending monetary authority controls to non-bank financial intermediaries.
(vii) The incidence of monetary policy for different sectors of the economy, particularly the market for residential mortgages.

Clearly, in the realms of monetary theory and finance, the implications of the growth of the non-banks are far reaching. However, before assessing the contribution of research in most of these areas, it is necessary to depart from our present concern with the microeconomics of asset choice and portfolio selection to the macroeconomics of the practical definition of money and the theoretical role of financial institutions in the monetary process.

3 Monetarism, Keynesianism and the money supply

The long debate over the theory of the money supply process in the UK has often been confused. The confusion has arisen partly as a result of the difficulty of reconciling the operations of the monetary authorities with either of the two major prevailing doctrines of economic management, though the Conservative administration in 1979 left no one in any doubt that its basic philosophy was monetarist.

There is a distinctly different role played by money in the interpretations of the working of an economy presented by monetarism and Keynesianism. Keynesianism views money primarily as an asset rather than a medium of exchange and regards credit flows and interest rate changes as of primary importance in the conduct of monetary policy and the transmission of monetary effects to the real sector. Keynesians therefore consider that the demand for money is very sensitive to changes in the yield on alternative (substitute) financial assets, the consequence being that the demand for money is both unpredictable and unstable. The increasing proliferation of financial assets contributes to this uncertain money demand. The money supply therefore *reflects* economic activity which responds to variations in credit flows and rates of interest. The monetarist school views certain financial assets (money) as possessing unique characteristics and therefore money itself is readily identifiable. The demand for money, it contends, is a stable and predictable function and will therefore be relatively insensitive to the yields on alternative financial assets. Furthermore, the demand for money is a stable function of permanent income and the economic problem becomes that of matching the supply of money with the demand for money generated by a particular level of economic activity. The supply of money is therefore determined exogenously by the monetary authorities and the monetarists claim to have improved the operational efficiency of monetary policy as a result.

Of course the distinction is crucial to the conduct of monetary policy. If the demand for money is not stable then there is no point in attempting to control its supply in an effort to control the economy. If the demand for money is extremely responsive to variations in the rate of interest, then any variation in its supply may simply alter interest rates rather than economic activity, providing of course that economic activity, via investment, is not very sensitive to interest rate changes. On the other hand, if the demand for money is *insensitive* to interest rate changes, then any restriction in its supply will deprive persons of liquidity and restrict their real expenditure, so influencing national income rather than, as the Keynesians would have it, causing persons to liquidate other financial assets. It is important, therefore, to determine the nature of the demand function for money in order to conclude whether control of the money supply is a necessary and sufficient condition for influencing economic activity.

Theoretical appraisals: The implications for monetary policy

A thorough theoretical investigation of the demand for money has been undertaken by Laidler (1977) in which he illustrates how money demand has a role to play in income determination through the conventional means of the IS (investment/saving) and LM (liquidity/money) framework. Without engaging in a discourse upon the IS and LM framework let it suffice to say that in the search for a level of national income which is consistent with full employment, the demand for money plays a crucial role in influencing the total quantity of money circulating in an economy. As the demand for money varies so will the quantity of money in circulation, shifting the LM curve and sustaining a different level of national income.

Laidler defined the aggregate demand for money as dependent upon (a) the level of income and (b) the rate of interest. He then proceeded to question the fundamental relationships inherent in deriving the LM curve, which describes the point at which liquidity preference is satisfied by the supply of money. He concluded that changes in the demand for money would, via the shifting LM curve, cause changes in national income and prevailing interest rates. More importantly, his analysis illustrates how the stability of the demand for money and the determinants of money supply are crucial factors to be investigated in assessing the appropriateness of monetary policy

> 'In short, if the demand for money is interest inelastic, fiscal policy is ineffective as an instrument of economic control, and monetary policy is all-powerful . . . the opposite is also the case (since) changes in the money stock are totally ineffective'. (pp. 33–4)

The extent to which the true nature of the demand for money lies between these two extremes is an empirical problem, the solution to which will determine the relative importance attached to fiscal and monetary policy at any point in time. By altering the assumptions concerning the stability of the demand for money and its relation to interest rates, Laidler generates different consequences for the national economy. His thorough analysis is a highly recommended reference for those wishing to pursue this matter further.

Of course, the role of money in income determination is not a new topic and was first mooted by Fisher (1911) and later refined by Robinson (1933). It is in the approach to monetary policy, which stresses the explanatory and controlling power of changes in the quantity of money, where the debate has raged since the early work of Friedman (1956). The view which Friedman propounded regarded money as the major determinant of economic activity. The money supply was determined by factors which emphasized its purposeful characteristics rather than merely its supply variations brought about by buying and selling bonds or varying interest rates, though these measures still had a role to play in the monetarist view. So, if a given level of national income requires a specific amount of money to sustain it, then this demand for money must be quenched if inflation is to be avoided and real growth achieved. The monetary authorities can operate directly upon the real sector to create or deny the required supply of money by the normal means of monetary policy. The money supply is therefore imposed upon the economic system, from the outside, by the monetary authorities, i.e. it is exogenously determined.

The role of velocity

There is another important factor which plays a crucial role in the monetarist school of thought. As a corollary of the demand for money, the velocity of circulation of money is assumed to be stable over time and indeed must be so if variations in the supply of money are to bear directly upon the money value of Gross National Product (national income). In any economy the total income of its members must equal total aggregate expenditure (including savings). However, since money changes hands and finances many different transactions daily, there is no reason why the amount of money in circulation should be equal to national income. Indeed, because money is a flow variable and finances many transactions, total income will always be greater than the supply of money in circulation. So, according to the pre-Keynesian quantity theory of money, the money supply (M) multiplied by the velocity of circulation (V) equals national income (Y) at current prices (P).

i.e. $$MV = PY$$

The income velocity of circulation of money is therefore:

$$V = \frac{PY}{M}$$

Now, the demand for money is bound to be the amount required to finance transactions. As a proportion of income the amount required will be the reciprocal of velocity i.e. 1/V. This implies that if the ratio of national income (at current prices) to money is four then the reciprocal of velocity ($\frac{1}{4}$) tells us how much income is required to sustain the demand for money and how much money is required to finance a particular level of income. Therefore:

$$M = \frac{1}{V} PY$$

The demand for money is equal to the reciprocal of the velocity of circulation multiplied by national income at current prices (GDP). The relationship between the demand for money and the velocity of circulation is clear; velocity is an important factor in determining the stability and predictability of the money demand relation. Variations in either can, according to the quantity theory, influence national income and prices, since the ratio of GNP at current prices to money supply is an indication of the speed with which money changes hands to finance exchange. Finally, as we shall see later, there has arisen some debate concerning whether the growth of certain financial institutions has influenced the demand for money or its velocity. Obviously, the answer is important, particularly to the monetarist school of thought[3].

Practical consequences

According to Newlyn (1964), Bell and Berman (1966) the Bank of England (1969) and Croome and Johnson (1970) monetary policy in the UK

---

3 See Friedman and Mieselman (1963).

immediately after the Second World War had indicated an implicit belief in Keynesian techniques. Certainly, the Radcliffe Committee dismissed the use of money supply variations as an effective tool of monetary policy. The assessment of monetary policy since the late 1960s undertaken in Chapter 4 did not contradict this view. It is important to note that the Radcliffe Committee's reason for dismissing the use of money supply variations was the explosion of money substitutes in the economy. The outcome, they believed, implied that any variation in the supply of money would have little effect upon interest rates since persons could substitute a whole range of financial assets for money. So the relationship between the money supply and variations in the general level of interest rates was, they believed, weakened by the growth of money substitutes. It is ironic that a committee with an obvious Keynesian bias should unwittingly contribute to the debate taken up by Gurley and Shaw (1960), with their contentions concerning the disruptive influence of non-bank intermediation. Not surprisingly, their original arguments found little favour in the monetarist environment of the United States, where the effective operation of the Federal Reserve System hinges upon the exogeneity of the money supply and other tenets of monetarism.

Whether or not the economy is managed along monetarist lines, as in the USA and West Germany, or Keynesian lines as it was in the UK, there is a distinct similarity in the monetary definitions adopted by different countries. The similarity results from the universal acceptance of the theoretical attributes of money, the distinction lies in the definition of the variable which retains those attributes. Because of the Keynesian view that certain assets at times take upon themselves monetary attributes, there is always some difficulty in identifying precisely the asset which is truly money. In different societies different assets assume importance under varying economic circumstances and so it is impossible to identify one asset which is always money under every circumstance.

Nevertheless, Kaufman (1969) has proposed three bases by which money may empirically be defined: first, by testing for cross-elasticities of substitution between financial assets; secondly, by discriminant analysis of time series characteristics; and thirdly by the ability of the variable to explain, statistically, aggregate national income. This reasoning was recognizably coloured by his monetarist beliefs and the work of Friedman and Mieselman (1963). However, irrespective of whether one is a monetarist or a Keynesian, there is no doubt a portfolio-adjustment approach is compatible with both in investigating the impact of changes in the money supply, by combining precautionary and speculative factors in the demand function for financial assets.

Of course, such academic investigations are important in that they deal with the complex theoretical problem of identifying money but for macroeconomic policy purposes a practical definition is required. In the

UK, the money supply is defined as the total of notes and coin in circulation plus sterling sight deposits held by the private sector. This is the narrowest definition of money usually referred to as M1[4]. The wider definition M3, includes M1 plus the interest bearing deposits of the *banking* system.

Furthermore, M3 is divided for reporting purposes into sterling M3 and M3 including deposits in the form of foreign currencies. The former, sterling M3, therefore includes wholesale deposits denominated in sterling, reflecting their increased importance since the early 1970s as a component of the money supply. Indeed, according to the Wilson Committee, between 1972 and 1976 wholesale deposits accounted for between one third and one half of the total sterling deposits of the clearing banks[5]. For a time there had existed an M2 definition of money which was abandoned in September 1972 when the previous distinction between private sector deposit accounts with the banks and discount houses and 'other' banking institutions was considered anachronistic.

The practical methods adopted by the Bank of England to control the supply of money have been explained by Savage (1979) as

'. . . based, not on a money demand relationship, but on the *ex post* accounting identity that (ignoring the necessary statistical qualifications and less important items) the change in the money supply is equal to the public sector borrowing requirement, minus debt sales to the non-bank private sector, plus the increase in bank lending to the private sector, plus external flows into the private sector, with a variety of different policy instruments being used to affect the elements in this identity'. (p. 48)

This analysis is supported by reference to an earlier article in which the Bank of England (1975) itself discusses the factors which influence the money supply. By presenting a simple money supply identity the policy options open to the monetary authorities become evident.

$$M = PSBR + L + X - D$$

Where M is the change in the money supply: PSBR is the public sector borrowing requirement; L is bank lending to the private sector; X is external flows to the private sector and D is sales of debt to the non-bank private sector. It should be noted that this is not a dependence equation but an accounting identity. To determine the impact of policy measures upon the money supply a demand for money equation would be required.

4 From May 1975, the term 'current accounts' was replaced by the more precise term 'sight deposits' which included money at call and money placed overnight, thereby allowing certain funds held by the discount houses to be included in the money definition.

5 See Evidence by the Committee of London Clearing Bankers to Wilson Committee, p. 273.

The policy instruments available to the government and their impact upon the money supply can be subsumed under the headings included on the right hand side of the above equation.

PSBR: the policy options are government expenditure programmes and a battery of techniques known collectively as fiscal policy, i.e. various forms of taxation. The borrowing requirement is the difference between government revenue and expenditure so its size is determined by policy instruments influencing both of those magnitudes.

L: bank lending is influenced, among other things, by interest rates and direct controls upon lending activity in the form of rationing, ceilings or minimum reserve requirements. HP terms or selective taxes can also be varied to influence the demand for credit obtained from the banking system.

X: this is dependent upon exchange rates and trade overseas, or at least the extent to which overseas trade is financed by sterling balances in indigenous banks. Similarly, any income for overseas operations which yields an inflow of wealth may be deposited with banks in Britain and can inflate the money supply. The financing of overseas trade via specialist trade credit or overdraft facilities is excluded. The policy instruments influencing this magnitude are controls and taxes upon imports and exports, limitations upon the exchange rate, the export of capital and the relationship between British interest rates and those abroad, since short-term capital flows (hot money) can have a disturbing effect on the money supply.

D: Finally, the sales of government debt to the non-bank private sector will depend upon the rates of interest offered on that debt compared to alternative financial assets, the maturity structure of the national debt inherited by an administration and the general expectations for the future path of interest rates. The unprecedented growth in PSBR witnessed in the mid-1970s led to the authorities adopting tactics referred to as the 'Grand Old Duke of York' by commentators. This implied periods of a sharp upwards movement in MLR to take the market off balance, unloading as much debt as possible as the non-bank private sector expected rates to gradually fall (and thereby yielding a capital gain). However, the continued use of this tactic is unreliable as investors learn from experience and it was one of the reasons why the Wilson Committee called for a reappraisal of the system of government debt financing. Effectively, sales of debt replace money in the personal sector portfolio with a less liquid asset, though the secondary market in government debt implies that liquidity is not sacrificed completely so far as the investor is concerned.

Clearly, the variables which interact to produce a change in the money supply present an enormous variety of policy options open to a government. In previous chapters concentration has been placed deliberately upon those policy measures which seek to influence financial intermediation in the UK. However, it was apparent that the policy instruments are directed primarily towards the banking system. This is because money, by definition, includes only the liabilities of the banks. One reason for this is that banking intermediation is endowed with a multiplier capability believed to be absent in non-bank intermediation. The concept of a monetary base ('high powered money') consisting of assets which constitute the cash reserves of the banking system alone implies a unique quality attributed to banking intermediation. This is investigated in the following section.

4 Banking multipliers and the role of non-bank intermediaries in the financial system

In order to appreciate fully the mechanics of how the supply of money is influenced by the authorities it is necessary to appreciate the balance sheet of a commercial bank. It is obvious how the authorities determine the supply of notes and coin because they are their sole creators. The creation of the other elements included in the monetary definitions is a little more complicated and requires elaboration.

If we consider the case of a simple economy with only one bank, the depositing of cash at a bank by a person creates a liability for the bank which now owes that cash to the individual. To the individual the form of his asset has changed from cash to a bank deposit. Of course different individuals save for different reasons and consequently the type of deposit liability created by the bank to suit the individual's requirements will display various liquidity and yield characteristics. Nevertheless, the sum of those deposit liabilities plus notes and coins in circulation must comprise the total money supply.

Payments between individuals in the normal course of exchange will not increase or decrease the money supply. If 'A' pays a cheque to 'B' then the former's deposit at the bank is reduced and the latter's raised by the same amount. The introduction of further individuals and banks into the discussion introduces the necessity to clear debts but the basic principle remains the same. However, in this limited context the importance of the provision of a loan by a bank to an individual must be stressed. In providing a loan a bank is creating an asset upon which it earns interest. On the other hand, the individual who obtained the loan now acquires a liability which is his loan repayment. Once the expenditure financed by the loan is made then the income received by the other agent in the transaction is deposited with the bank. Clearly, the bank has created a deposit by initially providing a loan. This deposit is not compensated for by a corresponding reduction in another individual's deposit elsewhere, so providing a loan has directly increased the amount of deposit liabilities of the banking system, or the money supply.

Obviously, the limits to this process are imposed by the demand for credit by the community on the one hand and the ability of the banks to meet the requirements of prudent financial management on the other. For example, in the simplest case of a bank with one depositor, consider the outcome if the bank had lent the full amount to a customer and was immediately afterwards faced with the depositor wishing to withdraw his money. The bank would be unable to pay and is in default. Of course, as deposits increase the likelihood of all deposits being withdrawn simultaneously diminishes. The bank learns what it is prudent to lend and how much to hold in reserve. Obviously reserves (R) are a leakage from the multiplier capability of bank loan (or credit) creation because they are unavailable for lending. The reciprocal of this leakage (1/R) reflects the amount by which a bank may multiply its original inflow of funds and is traditionally called the *money multiplier*. Thus if a bank, either traditionally or according to law, always keeps one-tenth of its deposits in the form of cash reserves then the money multiplier is 1/0.1 or ten. Any subsequent inflow of funds to the bank affords it the power to create credit up to ten times the magnitude of that original inflow.

Theoretical distinctions between banks and non-banks

The uniqueness of the banks in this respect has been stressed by Clayton and Wood (1962) and Harrington (1974). They each consider banks to be the *creators* of loanable funds and non-bank intermediaries *brokers* of those funds. Although they argued that the maxim 'every loan creates a deposit' was true for banks it was not necessarily so for the non-banks. Though the latter are capable of multiple credit expansion, they still rely upon the original creation of loanable funds by the banks. This reasoning led Clayton to describe the relation between banks and other financial institutions as the 'tiers of deposits' theory where financial intermediation served to proliferate secondary financial instruments only after the initial multiplier effect of bank lending had created primary financial instruments.

Traditional theory hinges on the assumption that other financial intermediaries hold their reserves on deposit at the banks. If an individual withdraws his deposit from a bank to deposit it with another (non-bank) institution such as a building society, then since the building society in turn deposits with the bank no change in the money supply has taken place. The name of the depositor has merely changed so far as the bank is concerned. Furthermore, since it cannot create its own future deposits, a non-bank institution can only lend a *proportion* of its inflow of deposits and must compete for extra deposits before providing further credit. A bank, on the other hand, effectively *creates* its own deposits by providing loans. Traditional theory therefore concludes that an increase in bank credit will lead to an increase in non-bank credit as the latter compete for and gain a share in the newly created credit. The reverse is not the case. An increase in non-bank credit does not enable an increase in bank credit. Bank credit is therefore considered to be high powered in that it is the precursor of non-bank financial intermediation.

It would, it seems, be safe to conclude that the control of bank credit creation is the panacea for all monetary economic problems. However, although the uniqueness of banking is not disputed, it is the impact of the switching of funds from bank to non-bank and vice-versa which is a bone of contention. Of course, switching is merely another way of describing a portfolio adjustment. According to Harrington (1974).

'As already seen, such switching would not cause any loss of deposits or reserves to the banks. There would be no decline in bank credit (and so M3), but there would be an increase in Non-Bank Financial Institution credit. Switching deposits from banks to NBFI, then, leads to an increase in credit and in consequence in aggregate demand'. (p. 557)

The obvious ramification of this argument, if it is correct, is that, in spite of the uniqueness of banking intermediation, the growth of the non-banks (which must reflect an increase in switching if they cannot create their own funds), could frustrate monetary policy, especially if that policy is directed solely towards controlling bank intermediation or the supply of money. Unfortunately, the difficulty of assessing the consequences of the growth of financial institutions lies in the difficulty of separating and identifying a multiplicity of complex financial relationships which exist in the financial system. Indeed Tew (1969) has likened this problem to unscrambling an omelette.

A final distinction claimed to exist between banks and other financial institutions concerns the near perfect redepositary ratio that banks possess compared with non-banking institutions. The redepositary ratio is a theoretical term which measures the likelihood that loans provided by the banks will return to the banking system in the form of deposits. It has already been demonstrated that a bank's ability to create money is a function of its marginal propensity to hold cash reserves. However, the full multiplier process depends upon loans and advances being redeposited elsewhere in the banking system. The redepositary mechanism needs to be almost perfect for the money multiplier to operate according to traditional theory. The greatest argument in favour of a near-perfect redepositary ratio is the sheer size of the banking system. However, as money flows through the financial system leaving a residue of secondary financial instruments in its wake, it is temporarily out of banking circulation. If one views the financial system as dynamic, then there will *always* be a proportion of funds originally created by the banks outside the banking system.

Whether or not this constitutes a leakage from the money multiplier and whether the proportion of funds involved is constant or changeable is the subject of some debate but surprisingly little research. Only Revell (1973) and Griffiths (1970) have devoted serious time to the problem of the redepositary ratio and the leakage caused by the non-banking institutions but have met with limited success in providing any answers. The issue still remains open.

Inside and outside money, wealth effects and intermediation

Much of the literature concerned with monetary economics is confusing. Terms such as high powered, base, inside and outside money abound. Inside and outside money can best be explained by resorting to the simple closed economy with one financial asset adopted by Gurley and Shaw (1960). The terms inside and outside are expressions used to describe the monetary impact of price changes upon an economy. Gurley and Shaw described the financial process in a simple economy as the 'gross money' and 'net money' doctrine and using this framework sought to explain the role of money and financial intermediaries in the financial system.

As we saw earlier every debt in a community is someone else's asset and this is the basis of the explanation of financial activity. The net-money doctrine holds that private debt cancels out private financial assets in both monetary and non-monetary form to leave a net residue of claims against the government and foreign sectors. This fund of net claims are 'outside' financial assets or the liabilities of outsiders to the private sector and can be of a monetary or non-monetary form depending upon the definition of money adopted. The total financial assets of the community net of these outside financial assets constitute inside financial assets. Obviously, those financial assets which are defined as money can be described in the same way. Gurley and Shaw concentrated upon the total of inside and outside money (gross money) and the flow of non-monetary claims to develop a theory of finance[6].

The influence of a price change upon the real wealth of a community can

---

6 A life insurance policy is a good example of a non-monetary financial claim since it is a legitimate claim upon a financial institution but cannot be used in exchange for goods and services: though it could be used as the basis for a loan.

now be examined. If prices actually fall, then the members of that economy will be better off in real terms given no change in their income. However, not only does the value of income increase but monetary and other fixed interest claims expressed in domestic currency also increase in value. Both the inside and outside components of gross money increase in value, reflecting the favourable wealth effect of the initial price fall upon the economy. Since consumption and the demand for financial assets depend upon the stock of real financial wealth in the community then the wealth effect of a price change can have profound implications.

However, it is at this point that the real importance of the distinction between inside and outside money becomes apparent. The increase in the value of inside financial assets as a result of the price fall will be exactly offset by the increase in the value of private debts which also constitute inside financial assets. This must be so if all inside debts are counterbalanced by inside assets. If an individual possesses a £100 bank deposit and this was on lent by the bank to a hire purchase company from which the same individual has a £100 loan, then the positive nature of the former is exactly offset by the negative effect (rise in the cost) of the latter. Now if the same individual possesses an asset which is held by an agent outside of the system then no offset occurs and the wealth of the private sector appreciates since, by definition, assets are not counterbalanced by an equivalent private sector liability. Therefore a price fall only benefits the economy in terms of increased wealth to the extent that outside financial assets are held. The implication is clear; the greater the proportion of outside financial assets to total financial assets the greater will be the wealth effect of a given price change.

The implications for domestic financial institutions is through the demand for financial assets. It was explained earlier that the demand for financial assets was a function of wealth, amongst other things. The wealth effect of a price change will alter the relative yields of inside and outside financial assets. In the case of a fall in prices the value of outside claims will increase and the demand for financial assets will react to this in favour of the appreciated value of outside financial assets. According to Goodhart (1975)

> 'Falling prices could, therefore, impart a financial stimulus directly, via the wealth effect, to private-sector demand for assets, without any need for reductions in interest rates. And at some point the increase in the value of "outside" assets would lead, with a given level of real income, to an expansion of real consumptions'. (p. 203)

The portfolio adjustment caused by such wealth effects directly influences the issuing of financial liabilities by financial institutions. On the assumption that the theory of wealth effects is correct then an inflationary climate as witnessed in the 1970s and 1980s would influence the demand for domestic non-monetary financial assets, of which the primary source are the non-bank financial institutions.

Although this theoretical issue is a complex one, it serves to illustrate the alternative interpretations which can be placed upon the development of a financial system and the factors which impinge upon the role of the non-banking institutions and the demand for financial assets. Clearly, an analysis of the growth of the non-bank financial institutions in the UK presents many contentious issues concerning the theory of finance, the role of money and the effectiveness of monetary policy. Many of the issues are, however, impossible to resolve theoretically.

5 Summary and conclusions

The object of this chapter has been to assess the major aspects of monetary economics pertinent to the study of financial intermediation and the consequences a changing financial system may have upon the traditional tenets of monetary theory. The characteristics of a financial asset were specified as liquidity, capital certainty and yield and these were shown to influence asset choice through the demand equation.

The shifting preferences of savers, who can be classified according to whether they save for precautionary or speculative reasons, and their subsequent asset choice, are influenced by the inherent liquidity of financial assets. If an individual is willing to switch between financial assets as relative yields alter, then this is regarded as an indication of the substitutability of financial assets. The topic of substitutability between non-bank financial assets and money can be considered central to the debate concerning the efficiency of monetary policy and, in particular, the appropriateness of the definition of money.

In earlier chapters, the general resort to increasingly monetarist methods in controlling some of the leading Western economies was commented upon. This explains the deliberate consideration of the essential distinctions which exist between the Keynesian and monetarist schools of thought in this chapter. Finally, the essential theoretical distinctions between banks and non-banking institutions were considered. Undoubtedly, in catering for the changing needs of savers the non-banking institutions have posed a serious threat to conventional theory. The following chapter considers some of the empirical efforts to test this contention.

Topics

1 Choose the range of financial instruments issued by any one institution of your choice in order to illustrate how financial intermediaries tailor their products to meet changing savings propensities.

2 Define liquidity and illustrate how the spectrum of financial assets corresponds to the varying trade-off between liquidity and yield.

3 Distinguish theoretically between banks and non-banking financial institutions. Why is this important to the conduct of monetary policy?

4 The definition of money in the USA has been gradually refined. Is this consistent with the monetarist viewpoint concerning the role of money and the application of monetary policy?

5 Define the velocity of circulation and explain why its constancy is crucial to the monetarist doctrine.

6 Examine the demand for money and its underlying importance in monetary theory. What is the role of substitutability in the debate between Keynesians and monetarists?

7 In view of the new approach to monetary control adopted in 1981, would you describe the underlying reasons for the changes as a shift in policy or a practical necessity?

8 Do you agree with the contention that non-bank financial institutions cannot act to create credit independently of the banking system? What are the consequences of your answer?

7 Empirical investigations into the role of non-bank intermediaries

1 Introduction

Investigating the fundamentals of financial intermediation in the previous chapters deliberately highlighted the growing importance of the non-banking financial institutions. This chapter pursues the same line of investigation but concentrates upon the empirical research undertaken on both sides of the Atlantic to clarify the issues raised in the previous chapter. Of course much research must inevitably be omitted, for in the end the choice of literature presented will always be subjective. Nevertheless, it is sufficient that a piece of investigative research should shed light upon some particular aspect of non-bank financial intermediation and its consequences in order to be included in the present chapter.

The specialist topics encroached upon by the subject of financial intermediation can be conveniently classified under several headings and the presentation in this chapter is structured accordingly. These are:

(i) The growth of the non-bank intermediaries and general trends in saving.
(ii) The demand for financial assets and money.
(iii) Substitutability and the effectiveness of monetary policy.

2 The growth of non-bank intermediaries and general trends in saving

Saving is that portion of income which is not put to the use of consumption. It was explained in Chapter 1 that there were different motivations for this activity which were classified according to the propensities of individuals. Saving, as a topic, is therefore critical in the study of economics both because of its relation with consumer behaviour and therefore demand and also because it has a macroeconomic role to play as a leakage from the circular flow of income and as such is a major influence upon the expenditure multiplier. However, in the present context attention is focused upon the repositories which cater for that saving. Obviously, the magnitude and nature of saving holds implications for the type of financial institution which will develop to fulfil the function of an intermediary. Savers are the surplus units which create the environment for the spawning of financial intermediaries.

During the 1970s saving patterns in the UK displayed changing tendencies as Townend (1976) and Falush (1978) noted. The conventional rules seemed somewhat to be undermined as the reduction in real income in the mid-1970s, caused by unprecedented inflation, was complemented by a real increase in saving. Some confusion arose because of the belief that saving must *always* be positively related to changes in wealth. In fact what actually happened was that one of the propensities to save, in this case precautionary saving, assumed a possibly temporary precedence over the others with the seemingly paradoxical outcome that persons were saving more when their real incomes were declining. Indeed, this saving pattern turned out to be prophetic as unemployment increased from 2.1 per cent to 5.1 per cent between 1974 and 1980, so justifying the caution of individuals.

Conventional wisdom held that a high rate of inflation would generally discourage saving and encourage a shift in its pattern towards real and away from financial assets. Dorrance (1980) pointed out that most members of the Organisation for Economic Co-operation and Development (OECD), including the USA, although to a lesser extent, have exercised savings patterns in the 1970s which have contravened conventional views. The evidence he presented confirmed that the private savings ratio in the 1970s was considerably higher than the 1960s for most developed economies. Furthermore, an increasing proportion of this saving was devoted towards the accumulation of financial assets.

One of the reasons for this change was the dramatic reversal of the belief that standards of living would continually increase, which had been fostered by the decline in the general level of retail prices between 1959 and 1968. Expectations concerning income and prices worsened considerably after the peak of purchasing power achieved in 1974 and was not attained again until 1978. Moreover, the general pattern of saving mirrored the change in private sector saving where the shifting pattern was most significant. According to Dorrance, an important aspect of the shift was that persons opted to save in a 'capital safe' form, i.e. in the form of deposits with financial institutions and claims on pension funds rather than in marketable assets, the value of which will vary. This tendency has been common to both the USA and the UK in the 1970s.

One surprising feature of the shift in savings patterns is that persons should opt to save in the form of fixed value assets which must, of course, depreciate most markedly in times of inflation. This is particularly surprising in the context of zero or indeed negative real interest rates which existed throughout much of the decade as the inflation rate equalled or exceeded interest rates. This runs contrary to the reasoning in the previous chapter which concluded that the demand for financial assets would be positively related to the yield on those assets. In 1974, the high level of saving in the UK existed in the face of large negative yields on such assets. The reverse happened in 1977 and led Dorrance to conclude that the relationship between saving (and therefore the demand for financial assets) and yields was 'perverse'. A reason he offered for this was that the demand for 'convenience' or liquid assets was assisted by social policy during the decade, the tax concession upon saving with the building societies is a case in point. Furthermore, Dorrance argued that there was a more important convenience motive in saving than there had been before and that persons in both the USA and UK were demonstrating a desire to hold a stock or fund of convenience assets since these can cater for those who required cash availability plus an interest yielding contingency reserve.

So far as life assurance and pension funds (LAPF) are concerned, Threadgold (1978) has highlighted the shift in saving towards contractual obligation and the consequences of this development for personal sector saving in general. In particular, he observed the net inflow of funds to the LAPF holding income constant in order to determine, amongst other things, whether persons were increasingly willing to substitute contractual for non-contractual saving. Deriving various consumption functions for a range of different classifications of real and financial assets, he attempted to determine whether, for the UK at least, increased contractual saving served to boost total personal saving in general and therefore contributed to the extraordinarily high savings pattern of the 1970s.

Previous research by Cagan (1965) and Katona (1965) had concluded that persons covered by occupational pensions may save more than other persons, partly as a result of a 'recognition effect'. The recognition effect implies that when an individual is forced to contribute to a pension plan the recognition of saving for old age suddenly dawns which intensifies a person's propensity to accumulate a stock of assets to be drawn upon later in life. However, despite the earlier work of other researchers, Threadgold concluded that demographic and economic factors hindered the proper observation of the relation between discretionary and contractual saving and, in spite of Munnell's (1976) conclusion to the contrary, observed only a small degree of substitutability between the two.

Finally, according to Threadgold, extra contractual saving added only 50 per cent of its magnitude to total aggregate saving. The reason for this was that the tax position of the individual and the peculiarities of his wealth portfolio would determine whether engaging in contractual saving would serve to create an upward shift in his total saving. Furthermore, the degree of awareness of and the valuation placed upon pension rights by individuals and the degree to which pension saving was compulsory would influence whether an individual's contractual saving replaced non-contractual saving or added to total saving. Obviously, if persons save more through pension contributions whilst maintaining their previous voluntary saving pattern then total saving must increase. If persons save through contractual pension schemes *instead* of saving voluntarily (i.e. the two are substitutable) then this will serve to reduce the impact of increased contractual saving upon total aggregate saving.

Of course there are a number of factors which impinge upon the propensity to save and which have not yet been mentioned. As well as taxation, the distribution of income is important in that the spreading of a given amount of wealth amongst a greater number may serve to reduce the total amount saved. However, Falush (1978) has pointed out the contradiction created by the behaviour of the savings ratio in this respect

'A more equal distribution of income and wealth, brought about by inflation and high taxation, should therefore produce a lower saving propensity, other things being equal. In so far as the actual rise in the saving ratio has contradicted this assumption, it is clear that many other factors played a part in swamping the negative effect on the savings ratio brought about by redistribution'. (p. 53)

The swamping of the redistribution effect was, according to Falush, created by a combination of a wage explosion after 1971, inflation and increased contractual saving. The only certain feature of saving is that no one single factor can explain its behaviour. The uncertainty created by the ignorance of the factors which determine saving and the demand for different types of financial asset is a problem which the financial intermediaries must face. It has been mentioned previously that they must tailor the issuing of liabilities to meet the needs of the community but if those needs cannot be predicted and are inherently unstable the problem is compounded. It is appealing to conclude that the meteoric growth of the non-banking institutions throughout the 1960s and 70s is evidence of their success in overcoming this problem. Certainly it has been argued by Goldsmith (1958) (1969) and Robertson (1964) that, at least in the USA the non-banks have been more successful in this respect. However, Goldsmith demonstrated that the ratio of banking to non-bank financial intermediary funds is lower in developed countries, suggesting that the growth of non-bank intermediaries is purely a wealth related phenomenon.

Nevertheless, the previous dominant position of the banks in the UK financial system may have served to breed complacency on their part. Furthermore, the increasing borrowing undertaken by respective Governments in the UK has increased the necessity to unload debt instruments upon the private sector. In the absence of any effective initiatives on the part of the monetary authorities in designing flexible financial instruments which combine capital certainty and yield in such a way as to attract saving, there had arisen an increasing need for non-banking institutions to develop new financial instruments on their own initiative, in order to intermediate between the issuers of public debt and the personal sector. In the light of these arguments the banks have been accused of responding too slowly to the changing financial needs of the community. However, in making such a statement the common and reasonable riposte is that the shackles imposed upon the banking community by monetary policy have precluded any major initiatives on its part. This topic culminated in violent debate between the banking community and the authorities at the end of the 1970s which has not yet been resolved.

Evidence concerning the growth of the non-banks was presented in Chapter 1 and need not be repeated here. Further discussion can be obtained from Gibson (1970), Revell (1973), Goodhart (1975) and the Wilson Committee Report (1980). The consequences of this growth are now of major concern. In the previous chapter it was noted that the consequences ranged from the effectiveness of monetary policy and the definition of money to the structure of the financial system. However, before proceeding to review the evidence concerned with these topics, it is necessary to consider the implications of the changing pattern of saving upon the demand for financial assets, for this provides the link with further topics to be considered later.

3 The demand for financial assets and money

Investigative method

It is apparent that the savings patterns of individuals, especially in the UK, have altered in recent years due to the influence of the rapidly changing economic climate upon their propensity to save. Since saving is that part of income not devoted towards the purpose of consumption, then it is the vital source of financial asset demand. Of course, there are assets in which persons may invest which are non-financial—such as property or land—these will in turn compete with other financial assets for a slice of total aggregate expenditure. The implication of this is that when empirically determining the demand for financial assets the return on other possibly non-financial forms of saving will influence an individual's portfolio selection. Unfortunately, one cannot be too precise concerning the true nature of the relationship since, as we saw in the previous section, persons have saved in a financial form in an inflationary climate whereas traditional theory would have pronounced that they save in the form of more *real* capital-certain assets. In fact the personal sector overcame the problem by investing more in capital-certain *financial* assets such as those provided by building societies.

Nevertheless, the principle that financial asset demand will be influenced by wealth, income and the yield on alternative assets is undoubted. The problem lies in identifying those conditions under which demand may behave perversely. Several studies concerning the demand for financial assets have attempted to improve the degree of statistical explanation in models by incorporating the yield on real as well as financial assets in the demand equation. However, in the present context the importance of explaining the demand for financial assets lies in the fact that it will provide clues concerning the behaviour of the demand for money, since money has become more prominent as the target variable for economic policy. Furthermore, in examining the choice between financial assets it should be possible to pronounce upon those assets which display monetary attributes. The implication of this is that the money supply may be ill-defined, with enormous repercussions for monetary management.

Of course, one can investigate the demand for financial assets at the personal and institutional level. Many studies concerned with the demand for financial assets have concentrated upon the portfolio choice of institutions. There are basically two approaches to this method of investigation based upon the theory discussed in the previous chapter. The first is the Markowitz (1952) approach whereby efficient portfolios are computed for an institution, i.e. portfolios which contain the ideal combination of risk and yield. The researcher compares the actual portfolio of an institution with Markowitz efficient behaviour in order to explain the departure from the optimum position. For example, the institution may err on the side of caution in its portfolio selection because it is catering for investors who prefer capital-certainty to yield. This would be reflected in the measured deviation between the actual and the efficient portfolio. The second approach is to specify the objective function of the institution under investigation, say to maximize income, and determine an optimization procedure that the institution is expected to follow. The latter approach has been adopted by Goldfield (1966) and Pierce (1967) in their studies of commercial banks in the USA.

However, some researchers, notably Parkin (1969), chose neither of the above approaches, deriving strong empirical relationships to explain actual portfolio choice. In this case, he concentrated upon discount houses, describing how they achieved desired portfolio and debt positions and how they respond to changes in economic circumstances. The advantage of the approach adopted by Parkin is that, being based upon the uncertainty choice philosophy, changes in the portfolio are explained entirely by variations in interest rates. Given the objective function of utility maximization, any new combination of assets which will improve utility will be selected, subject to operating constraints.

This method is important because it reveals a truism in the study of the demand for financial assets (portfolio selection). Only when the original size constraints of a portfolio have been defined will the relative yields determine the make-up of the portfolio. That is, before the content of the portfolio can be determined the limitations upon its size must be defined. This is where aggregate saving is important since it limits the size of institutional portfolios which must equate with the sum of individual, corporate and asset portfolios.

Institutional research

In the context of institutional research, so far as building societies are concerned, most early studies tended towards a narrative of their development. Cleary's work (1965) is the most extensive in this respect. In the previous decade however, more rigorous econometric investigations into building society behaviour have taken place, notably by Oherlihy and Spencer (1972), Ghosh and Parkin (1972), and later Ghosh (1974) again.

Oherlihy and Spencer sought to explain the major financial flows in building society balance sheets by concentrating upon the two key interest rates which they control i.e. their borrowing and mortgage rates. The study pointed to the desirability of considering withdrawals and deposits as separate items rather than concentrating upon the net item, which was the normal method used to explain building society behaviour. The method typically under-estimated inflows of shares and deposits when the authors attempted to forecast the future. One major complication was the 'stickiness' of the recommended rate on shares and deposits which they discovered was much more difficult to forecast than the mortgage rate. Nevertheless, they did discover that gross receipts were responsive to variations in income in the community, notably through variations in the rate of income tax, changes in Minimum Lending Rate and the rate offered on shares and deposits. This, of course, is entirely consistent with the previous theoretical exposition of the demand for financial assets. The authors merely investigated the issuer of financial liabilities which have become a significant element in the personal sector's asset portfolio. It is obvious that national income, the yield on alternative assets (then represented by MLR) and the rate offered by the building societies combine to determine the demand for building society shares and deposits.

The difficulty of applying a utility maximizing approach to building society behaviour was pointed out by Ghosh and Parkin who noted that it is unsure whether the building societies in fact attempted to maximize anything. Cleary had already explained that societies decide which purposes they exist to serve quite independently, subject of course to occasional interference from legislators seeking to ensure that the purposes chosen are compatible with the public interest.

The prime function of a building society is to provide funds for house purchase. Accordingly, their interest rate structure is devised to attract sufficient funds in order to fulfil this function rather than maximize the inflow of funds. This complicates the problem of explaining building society behaviour since the conventional objective function of profit maximization is inappropriate. This should serve to remind any researcher that methods of analysis are rarely universally flexible and must be tailored according to the economic agent under investigation.

To overcome this problem, Ghosh and Parkin opted for growth as a reasonable objective of building societies, subject to the constraint imposed by security. The objective function they translated into a desire to accumulate reserves. By this reasoning the authors could then adopt the traditional means of investigation since the objective function of maximizing utility (reserves) was rationalized.

The above investigations have been cited to illustrate the theoretical validity of the assumption underlying portfolio selection. However, they dealt primarily with the institutional role in the flow of saving. In effect, institutional effort to attract funds is the mirror image of aggregate saving. Whether persons opt to save in one form or another will depend upon their own objectives (propensity to save) subject to consideration of wealth, income and yield. The similarity with the institutional portfolio choice problem is obvious and confirms that the theory of portfolio choice (financial asset demand) is applicable to all economic agents, collectively and individually.

The personal sector is the sector with the greatest financial surplus and is therefore the major source of saving. However, the portfolio of the personal sector necessarily includes the vital element of money since it is this sector which engages in consumption and saving simultaneously, serving to distinguish the portfolio problem from that facing financial institutions. One cannot therefore discuss the personal sector's demand for financial assets without considering the demand for money and also some would argue, for consumables.

Slovin and Sushka (1977) have pointed to the importance of the non-bank financial institutions in this respect

'Both early Keynesian and quantity theory approaches to macroeconomics emphasized the importance of either the short term rate of interest or the quantity of money in determining the level of economic activity, and ascribed little macroeconomic influence to either the behaviour of non-bank intermediaries or other major participants in the financial market'. (p. 100)

In consequence, the focus of attention in the field of monetary economics necessarily shifted away from the supply and demand for money to the whole spectrum of financial assets and the portfolio mix problem. This was a direct consequence of the growth of non-banking institutions and the profound effect their liabilities had upon relationships in the financial sector. In each different economy these relationships require investigation because the structure of the financial system impinges greatly upon the demand for financial assets. Markedly different financial systems will therefore display entirely different relationships between income, wealth, yields and the demand for financial assets, including money. The portfolio approach to asset demand is generally believed to be the most convenient method of undertaking the required investigation.

Macroeconomic research

The importance of investigating the demand for money stems from the implications it holds for the theory which underlies monetary policy. If the demand for money is unstable, which would be indicated by erratic switching by savers between different forms of saving and money, then the monetarist assertion concerning the uniqueness of money may be challenged. But this can only be observed by studying the personal sector demand for money and other financial assets and the portfolio response in the face of changing relative yields and wealth in general.

It is no accident that the major source of studies concerning the uniqueness of money is the USA from where the 'high powered money' doctrine sprang. Friedman and Mieselman (1963) were the first to suggest the inclusion of other financial assets in the money supply definition, especially since they had discovered that time deposits were extremely close substitutes for money. However, they devised a test which should be applied before other financial assets were included in the monetary definition. The test was simply the highest correlation obtainable of the sum of a group of financial assets with National Income. The starting point would be to correlate a given financial asset, say time deposits, with Income. This would be repeated systematically including other financial assets one at a time. When the highest correlation between Income and a group of financial assets was achieved then that group would constitute the appropriate monetary definition. By inserting their own wider definition of money into the usual income determination models they achieved a better explanation of variations in National Income.

A later study by Kaufman (1969) discovered that the deposits of the Mutual Savings Banks showed approximately the same correlation pattern as commercial bank time deposits. However, these studies focused primarily upon the money definition and the ability of wider definitions of money to explain National Income statistically. Scant consideration was given towards the question of the *relationship* between money and other financial assets but this situation was quickly remedied from then on and throughout the 1970s. Indeed, a plethora of studies has been undertaken, which make conclusions difficult to reach and always tentative. This intense period of monetary research in the 1960s was confined largely to the USA.

Studies by researchers such as Feige (1964), Lee (1966), Laumas (1968) and Chetty (1969) were directed towards the relation between money and other financial assets and testing for substitutability between the two. They each, to a different extent, considered certain financial assets to be good substitutes for money, thereby destabilizing the demand for money relation and bringing monetarist beliefs into question. Chetty believed that by determining degrees of substitutability between different financial assets and money they could all be weighted appropriately in an extended monetary definition. The object of extending the monetary definition was that it was considered to be a better reflection of the expenditure capability of the economy and therefore a more appropriate target to be aimed for in the conduct of monetary policy. Chetty concluded that cross-elasticity of substitution was the preferable method of analysis, a method which was to be adopted widely thereafter with varying degrees of success[1].

The proponents of the view that certain financial assets are good substitutes for money adhere to the Radcliffe Committee's opinion that this development was a direct result of increasing non-bank intermediation with the consequence that the demand for money was destabilized. However, there are many detractors from this view such as Friedman and Mieselman (1963), Feige (1964), Hamburger (1968), Timberlake and Fortson (1967), Feige and Pierce (1977) and many others. A brief comparison of several studies should serve to illustrate the common methodology adopted and the quite different viewpoints propounded on this topic.

Substitutability studies

Lee's work probably demonstrates the extreme view in attributing 'moneyness' to certain financial assets. His research implied at the outset that non-bank liabilities were substitutes for money because

> 'both sets of institutions (i.e. banks and non-banks) issue liabilities, and both use their monetary receipts for the purpose of creating credits—thereby transmitting loanable funds through financial markets'. (p. 442)

In order to test his proposition Lee derived money demand equations structured in an identical way to the financial asset demand equation described in the previous chapter. In this case, the narrow definition of money (M1) became the dependent variable and the independent variables were permanent income, a weighted average interest rate on SLA shares and Mutual Savings deposits and another weighted average of the rate on short and long dated government stock. Permanent income derives from the Permanent Income Hypothesis propounded by Friedman, which states

---

1 In such analysis the choice of appropriate interest rate is always a difficult decision. A weighted average is sometimes adopted as the solution. See Christ (1963) and Lee (1967) in this respect.

that consumption is a function of the present value of all the future income a consumer expects to obtain in his lifetime. Thus temporary variations in actual income are believed to be relatively ineffective according to the monetarist school. This reasoning substantiates their view that fiscal policy is a relatively ineffective measure for determining expenditure since it is permanent rather than actual income which determines consumption. It follows that policy should necessarily be directed towards influencing *expectations* regarding future income and its present value. Each of the yields was included in the model after the yield on demand deposits had been deducted. This refinement was undertaken in order to detect how the demand for money had responded to the rate of interest offered on non-monetary liabilities. Of course, conventional theory has it that the demand for money (cash) will be inversely related to the rate of interest. Lee's results displayed the correct negative signs between the dependent variable (money) and the rates of interest included in the model.

More importantly, however, Lee discovered that variations in the yields on non-monetary liabilities influenced the demand for money. If persons are willing to hold less cash when the rate on, say SLA funds, increases, then those persons must regard the two as substitutes in their asset portfolio subject, of course, to the proviso that their propensity to save remains the same. Lee also concluded that changes in the *quality* of non-bank financial liabilities had reduced the demand for money and stated his affinity with the Gurley and Shaw viewpoint. His study is important because it contained complementary analyses of the demand for a whole range of financial assets in order to determine where substitutability was most evident. Indeed, he found strong support for the proposition that SLA shares were good substitutes for both demand and savings deposits at banks. If this is indeed the case, then an extended definition of money which includes the latter and excludes the former is, he argued, questionable. This is especially so when one considers that he found SLA shares to be better substitutes for bank demand deposits than were the bank's own time deposits!

On the other hand, Timberlake and Forston (1967) undertook an analysis using a similar method but adopting entirely different criteria to assess the implications of the growth of non-banking intermediaries. In this case they specified equations with National Income as the dependent variable in the following manner:

$$Y = a + bM1 + b1S1$$

Where Y is Income, M1 is currency plus demand deposits and S1 is whatever non-bank savings deposit is chosen for investigation. In the equation b and b1 are regression coefficients and a is the constant.

Their objective was to determine whether the degree of explanation regarding variations in National Income would be improved by including non-monetary liabilities alongside money in the equation. They discovered that even the inclusion of bank time-deposits in the model (as S1) did not significantly improve the degree of explanation for the period 1953–65. They found no evidence, therefore, to support the inclusion of non-banking liabilities in the monetary definition.

Nevertheless, Laumas (1968) disagreed with their contention and extended the analysis to include MSB deposits, Postal Deposits and SLA share capital. He found that they each possessed varying degrees of 'moneyness'. Feige (1964) however, disagreed entirely and favoured the narrowest possible definition of money, refusing to extend the money definition beyond currency. Using cross-sectional data he found no evidence at all to substantiate claims for substitutability between non-bank liabilities and money and concluded that the non-banking institutions had no impact upon the demand for money. It follows that if the demand for money is predictable and stable then the monetarist viewpoint is substantiated. Over a decade later Feige combined with Pierce (1977) to produce an extensive literature review which did little to detract from his original standpoint. They concluded that there is sufficient empirical consensus in favour of an *absence* of sufficient substitutability between bank and non-bank financial assets.

However, although these studies are interesting and informative, they naturally concentrate upon American experience. In the UK the financial system is different and, some would argue, the demand for money is more unstable as a result. Certainly Smith (1978) and Bhattacharya (1978) have presented strong evidence concerning the substitutability of other financial assets for money and non-banking for banking financial assets. The present author also has provided evidence supporting the existence of occasional shifting in the personal sector's asset demand functions which may serve to destabilize the demand for money. Earlier, Slovin and Sushka (1974) had demonstrated that regulation 'Q' in the USA had created a structural shift in the demand for financial assets.

The method of analysis undertaken in the UK stems from the previous research undertaken in the USA. Writers such as Kern (1972), Lomax (1973) and Smith (1978) concerned themselves with extended definitions of money, i.e. definitions which included more and more liquid financial instruments until the definition included all liquid financial instruments. Kern believed that the policy of Competition and Credit Control, while increasing the degree of competition in financial markets, had achieved this at the expense of increasing the difficulty of monetary control. Although concuring with this view, Lomax considered the major difficulty to be the reserve asset system when compared with the monetary base system already adopted in the USA. Nevertheless, after 1971 a spate of studies in the UK concerned themselves with the departure between the two monetary series M1 and M3 which some, such as Parkin (1975) believed resulted from the increased popularity of Certificates of Deposit while others, such as Stevenson and Trevithick (1977) and the present author, believed the divergence to be evidence of a structural shift in the demand for financial assets. Certainly, later in the decade the behaviour of savings indicated that some profound change in savings patterns had taken place but the cause of this change can, as we have seen, be ascribed to several factors.

Like the USA, much of the debate in the UK has been concerned with whether the adopted monetary definitions are appropriate. The reason for questioning the appropriateness of the money definition stems from the growth of the non-banking institutions and the increasing proportion of non-bank financial assets in the personal sector portfolio, with seemingly no loss in expenditure capability. Economists have naturally questioned whether the money supply is still representative of expenditure potential and, further, whether monetary control is a sufficient condition for managing the level of a National Income.

Smith concerned himself with these problems and studied the relationship between five monetary definitions over the period 1924–1977. The interesting feature of his paper is that M4 and M5 included building society, Trustee and National Savings Banks' deposits. He concluded that discrepancies in monetary series tend to reflect short-term factors and, more importantly, that wider series should be defined and reported by the monetary authorities since his model testing obtained better statistical explanation when using M5, the most extended definition. This, he believed, was evidence of the increasing substitutability between the deposits of banks and other financial institutions.

In a rigorous econometric investigation of the demand for financial assets in the UK, Bhattacharya (1978) discovered that the deposits of building societies and Trustee Savings Banks were particularly good substitutes for money. Using a multi-period model and including real assets as well as financial assets in the analysis, he generated elasticity co-efficients between the demand for building society, TSB deposits and wealth as indirect evidence of a substitutability relationship. His analysis confirmed the early findings of Barrett, Gray and Parkin (1972) that

'Variations in the quantity of money would largely be absorbed by small variations in the rate on, and large variations in the quantity of building society shares and deposits, thus reducing the impact of monetary policy on interest rate levels and hence on aggregate demand'. (p. 518)

In the light of this evidence it seems surprising that Mathews and Ormerod (1978) should discover no alteration in the nature of the relationship between the standard definitions of money and National Income. Furthermore, the Bank of England (1972) survey on demand for money studies concluded that interest elasticities of the demand for money rarely exceeded −0.5. Thus, at best, variations in interest rates could account for 50 per cent of the demand for money, leaving another 50 per cent of its variation to be accounted for by other factors—such as the competitiveness of other financial assets.

A solution to the problem of defining and identifying substitutability has not yet been obtained. Some authors have avoided the complexities of analysing the relation between the demand for money and other financial assets by refining total asset demand into more descriptive categories. One of the first to do this was Farr (1971) who recognized the difficulty of obtaining a valid explanation of the behaviour of the demand for money when two entirely distinct categories of money were rolled into one, thus obscuring any sensible relationship between that demand and wealth, income and yield. The solution, she believed, was to separate the definition of money into 'basic' (transactions) and 'store of value' money whereby the latter is held in anticipation of some transaction at a known or unknown future date.

The aggregation of two types of money asset complicates the problem of control by the monetary authorities. Some have argued that extending the money definition would compound this problem since the responsiveness of the wide range of assets to interest rate variations and other monetary weapons would by no means be uniform.

Certainly Farr believed that since different types of money assets and non-money assets are held for different reasons then the aggregation of such money and non-money assets is undesirable. She believed this to be the reason why no satisfactory models empirically defining money had been discovered. In particular, the transactions demand for money had never been correctly specified. It is not surprising, therefore, that Dorrance (1980) should have concluded that the identification of 'convenience assets' is crucial to understanding the portfolio behaviour of the personal sector. Unless the convenience motive is correctly defined we shall be unable to explain fully the savings patterns witnessed in the 1970s. It should be stressed, however, that the convenience motive is not a new propensity to save, merely an explicit recognition that, in high income economies, certain propensities assume a greater significance than others. In the British case 'convenience' was of overriding importance during the last decade, according to Dorrance.

The importance of correctly identifying the nature of the asset(s) under investigation cannot be stressed too much. Consider the money supply itself. If persons opt to hold more cash in their day-to-day activity then, assuming the Government provided the extra currency, money supply has increased. However, if the increase in the money supply was the result of the provision of extra loans by the banking system or persons opting to make fuller use of overdraft facilities then, although the expenditure effect is the same, the implications for policy are quite different. In the former case, transactions demand for cash has increased, in the latter case this may not be so—the funds may have been required for security or speculative purposes. The importance of distinguishing between the two is that the method adopted to combat such increases in the money supply by the authorities will be quite different. Raising interest rates may well dissuade persons from speculating and reduce that increase in money supply created by bank lending. But is it safe to conclude that the transactions demand for cash responds in an identical manner to a rise in interest rates? Clearly it is not, especially when one considers the evidence which demonstrates that the demand for money is only 50 per cent explained by variations in the rate of interest. If one believed, as a monetarist must, that the elasticity of demand for money approaches unity and is a stable function of Income then the distinction between the two types of money supply would be unnecessary. However, the absence of convincing evidence in this respect has caused certain British economists to adopt a more selective approach to the demand for money and other financial assets.

It may seem paradoxical that those who argue for the more selective approach to asset demand are often those who also wish to extend the money definition. The reason is quite simple. If one holds the view that saving displays distinct and changing behaviour patterns which impinge directly upon the demand for money then the blinkered focusing of policy upon one sacrosanct monetary magnitude may be misdirected, bringing the whole of monetary policy into question. This does not of course render policies such as a monetary base system untenable, for the adoption of such a system requires explicit recognition that the major part of national expenditure is financed by money created within the banking system. The base system is merely an efficient method of controlling money created in this way. Those wishing to extend the money definition are not convinced that money created within the banking system is the sole source of expenditure and accordingly emphasize the closeness of other financial assets to money and the independence of the non-banking institutions to support their case.

4 Substitutability and the effectiveness of monetary policy

The whole question of the substitutability of certain financial assets for money is a direct consequence of developments in the financial services industry. In particular, the rapid growth of the non-banking institutions created the proliferation of financial instruments which highlighted the problem and has culminated in the questioning of traditional monetary theory and the conduct of monetary policy. If non-bank financial assets are liquid instruments which may, under specific conditions, serve to replace money, (however defined), in the asset portfolio of the personal sector to such an extent that expenditure is maintained in the face of a monetary squeeze, then the efficiency of monetary policy is weakened. The link between variations in the supply of money and National Income (if any), is then threatened.

There is little doubt to some that financial intermediaries are generally a precursor of economic growth because, in fulfilling the intermediary function, growth is accelerated. The process has been described by Polakoff *et al* (1970)

'It is now fairly obvious, therefore, that their [intermediaries] growth and proliferation, to the extent that they result in a greater and more varied assortment of claims than would be possible in their absence, encourage higher levels of saving and investment at each level of income'. (p. 14)

As we have seen, since intermediaries obtain funds from the public by offering a yield on the liabilities they issue and use the funds to maintain their own asset portfolio, then the proliferation of these institutions produces a greater than proportionate increase in the number of debt instruments. It was also stressed in the previous chapter that the non-bank institutions must compete for funds since they do not possess the money creation capacity of the banks. It is therefore in the interests of some non-banking institutions to provide liabilities as similar to banking liabilities as possible whilst retaining the important elements which serve to distinguish them from bank deposits. Since fiscal policy has afforded tax advantages to certain institutions, their ability to pursue this objective has been reinforced. It is not surprising, therefore, that those non-bank institutions which issue liabilities said to be substitutable for money are those which have enjoyed both tax concessions and the avoidance of controls upon banking intermediation.

Much of the research concerned with detecting these propositions has been directed towards identifying switching between assets, particularly that between certain non-bank and banking financial assets. It is obvious that if the relative yield, between two assets is the determinant of choice in an individual's portfolio selection, then the other characteristics of the two assets must be considered similar if not identical. Therefore much research has concentrated upon the relative yields of non-bank and banking financial assets and the extent to which persons will switch from one to the other in the face of changes in those yields.

The separation of research into that conducted to investigate substitutability from research devoted towards analysing the demand for financial assets (including money) is impossible. The reason is that an asset demand function is the conventional method adopted to determine substitutability, excepting of course those studies which adopt models of income determination[2]. Normally therefore, the study of financial asset demand and substitutability are complementary.

Building society deposits, bank deposits and switching

Probably the most controversial area concerned with substitutability is the relationship between building society and bank deposits, since the former are generally considered to be the closest existing substitutes for money in the UK. In terms of the liquidity spectrum of financial assets, building society deposits are supposed therefore to be next to bank deposits. The only real distinction between the two is that building society deposits cannot be transferred immediately by cheque and therefore do not fulfil the complete role as a medium of exchange. However, most of these deposits can be withdrawn on demand with the additional benefit that the funds are accessible for longer periods.

Many would argue that switching from one type of deposit to another is irrelevant in the context of monetary control, or at least the control of £M3. To reiterate, the argument offered is that when a sum of money is transferred to a building society no change in £M3 takes place. The name on the bank deposit merely alters from the individual to the building society. Even if the building society lends a proportion of the funds switched, the recipient of the mortgage purchases property from someone who will eventually deposit with a bank. However, as anyone who has purchased a house will know, the receipt of payment for a property is very often the trigger for another purchase elsewhere. If switching facilitates house purchase, then the credit creation capacity of building societies is dependent upon their competitive ability in the savings market. If the supply of housing does not respond to the increased demand facilitated by switching then the process is inflationary. This is particularly important if controls are imposed upon the growth of the money supply or upon the banks' ability to compete for savings, since the squeeze on banking intermediation may be offset by the growth in non-banking intermediation. Since the latter could be inflationary then the squeeze on the money supply as part of a counter-inflationary package is to some extent nullified.

Another important consideration is the source of the switched funds. For example, switching from banks to building societies is said to have no impact upon £M3. However, because of the redepositary argument outlined in the previous chapter the converse is not the case. A switch out of building society deposits into bank deposits again has no influence on £M3, but building society deposits will fall. So the relationship is asymmetric.

Llewellyn (1979) however, has pointed to the problems with this argument. The implications can be enormous depending upon whether the

---

2 See Timberlake and Fortson (1967).

switching is into or out of the public sector. For example, if the societies attract funds from National Savings or gilt-edged stock then the monetary authorities may have to issue further Treasury bills to cover the deficiency. If a reserve asset or monetary base system defines Treasury bills as part of high powered reserves then bank credit creation may increase. Thus, depending upon the nature of switching a change in the money supply may result. Indeed the disposition of funds by the societies may similarly influence the money supply.

The implications are threefold. If monetary policy is geared towards the encouragement of switching funds from the non-banks into the banks' tills whilst the banks' own lending is squeezed then non-bank as well as banking intermediation is restricted. If banking liabilities (M3) are controlled alone, and at the same time non-banking institutions enjoy competitive advantages over the banks, then switching under certain conditions may frustrate monetary policy.

Finally, the precise nature of the switch into or out of building society deposits whether from the banks or some other source is important, since this holds a direct implication for public financing and bank lending. It is obvious that a policy of monetary control, no matter what system is adopted, must be complemented by the control of non-banking intermediation. It seems ironic that policies designed to encourage the growth of thrift institutions for social reasons may have acted to reduce the effectiveness of monetary policy.

The debate over monetary policy

As usual in the field of money and finance, there are detractors from the view that certain non-bank institutions can immunize themselves against a general credit squeeze by competing more vigorously for savings. Bloch (1970) has demonstrated that under certain circumstances those intermediaries providing housing finance are in fact influenced to a greater extent than banks by the conduct of monetary policy. For example, a tight monetary policy is generally accompanied by high interest rates as the authorities 'crowd out' the private sector and attempt to choke-off the demand for money balances. In response, the banks will trade in primary securities holding the higher yielding assets to maintain the profitability of their portfolios. Unlike the banks, however, those institutions heavily committed to providing mortgage finance (for which there is no secondary market), cannot adapt their portfolio and must attempt to vary the yields on existing assets. The restrictions upon holding primary securities serves also to compound this problem. Although there seems at first glance to be little problem for savings and loan associations and mutual savings banks in the USA, and building societies in this respect in that they can vary their mortgage rates, the rising cost of mortgages may serve to reduce demand for housing finance, contracting the credit creation potential of these institutions.

An early study by Pesek and Saving (1967) in the United States attempted to resolve the issue concerning the substitutability of non-bank financial assets for money before the debate had properly begun in the UK. In their view, the issuing of debt by institutions other than banks could never be anything else but bonds. The rate of interest paid on these bonds, they argued, will *always* be below the short-term market rate of interest, the difference being due to the value of additional services provided by the non-banking institution. They argued that this difference was the acid test of a non-banking institution.

The short-term rate of interest in any economy is regarded as the true cost of money at any point in time. The fact that non-banks can compete for saving by offering yields below the true cost of money is an indication of the extent to which those bonds differ from money and a measure of the value individuals place upon the function of a particular institution. In simple terms, if one is prepared to sacrifice the short-term yield obtainable by lending money in the open market in order to lend to an institution (invest in a bond) at a lower rate then the two cannot be considered substitutes. Persons may switch from banks to non-banks in recognition of the declining value of the services provided by one institution compared with the other not because they are indifferent between non-bank deposits and money. According to this reasoning, Pesek and Saving regarded the substitutability hypothesis as untenable. Although they recognized the store of value property of certain non-bank financial assets they did not consider this a sufficient condition for regarding non-bank financial assets as money.

A later critique on the empirical definition of money by Mason (1976) in the UK, considered the whole approach to substitutability confusing and at worst obsolete. He believed saving to be quite a distinct category of economic activity unrelated to the creation and definition of money.

'Saving is only remotely related to money because, aside from misers, who are presumably irrelevant, savings are held primarily in income earning assets, at least some of which would not be included in the money supply—however money might conceivably be defined'. (p. 529)

Mason (1976) contested the view of one of the world's leading monetary economists, Harry Johnson (1972), who had concluded that the definition of money was an empirical issue. In Mason's view the definition of money is an unchangeable theoretical construct in economics, what was contested was the *identification* of those financial instruments which fulfil that function. Although seemingly innocuous, this comment highlights the problem in this field of economics, since it is obvious that at certain points in time certain assets obtain monetary attributes. However, it would be meaningless to regard everything of value as money. The subtle philosophical distinction between the concepts of value and money, as with income and wealth, must be fully understood in order to provide a reliable framework for empirical research. The problem is compounded because the rationale adopted for choosing certain assets as an empirical counterpart to the definition of money will vary from one financial system to another and especially between economies at different stages of economic development.

The financial services industry

In an effort to explain the growth of non-banking intermediaries in terms of marketing and organization, Greenbaum and Haywood (1971) pointed out the importance of identifying those institutions whose business is as an intermediary and those who intermediate as a by-product of their main business activity. They segregated the evolution of the financial services 'industry' into two distinct areas. First, one can investigate the structure of the industry which produced the financial claims and secondly an investigation can concern itself with the menu of intermediary financial instruments available to wealth holders. They noted that very often research had concerned itself with the latter with little regard to the former.

Their paper is interesting in that it provides a theoretical justification for growth of financial intermediaries and the consequent explosion of financial claims. The parallel to technological change in the financial sector is the narrowing of the spread between what the intermediary pays others to hold its liabilities and what it charges others for holding their liabilities. A greater turnover of claims and improved administrative efficiency effectively enables intermediaries to shave the margins they require to fulfil their function. Furthermore, since the demand for any financial asset will be a positive function of its yield and a negative function of the return on competing assets, then the increasing information fed by the financial services industry to the community, combined with the erosion of real returns because of inflation, will serve to foster an increasing awareness of switching and amplify the 'positive substitution effect' between financial assets. This line of reasoning is interesting; it offers sensible reasons for the growth of financial intermediaries other than that persons regard their liabilities increasingly as money.

Another interesting parallel to the industrial world to which they drew attention was that the diversification of financial instruments is representative of taking advantage of investment opportunities. In identifying market segments, where a particular combination of capital-certainty and yield is desired, financial institutions are effectively taking advantage of investment opportunities. The extent to which they can flexibly devise new financial instruments is a measure of technological innovation in the financial services industry. This, combined with government regulation, provides the dominant influence upon the structure of a financial system in much the same way as technological change, such as the microchip, and government industrial policy dictate industrial structure. Since regulation impedes the ability of financial institutions to compete on other fronts, it is natural that innovation in the financial services industry should take the form of increasingly ingenious ways of maintaining wealth. This, according to Greenbaum and Haywood, is a major contributory factor to the proliferation of financial instruments witnessed today.

Focus of debate

So far we have considered substitutability and have related this topic to the growth of non-banking institutions. It has been mentioned that the importance of the whole debate lies in its implications for the effectiveness of conventional monetary policy. The first of the two related aspects to this particular problem is whether substitutability is sufficiently evident to influence the stability and predictability of the demand for money. To do this one must observe whether the proliferation of financial instruments has influenced the velocity of circulation of money. Clearly, the behaviour of both the demand for financial assets and the velocity of circulation are crucial to the monetarist school of thought. Furthermore, the demand for money is itself represented by the velocity of circulation. The reason why velocity is assumed to be constant over time is that the demand for money is assumed to be invariable, except in the short-run. Velocity is therefore a measure of the demand for money. What must be considered is whether fluctuations in the demand for financial assets is evidence of a shifting demand for money, which in turn must manifest itself in variations in the velocity of circulation.

The second aspect is concerned with the implications of the first for monetary control. Certainly the control of monetary aggregates involves a knowledge of financial relationships which are continually shifting. The structural shift in the demand for financial assets in the early 1970s and the divergence in the monetary series in 1980 illustrated that the monetary series may be inadvertently influenced by fairly innocent manoeuvrings by the monetary authorities. In 1980 the suspension of the 'corset', or supplementary special deposits scheme, caused the redirection of a significant amount of banking intermediation into a measured series only to create an explosion of £M3 whilst M1 reflected the tight monetary stance adopted at the time. It is not surprising that wider series, including a new definition M2 for retail banking deposits, and the introduction of an embryonic monetary base system should result from the disillusionment with the traditional series. But, as Grantham, Velk and Frass (1977) have argued, the problem is a perennial one:

'The capacity to form unanticipated contractual arrangements means that the monetary authorities can never shut off the supply of new monies. Indeed, attempts to prevent money creation by regulating monetary activity creates new kinds of incentives to invent private means of payment'. (p. 355)

It is undoubtedly the case that attempts to confine money creation in a dynamic system in the manner adopted in Britain since the 1960s have been self defeating. Once a leakage in the system is plugged new incentives are created from which other leakages appear. The proponents of the monetary base system recognize this and defend their basic proposition that once the source of money and credit (the monetary base) is controlled, dynamic activity will take place only within limits prescribed by prudential financial management.

Certainly, the increase in the range of monetary targets during 1981 was implicit recognition that £M3 in itself was not sufficient as a single monetary indicator. The official reasons offered at the time were concerned with the technicalities of public financing and the temporary effects of the dismantling of outdated measures. No explicit recognition of the role of other, non-banking, financial institutions in the effectiveness of monetary policy was made, an omission which some, such as Tobin and Brainard (1963) in the USA, Clayton, Dodds, Ford and Ghosh (1974) in the UK and Patinkin (1972) would have found alarming.

Patinkin (1972) is particularly notable for his contribution to the debate concerning the impact of non-banks upon the efficiency of monetary policy. His assertions stemmed from the argument that the liquidity of financial assets is unlikely to remain fixed over time. If this is the case, the changes in liquidity will directly influence the demand for and supply of money. However, he departs from the traditional view concerning the role of non-banks in this respect, i.e. that they weaken the assumed relationship between the money supply and interest rate variations. He considers their impact to be purely upon the velocity of circulation of money. Thus, since non-bank intermediaries are brokers rather than creators of money, increasing non-bank intermediation will widen the disparity between actual expenditure and money supply (i.e. increase the velocity of circulation of money). We have seen that the velocity of circulation is a crucially important element in the monetarist doctrine and as such is assumed to be constant in the long-run. Therefore, if Patinkin is correct, the existence of non-bank financial intermediaries will serve to impair the efficiency of monetary policy by virtue of the fact that they introduce another uncertain link in the chain of monetary influence[3].

3 Of course the outcome will in turn weaken the relation between interest rates and the money supply. Patkinkin's argument was directed mainly towards the *process* by which this would occur.

Concentration upon the substitutability debate has allowed us to focus attention on two related topics concerning the reduced efficiency of monetary policy as a result of non-banking institutions. First, they may serve to influence the velocity of circulation of money and so destabilize the demand for money. Secondly, they may serve to reduce the central role of money by providing interest bearing substitutes, creating confusion concerning the break between money and other financial assets in the liquidity spectrum.

So far as the velocity debate is concerned, Pierce and Shaw (1974) have demonstrated the importance of recognizing the theoretical distinction between the *creation* and *transmission* of credit. Credit creation adds to total credit flows within the economy, whereas credit transmission merely recognizes the brokerage role of intermediaries. Obviously, it is almost impossible to classify intermediaries according to whether they are creators or brokers of credit so that the distinction is unlikely ever to find practical application. Furthermore, it is likely that most intermediaries undertake both activities. As such, then the ability of certain intermediaries to distance themselves from monetary control may be reflected in their ability to transmit funds in the face of a credit squeeze (i.e. to those financing activities least influenced by the policy). The upshot of this manoeuvre would be an increase in the velocity of circulation of money since monetary contraction may not cause a proportionate contraction in income. On the other hand, if the theoretical explanation of the intermediary function as a credit creator is correct then, as indicated in the previous chapter, the money supply is the sole source of credit creation and non-banking intermediation cannot be said to be independent of monetary control. A contraction of the money supply will contract credit creation so that aggregate expenditure declines, precisely in accordance with monetarist beliefs.

The subtle distinction between the transmission and creation of credit is unlikely to find an empirical counterpart but is a quite valid one, enabling the impact of non-banking intermediation upon the efficiency of monetary policy to be understood. In practice, however, the important factor is the source of funds which the intermediaries attract. Pierce and Shaw correctly pointed out that only when funds would have been idle or used to purchase goods and services but were instead attracted into a financial institution will credit be created. Funds attracted from one financial institution to another (switching) do not necessarily add to total credit but may merely transmit those funds elsewhere.

5 Summary and conclusions

The monetarist view concerning the operation of a financial system holds that the velocity of circulation, which can be described as the reciprocal of the value of money balances expressed as a fraction of national income, is determined by social custom and habit which do not respond in the short run to variations in the quantity of money. According to Kaldor and Trevithick (1981), it is the desire of persons to hold a proportion of their real wealth in the form of money which is the real determinant of the velocity of circulation and this in turn reflects the different time frequencies with which money is received and spent. Furthermore

'It depends also on the desire of individuals to keep some part of their wealth in the form of general purchasing power (Keynes's precautionary motive for holding money) or in order to be able to take quick advantage of future opportunities for profit making the occurrence of which cannot be precisely foreseen in advance (Keynes's speculative motive)'. (p. 4)

It is evident that throughout the 1970s precautionary saving increased and this has been provided as the major reason for the increase in the savings ratio during this period. Furthermore, research on substitutability has concentrated upon the switching between financial assets, which may also be evidence of an increasingly speculative element in personal sector financial asset demand. The two may have combined to increase the amount of real wealth held in a financial form, which is tantamount to saying that the demand for financial assets has increased. This can be regarded as conflicting with monetarist theory only if money, as a component of wealth portfolios, has suffered the same experience. However, as pointed out in the early section of this chapter, the shifting demand has concentrated upon non-banking financial assets since saving has been directed towards this end, reflecting the growth of the non-banking institutions. In this case one could turn the argument around and regard the growth of non-banking institutions as confirmation that the demand for money is in fact stable in the long run.

A monetarist would argue, therefore, that the holding of non-bank financial assets is unrelated to the demand for money because the two are not substitutes. To argue in opposition that monetary velocity has been altered by the intermediation of non-banks in response to the increased demand for non-bank financial assets still relies upon there being a substitutability relation between money and other financial assets. It seems that from whatever angle one approaches the topic of the efficiency of monetary control one eventually reaches the substitutability question. This accounts for the enormous amount of time devoted to this topic by economic and financial researchers and the space devoted to its investigation in the present chapter.

It should be apparent to the reader that there is no universal agreement concerning the theoretical role of the non-bank financial intermediaries. Some regard them as creators of money through providing perfect money substitutes, others as brokers of credit. The distinction is important for it determines whether one can account for their existence within the confines of conventional theory, where the money multiplier is the source of expansion and contraction of the money supply and financial activity, and non-banking intermediation is a financial transmission service which cannot immunize those responsible from the manipulation of the banking system. It is only relatively recently that consideration has been given towards the possibility that non-bank credit may be independent of monetary manipulation and even self-perpetuating. The purpose of this chapter has been to make the finance specialist aware of this contentious area and its implications for the conduct of monetary policy.

Topics

1 Consider the contention that increasing contractual saving was responsible for the general increase in personal saving witnessed towards the end of the 1970s.
2 Why should the problem of portfolio choice be any different for an institution compared with an individual? What are the consequences for analyses of the demand for financial assets?
3 Discuss the particular problems associated with investigating the behaviour of building societies using a variation on the financial asset demand equation.
4 Discuss the different methods of testing for evidence of substitutability between financial assets. Why has the technique of cross elasticities proved so common and yet so inconclusive in this respect?
5 Consider the proposition that non-banking institutions can immunize themselves against a contractionary monetary policy by competing more vigorously with the banks in a period of credit squeeze.
6 Precisely how may non-bank financial intermediaries 'weaken the assumed relationship between the money supply and interest rate variations'? (p. 167) If the quote is correct does the increasing size of non-banking institutions strengthen or weaken the monetarist viewpoint?

8 Monetary policy and competition in the financial system

1 Introduction

In Chapter 6, it was stated that the study of the variables which influenced the demand for money, such as wealth, interest rates and expectations, stemmed largely from earlier work by economists like Pigou, later refined by Keynes and Robinson and more recently by a welter of modern monetary economists. The empirical investigations considered in the previous chapter examined the same topics, though two quite separate schools of thought were identified. There are those who treat money as the important deterministic variable in the economic system and those who believe that the provision of substitutes for money has weakened its central role. The two schools of thought were labelled the monetarist and Keynesian views respectively and it was particularly emphasized that the behaviour of the demand for money was fundamental to the arguments of both.

The growth of certain non-bank financial institutions in the UK is a corollary to the theoretical discussion of the two preceding chapters. In discussing the implications of their growth for the conduct of monetary policy little has been said concerning the nature of competition in the financial service industry. Of course, this will in turn indirectly influence the conduct of monetary policy but more for practical rather than theoretical reasons. It is simply that, by influencing the structure, conduct and performance of the financial system, the non-bank institutions hinder the continuance of the status quo and cause policies to be initiated which further influence the financial system. The Wilson Committee, which reported in 1980, recognized the importance of the non-banking institutions and the following draws heavily upon its conclusions.

2 The UK financial system in the 1980s

In Chapter 1 it was stated that the various financial institutions which make up the British financial system had quite different beginnings; some had begun as money-lenders, others as brokers in particular transactions. The metamorphosis has created what can be observed today, a very dynamic system composed of institutions which still retain their origins either in their title or actual business, but where the distinction between the different types of institution has been eroded gradually over time. The financial institutions exist in a market where competition prevails both for the supply of funds and for lending opportunities. Specialism still manifests itself most strongly in the provision of lending facilities, but the spread of universal type financial institutions, exemplified by some German banks, is weakening even this.

Competition between institutions takes the form of price competition, either in the yield they offer or the price charged for money transmission services and the quality of the service provided. On occasion, price competition has been imperfect because of collusion between institutions such as the banks' interest rate cartel, which was disbanded by the policy of Competition and Credit Control in 1971, and the building societies' recommended rate system which was questioned by the Wilson Committee and gradually began to lose favour in 1981. However, these two examples refer only to competitive manoeuvres between types of financial institution. It should be remembered that the sharpest point of competition will always exist between the same type of financial institution operating in the same market. In this case, the salient feature of competition has been the creation of new financial instruments, their individual characteristics dictated by the prevailing economic climate and an institution's perception of the savings propensies of its target market.

While admitting that efficient competition in the financial system is a laudable objective, the Wilson Committee noted that certain functions would best be accomplished co-operatively in order to avoid duplication and to share the capital cost of expensive technology. The clearing arrangements are a case in point. Furthermore, the Committee drew attention to the futility of attempting to achieve effective competition by over-regulation. While the the policy of Competition and Credit Control sought, amongst other things, to increase the degree of competition in the financial system, it can be argued that it did so at the expense of the banks. The nature of regulation holds important implications for the effectiveness of competition. The authorities have the power to influence directly the extent and nature of competition by deciding upon the incidence of monetary control and the fiscal treatment of different forms of saving.

There is no doubt that the conduct of monetary policy and the pattern of fiscal policy have been the most important influences upon the financial system in the UK in recent years. High public sector borrowing during the 1970s increased the significance of public sector debt and those institutions responsible for channelling funds towards holding that debt. It is not surprising that the structure of taxation was such that it encouraged the growth of pension funds and life insurance companies and even less surprising that the decade should have experienced sporadic periods of rapidly accelerating interest rates. At the same time, private financial institutions were continually seeking economies of scale and, reinforced by developments in computer technology, diversifying their activities. The disenchantment with Keynesian economics, which some believed had produced less than full employment at the expense of recurring inflation, brought about a greater focus of attention by the policy-makers upon monetary magnitudes and financial relationships. The consequence was a period of unusually pronounced monetary tightness. Interest rates remained high until the return to real rates of interest provided scope for their reduction. The intention was to squeeze inflation out of the economy, at any expense in terms of unemployment, so that a period of relatively low price increases and low rates of interest could begin. Productive potential, and so real incomes, would temporarily suffer but expectations and convenience would continue to dictate the demand for financial assets.

In this respect, although it is true that increasing real incomes contributed to the growth of assurance and pension funds it does not necessarily follow that the converse is the case. Because of the fiscal priority attached to pension and life insurance contributions and the increase in precautionary saving, any reduction in real incomes brought about by monetarist policies tended to bear most strongly upon the demand for real assets and was a contributory factor to the severity of the recession in the early years of this decade. These factors, plus the fact that the incidence of contractionary policy fell most heavily upon the corporate sector, combined to maintain personal sector saving and is the reason why the recession had a disproportionate impact upon the real compared with the financial sector.

While recognizing that one can continue indefinitely to discuss the interplay of factors bearing directly upon the British financial system, Rose (1980) has identified four major factors which served to shape the financial system throughout the 1970s. These were (a) inflation, (b) monetary policy, (c) internationalization and (d) government regulation. Inflation is important in that it leads to high nominal rates of interest and contributes to uncertainty in the long-term. As a result, the market for long-term corporate fixed interest bonds evaporated during the 1970s. It also contributed to the Government occasionally offering unnecessarily high rates of interest on long-term borrowing, belatedly recognized in 1981 when the first indexed gilts were issued after the March budget. Rose believes that the growth of variable-rate medium-term lending by the banks and the prevailing high level of interest rates which has 'crowded out' the private sector combined to increase the share of industrial financing undertaken by the banking sector. Although this trend could alter in the 1980s, an increasing role played by the banks in making investment decisions by British companies must be beneficial in the long term.

The impact of developments in monetary policy and supervision has already been dealt with elsewhere[1]. However, Rose considered the increasing internationalization of the markets for short- and medium-term funds to have had a profound effect upon the banking system in recent years. In particular, the increasing proportion of non-resident sterling deposits has severed the relationship between advances and resident sterling deposits. This required monetary aggregates to be revised to include deposits other than the sterling deposits of residents in order to measure precisely the liquidity and lending capacity of the banking system. The increasing internationalization of banking has also influenced the nature of competition within the banking system. The removal of exchange controls and the computerization of monetary transmission services have reduced the importance of geographical location and removed the dependence of lending in a foreign currency.

Of course, the internationalization of banking not only creates problems in the monitoring and control of domestic lending for the purposes of monetary policy. Many forms of deposit insurance exist in other countries to protect the individual depositor (and the financial system) from the consequences of default. However, no agreed code of practice exists between countries. This is particularly important in the context of multinational banking and the growth of Euro-currency markets, which in any case often exceed the stipulated maxima of formal deposit insurance schemes. Any bank which deals in foreign currencies, both raising and lending funds abroad, can be referred to as international. A multinational bank is one which conducts its international operations from offices established in other countries. Euro-currency markets, i.e. markets in currencies deposited outside their country of origin, are a corollary to multinational banking and both have created problems concerning the regulation of international banking practice.

The special problems created by the recycling of surplus OPEC funds have facilitated the spread of multinational banks. These have acted as intermediaries between OPEC nations and those countries experiencing deficits as a result of the OPEC pricing policies. Furthermore, Euro-currency deposits have often been exempted from national monetary controls in the form of minimum reserve requirements, highlighting the need for an international consensus on prudent banking regulation. While the Committee on Banking Regulations and Supervisory Practices, under the auspices of the Bank for International Settlements, has attempted to do this, it is, according to Dale (1981), difficult to envisage a true consensus appearing until the obvious conflicts of interest and inconsistencies in reporting standards have been resolved.

In Chapter 1, evidence was presented which illustrated how the banks had experienced a decline in their share of total deposits made by the

[1] See Chapter 4.

personal sector. Since 1971, however, the banks have recovered some lost ground, mainly at the expense of National Savings. Rose (1980), has pointed out several other important aspects of competition for personal sector deposits which provide an insight into this development. First, deposits themselves now play a smaller part in the total financial system. The deposits of all financial institutions accounted for 58 per cent of *total* financial intermediary liabilities in the 1970s compared with between 65 and 70 per cent in the 1930s. Secondly, he points out that the recovery of market share by the banks and the continued growth of building societies have combined to erode the overall market share of National Savings. This had reached such a pitch by the 1980s that there remained little scope for the further expansion of either unless at the other's expense.

According to Rose, the financial institutions' share of the lending market tends to influence the deposit market share rather than the converse. That is, it is a common fallacy that institutions seek to attract as many deposits as possible and then begin to compete for lending opportunities. In fact, the truth is that it is easier for interest rates to be manipulated to attract deposits than it is for lending programmes to be revised. There is no point in attracting funds unless they can be lent at a profit. Lending activity is where institutional specialization lies and the securing of deposits is a secondary activity, whether lending programmes are prescribed by law (as with the building societies) or not. The assertion made by Rose that lending and deposit market shares are distinct is confirmed by the evidence. While it has already been shown that the deposit market share of the banks declined up until the early 1970s when the decline was halted, the evidence on the percentage shares of sterling advances to private and overseas sectors by the banks and building societies suggests a quite different conclusion.

Table 8.1 Percentage shares of sterling advances to private and overseas sectors by UK banks and building societies 1971–1979

Year	Total for all banks	Building societies
1971	40	60
1977	47	53
1978	47	53
1979	48	52

Source: 'The Banks and their Competitors', Institute of Bankers, 1980.

Table 8.1 illustrates how the banks' share of lending has increased from 40 to 48 per cent over the period whereas building society lending has declined from 60 to 52 per cent. It may seem inexplicable that the banks have managed to expand lending while not correspondingly increasing resident sterling deposits. The answer, of course, is that the upsurge in non-resident sterling deposits has financed the banks' increased lending activity.

Both the legislative constraints upon building society lending and the abolition of bank lending controls have meant that the relative shares of the banks and building societies in the lending market have not mirrored developments in the deposit market. Since the increase in bank lending activity has been concentrated in the business and household sector, the recessionary period of the 1980s, with declining real incomes, can be expected to slow down the rate of growth of loan demand. Another factor pertinent to the relative shares obtained in the lending market, which, Rose points out, is directly related to the intended decline in the Public Sector Borrowing Requirement. It was mentioned earlier that the increase in the PSBR had facilitated the growth of life asurance, pension funds and various gilt-edged funds. If the total borrowing requirement is reduced then this will release funds which are likely to find a home in the new issue market or possibly a revived long-term corporate bond market. Either way, this could impair the lending market share enjoyed by the banks. This would intensify competition in the lending markets and Rose envisages a spillover into the personal sector lending market, which in turn implies even more intense competition for personal sector deposits.

The clearing banks

The clearers have undoubtedly borne the major brunt of the intensified competition in the financial sector, particularly because domestic retail banking is the major contributor to their business. Indeed, after the intensely competitive decade of the 1970s domestic retail banking still contributed 60 per cent to the clearers' profitability. Their share of sterling deposits with UK banks had fallen from 74 per cent in 1962 to 49 per cent in 1979. And, while the clearers' total deposits increased by 420 per cent over this period, total bank deposits increased by 690 per cent and building society deposits by 1,100 per cent!

Naturally, the wind of competition has forced the clearing banks to expand their activities in fields other than retail banking and a continuation of this expansion into international banking and other financial services is likely to take place in the present decade. Lord Armstrong (1980) predicted a polarization into three types of activity. First, he envisaged a consolidation of the clearers' retail banking operations. Secondly, lending overseas and particularly the involvement in Euro-currency markets was expected to increase. Furthermore, the changing pattern of trading in the UK required more export financing and advice than previously, such as the provision of performance bonds and advice upon project finance and trading conditions in other countries. Thirdly, the clearers have diversified their activities into leasing, factoring, insurance and merchant banking. The advantage of these activities is their relative independence from interest rate movements, which provides counter-cyclical activity in their banking operations. The sheer size of the clearing banks' operations gives them a natural advantage in the marketing of their services. Since they already bear the fixed costs of over 11,000 branches and the variable costs of 150,000 staff and sophisticated accounting and information systems, their access to markets, and so their ability to identify lending opportunities, is second to none. Indeed it is this established presence which has enabled the clearers to increase their lending programmes successfully, particularly the provision of medium-term finance to local businesses, since the banker/customer relationship has developed over a number of years and the local manager is in touch with the peculiarities of local financial demands.

However, while the extensive branch network and a large trained staff have their advantages, they also provide a constraint upon change. The geographical shifting of business and population patterns may render the situation of certain branches inappropriate. New technology may be difficult to introduce because of the physical constraints imposed by the capacity of premises or, more seriously, by the unwillingness of a labour intensive (and unionized) industry to convert to a highly mechanized (and capital intensive) one. In short, the present infrastructure of the clearing banks imposes a degree of inflexibility which can always pose problems for any industry. In banking, however, the problem is particularly pronounced when a fall in interest rates can seriously reduce income without a corresponding reduction in overheads since branches are difficult to close and labour difficult to shed, at least in the short run. In his paper on challenges to clearing banks in the 1980s, Lord Armstrong recognized this inflexibility in the operations of the clearers and concluded that this was the reason why they had lost ground to the wide diversity of competitors who could offer more narrowly defined facilities because of their relatively lower fixed operational costs. Nevertheless, he believed that the 1980s held several opportunities for the clearers

    (i) The 'unbanked' population.
   (ii) Increasing the range of lending facilities.
  (iii) Improving the funds transmission mechanism.
  (iv) Reducing the average unit cost of financing transactions.

Since approximately 50 per cent of the UK population do not have a bank account there is scope for expansion in the deposit market[2]. However, as was said earlier, there is no point in obtaining funds which

2 In 1980 the 'unbanked' market was estimated to consist of a potential 11 million accounts with a cash throughput of £40 billion per annum.

cannot be lent. Thus an extension of the range of lending activities by the clearers is required, such as into the area of mortgage finance. He correctly anticipated the increasing automation of routine banking money transmission services both speeding up and reducing the administrative costs of day to day banking. In analyzing the potential markets for banking services, Lord Armstrong felt that the future for the clearing banks held great prospects. In particular, the distinction between three categories of customer needs to be appreciated. These are domestic, international and related services. Only when this distinction is recognized can the marketing strategy of the clearers be tailored to the requirements of their different clients and it is fundamental to the effective improvement of the branch network.

Competition between banks and building societies

The importance of the building societies was investigated in Chapter 3. They are the largest holders of personal sector deposits in the UK, overtaking the banks in the mid-1970s and the insurance companies in 1977. Almost one half of total personal sector liquid assets is held with the societies, while one third is held with the banks. As far as lending is concerned, the societies still perform their primary function of providing housing finance and, despite recent increases in mortgage lending by the banks, still provided over 86 per cent of all mortgage finance in 1980.

The societies have tended not to compete with other money transmission services but rather to concentrate upon attracting savings in much the same way as savings banks in other European countries. Indeed, the British building societies operate identically to savings banks in the deposit market but their lending programmes are severely restricted. As a result of their specialization they have tended not to compete with the banks as effectively for lending opportunities as they have for deposits. Consequently, the banks and building societies have learned to co-exist and this is mirrored in the fact that nearly 40 per cent of the population hold accounts with both institutions.

On the face of it, the lending activity of building societies may seem more risky than conventional banking because loans are provided with a maturity of (nominally) twenty-five years while 90 per cent of deposits can be withdrawn very quickly. However, as Leigh-Pemberton (1979) has pointed out, personal sector saving in aggregate is inherently stable. Furthermore, the average length of a lending term is in fact only eight years. When one considers that the societies are also lending upon the security of property then the risk attached to their management diminishes. Leigh-Pemberton believes that, in spite of the theoretical advantages of diversification, bank lending is considerably more risky with both deposits and lending activity subject to great volatility. The consequence is that banks must take greater precautions than the societies in that they must maintain a higher degree of liquidity. If the liquidity ratio is defined as the proportion of liquid assets (cash, bank deposits, CDs, central and local government debt) to sterling deposit liabilities the banks hold 33 per cent of their assets in liquid form on average, whereas the societies hold approximately 22 per cent. Of course, the banks have previously been required to hold non-interest bearing assets and are constrained by other balance sheet ratios which were discussed in Chapter 5. Leigh-Pemberton has argued that these constraints affect the margins which the two institutions need to maintain between deposit and lending rates. The excessive liquidity costs imposed upon the banks by both the nature of their business and the conduct of monetary policy serve to impair seriously the banks' ability to compete effectively with the building societies.

Furthermore, the tax privileges enjoyed by the building societies not only include the composite rate agreed between themselves and the Inland Revenue but also they are normally charged a lower rate of corporation tax than other financial institutions and firms. The banks presented these arguments, combining them with statistics to support the imperfections which exist in the savings market which, they said, arise as a result of an iniquitous system of fiscal controls.

But what counter-arguments can be offered on behalf of the building societies? *The Building Society Gazette* and other financial publications were replete with counter-offensives to the clearing banks after their evidence was presented to the Wilson Committee. Williams (1980) has collated these arguments in a competitors' view of banking in the UK. He argues that there is little substance in the arguments concerning the fiscal advantages attached to saving with and borrowing from the building societies. The composite rate of tax is merely a question of administrative efficiency so far as the Inland Revenue is concerned, since if it did not collect the tax from the societies, it would be forced to collect it directly from millions of individual taxpayers. This rate of tax merely reflects the trade-off between administrative cost and reduced tax revenue, because the net revenue to the Government, it is argued, would not be any greater if it fully taxed this form of saving and incurred the expense of collecting the tax itself.

It is further argued that the composite rate is itself a disadvantage to the building societies who seek to attract young and older people who pay no tax at all. Furthermore, the societies are subject to statutory constraints upon their activities. As we have seen, they are constrained in their lending activity to the provision of mortgages and tax relief is limited to a current level of £25,000. Williams contends that the statutory requirement to value any security on which they lend (property) and the requirement to publish details of their operations are further handicaps which the banks avoid. The result he envisages is the societies exerting pressure upon the authorities to obtain fiscal neutrality in order to compete on equal terms with the banks.

Williams recognized the inappropriateness of the distinction between building society accounts and bank deposits in the definition of the money supply. Building society lending is a major source of credit and can be substituted for other forms of credit. In other words, when a person moving house decides not to use all the equity tied up in the first to finance the purchase of the second and realizes some of this capital in order to purchase a car then credit substitution has taken place. There is little difference therefore between the relationships of bank finance and building society finance with expenditures in the economy. This strengthens the argument considered in Chapter 6 concerning the substitutability between the savings held with certain financial intermediaries and the banking system.

Indeed in January 1982 the Bank of England issued a directive on the issue of mortgage lending by banking and licensed deposit taking institutions. It sought to tighten up the guidelines covering the provision of mortgages by asking the financial institutions to ensure that any increase in the size of a mortgage is used for its proper purpose rather than credit substitution. The guidelines were a purely precautionary effort to ensure that the switching of mortgage lending away from the building societies would not be inflationary.

It has already been stated that the problems associated with monetary control and the role of the non-bank financial intermediaries were highlighted by the rapid growth of the non-banking institutions. The growth rate achieved in the 1970s by the building societies is not expected to be maintained through the 1980s, when a consolidation of their position and changes in the fundamental nature of their operations are more likely. One can expect that, by the mid-1980s, the relationship between investing and mortgage rates will have been severed and the cartel on rates a thing of the past. Furthermore, the freedom extended to the societies in the provision of finance is likely to be expanded, as with their American counterparts the SLAs, but if this is the case it is also likely that they will be incorporated into the framework of monetary control. Should a change of government take place in the UK during the first half of the decade then social priorities rather than monetary efficiency may well take precedence and the debate concerning fiscal inequity continue unabated.

3 The fiscal inducements to save: The Wilson recommendations

The Wilson Committee noted the sharp increase in personal sector saving in the previous twenty years, rising from $4\frac{1}{2}$ per cent of GDP in 1958–62 to over $10\frac{1}{2}$ per cent in 1979, equal to over half of the total saving in the economy. The reasons for increased personal saving have already been discussed. However, the Committee noted that it is not only shifts in the nature of personal behaviour which account for the increase. The changing characteristics of particular financial intermediaries and the variety of incentives and disincentives created by the Government, deliberately or otherwise, serve to influence the final choice between financial assets. Undoubtedly, fiscal measures are of paramount importance in this respect. The Committee recognized the influence of fiscal and other incentives upon saving and, in particular, on competition between the banks and building societies

'The most important of the latter [controls] are probably of a fiscal kind. Other examples include the imposition of different prudential require-ments on different types of intermediaries and the exercise of monetary policy in ways which effectively discourage savings from being held in the form of bank deposits in favour of other outlets with similar liquidity characteristics which fall outside the operational definition of the money supply, principally building society deposits'. (para. 679)

The Committee noted that government controls affect both the end use to which savings are put and the channels through which they flow. The former determines the final impact of saving upon the real economy, while the latter holds implications for the effective conduct of monetary policy by altering the competitive relationships within the financial system. While it is true that various government policies influence the lending programmes (and therefore asset portfolios) of financial institutions, we have concen-trated our attention upon the direct financial inducements or otherwise which influence financial asset choice and therefore the performance of different financial institutions.

Of course, there will always be some difficulty in ascribing cause and effect relationships between fiscal measures and particular forms of saving. The Committee noted, and this has been witnessed on several occasions during the discussion of the research in the previous chapter, that the various tax incentives designed to switch saving from one form to another may well influence total aggregate saving. There will always be some uncertainty in assigning cause and effect while the final choice of financial assets depends upon the interplay between personal preference and rational economic criteria.

Nevertheless, the three areas which are the most obviously influenced by fiscal measures are saving through building societies, life assurance and pension funds and lending to the government. We have already noted the fiscal advantages enjoyed by the building societies. However, just as important are the fiscal advantages enjoyed by a mortgagor, specifically the tax relief upon the mortgage interest repayments, the absence of capital gains tax upon the sale of a home and the exemption from stamp duty up to a certain minimum price level. Indirectly, these factors encourage saving with the building societies and, to a lesser extent, with other institutions providing finance for house purchase in order that in the future the saver may benefit from these advantages and enjoy home ownership. The Wilson Committee noted that the ideal of home ownership was a political rather than a financial consideration. On the other hand, the main justification for the composite rate of tax (which stood at 21 per cent in 1979–80 while the basic tax rate was 30 per cent) was administrative convenience to the Inland Revenue.

The Committee contended that the arrangements undoubtedly distorted competition between financial institutions and that if we were to start anew in designing a financial system, such distortions should be avoided. However, in spite of the anomalies, the Wilson Committee made the general comment that reverting to an entirely different basic philosophy would have disastrous consequences upon the stability of the financial system, since existing financial relationships reflect the capitalization of the inducements and disincentives by savers in the economy. Nevertheless, it did protest at some of the measures and agreed with the Inland Revenue's resistance to extending similar facilities to the Trustee Savings Banks.

The Committee recommended the termination of the composite rate system and that some consideration be given to equalizing the tax treatment of saving with different deposit taking institutions. Furthermore, they recommended that the societies should in future pay corporation tax at the standard rate. Finally, the Committee recommended the abolition of the 'recommended rate' system, a cartel arrangement by which the societies agree to limit interest rate competition between themselves. Although to date no firm action has been taken on these matters, the inability of the Building Societies Association to maintain control has meant the slow crumbling of the recommended rate system in the early 1980s.

Saving through life assurance and pension funds has benefited significantly from tax relief. Not only are contributors allowed to deduct contributions from gross pay before their tax liability is assessed and entitled to a tax free lump sum option at retirement, but no tax is levied on the investment income or capital gains of an exempted fund. The Wilson Committee described pension arrangements as deferred pay and found difficulty in justifying the tax-free nature of the lump sum payment since the deferred pay (pension) is normally taxed as earned income. Life assurance premiums also qualify for tax relief up to a specified limit. As we saw in Chapter 2, premiums are paid by a policy holder net of a deduction which is equivalent to the relief on half of the original premium at the basic tax rate. In April 1981, the deduction was 15 per cent, representing a basic rate of tax at 30 per cent. The justification for premium relief was the social desirability of saving for the future and providing for dependants. Furthermore, the nature of pension and assurance liabilities is such that the life assurance and pension funds are well placed to fill the gap in the market for long term corporate finance if it recovers in the near future.

One anomaly the Wilson Committee pointed out in this regard is the obvious fiscal advantage of engaging in long-term contractual saving through either of the above channels compared with private arrangements by individuals pursuing the same objectives. Recognizing the laudability of such savings schemes, the Committee recommended that the fiscal advantages be extended to all forms of long-term contractual saving subject to the same conditions. The main beneficiaries of such changes would be other competing institutions such as building societies and unit trusts who at present have to arrange such schemes through insurance policies to derive the fiscal benefits.

The final area of saving which derives major fiscal advantages is saving through holding government debt. The two major advantages of lending to the Government stem first from the exemption of gilt-edged securities from capital gains tax if held for over a year and their transfers are exempted from stamp duty. Secondly, as we saw in Chapter 2, national savings schemes are usually wholly or partly tax exempt.

The tax exemption on gilts was introduced in 1969 to facilitate switching between stocks by maintaining an active secondary market in government securities. At the same time, an active secondary market increases the effectiveness of open market operations by the Bank of England since the buying and selling of bonds by the Government at varying yields is quickly transmitted throughout the capital market. The major objectors to this system are the local authorities and major industrial borrowers who cannot offer similar concessions. The Committee recommended that the tax arrangements for government borrowing should generally be brought into line with other forms of saving and that if the special arrangements for small savers are seen to be necessary in the case of national savings the same arrangements should be available to other competing institutions.

Finally, the Committee recognized that a taxation anomaly had prevented the effective development of bond or gilt funds in the UK. Income on bonds held through a unit trust was, until recently, liable to corporation tax whereas an individual, if he held them privately may only have to pay the basic tax rate, which is usually much lower. The ability of a trust to write off management expenses against this income was never sufficient to overcome the differential, thus discouraging the setting up of bond funds in the UK. With the removal of this anomaly from March 1980 it is feasible that bond funds may begin to flourish in the UK during the 1980s.

There is little doubt that the members of the Wilson Committee realized the profound effect that fiscal controls had had upon competition in the financial system. However, this is not a purely British phenomenon. Distortions in a financial system are often contrived in order to achieve some political goal and as this is an undeniable prerogative of government it is with us to stay. Nevertheless, this does not mean that the system in the UK cannot be simplified, or at least made more uniform, so that savers may readily obtain the information required to make the appropriate choice of financial asset. The increasing complexity of the fiscal arrangements can only create confusion and, in some cases, abuse.

The supervision of financial institutions

The regulations designed to supervise the operations of financial institutions vary according to economic circumstances and the roles of particular institutions in the financial system. As certain institutions increase in significance they naturally fall under the close observation of the authorities. The type of supervision will vary, depending upon the existing procedures which have been developed historically by the financial institution to maintain its own particular code of practice. Often the question with which the authorities are faced is whether the increasing significance of a particular type of financial organization merits the instigation of a new, more stringent, code of practice or whether the existing arrangements are strong enough to weather such changes.

In particular, the events of the late 1960s and early 1970s provided a rude awakening in respect of highlighting the inadequacy of relying upon non-statutory controls to regulate certain financial activities. In the early 1970s, bank lending on the basis of property as collateral reached a peak. At the same time there were many (sometimes dubious) property developers willing to borrow. This two-way relationship was self-reinforcing, cemented by the inflation in property values and exaggerated by competition between banks. Increasing property values were used to secure loans which in turn were used to purchase property in a typical inflationary spiral. Late in 1973 the critical point was reached when it was suddenly discovered by large financial institutions (and in many cases private individuals) that they had over lent on the basis of property values. Obviously, those financial institutions who were heavily lent on the basis of previously appreciating property discovered that borrowers were unable to pay and forced to realize property for less than the debt incurred. This weakened the asset portfolios of many institutions and, in the case of the banks the 'lifeboat'[3] was sent out by the Bank of England in order to avoid a major catastrophe.

Banking supervision

The 'domino effect' of banking failure is well-known, i.e. the effect upon

3 Explained on pages 186 and 199.

the economy of a single banking failure is disproportionate to the original failure, as Friedman and Schwartz (1963) and Goodhart (1975) have demonstrated. It was in the shell-shocked atmosphere created by the collapse of the property market in the 1970s that the Wilson Committee was appointed[4]. The perennial problem of regulating banking activity was defined succinctly by the Committee

'The dilemma for the regulatory authorities, whether statutory or non-statutory, is to devise effective methods of regulation which do not so stifle competition between the financial institutions as to lose their customers the advantages usually associated with it in terms of price, innovation and quality and variety of service. Ideally, regulation and competition should be complementary, the one providing a framework within which the other can then be allowed to operate safely'. (para. 1071)

The solution in the USA was the Federal Deposit Insurance Scheme which is run under the auspices of the Federal Deposit Insurance Corporation set up by the Glass-Steagall Act of 1933. In fact the FDIC tries to protect all the deposits of a bank by whatever expedient means available. For example, when the National Bank of San Diego experienced difficulties a take-over by the Crocker Bank was arranged by the FDIC. Though the basic element of financial security was ensured by the arrangement there is no doubt that banking competition in Southern California was reduced as a result. This highlights the problem of incompatibility which may often arise between the objectives of ensuring security and maintaining effective competition in banking. Banking supervision in the USA is further enforced by the Comptroller of the Currency whose office enforces codes of conduct for prudential banking, for example by restricting the proportion of loans which may be afforded to a single borrower and of loans to shareholders and officers of the bank. The statutory regulations are supported by informal controls which may be invoked from time to time to encourage lending to specific sectors or discourage loans to certain persons or indeed countries. For example, the banks were advised to restrict lending to Italy during 1974 and naturally constrained further lending to Poland in the early 1980s when it was discovered that loans granted during the 1970s could not be repaid.

For several reasons, the conduct of financial business is less secure than the provision of tangible goods and services. First, persons tend to rely upon finance as the basis for all other expenditures with the additional factor that financial obligations often account for a large proportion of total expenditure. Secondly, and more importantly from the point of view of security, financial services are often more difficult than other products

---

4 Although it was finance for industry, as against property, which was the primary reason for its appointment.

and services to test (and value) at the time of purchase. The Wilson Committee emphasized that, as a result of these basic traits of the financial services industry, it is sometimes possible for an institution trading unprofitably to conceal the fact for a number of years, while undercutting competitors by under-providing for liabilities which have to be discharged at some future date. This was the reason for the apparent success of the Vehicle and General Insurance Company before its demise in 1971 and it certainly contributed to the later banking crisis.

The UK approach to the regulation of banking has traditionally been based upon informal but very close supervision by the Bank of England. The informality attached to banking supervision was so entrenched that there was, until the 1979 Banking Act, no official rigid definition of 'bank'. However, the inflow of foreign banks from the mid-1960s and the setting up of fringe or secondary banks to evade ceilings highlighted the disadvantages of the informal and often voluntary system of controls. While the 1971 policy of Competition and Credit Control recognized and attempted to remedy some of the competitive defects and certainly increased competition in money transmission services, it did nothing to compensate by way of introducing appropriate prudential requirements to complement the increased competition.

The cruel timing of the property collapse in December 1973 revealed the imprudent operations of many banks. The Bank of England scheme, colloquially termed 'the lifeboat', fortunately prevented the domino effect which is usually associated with banking crises. The scheme operated by the depositing bank and clearing bank funds with threatened institutions. The total deposited in this way reached a peak of £2 billion at one point during the crisis. The basic problem had been compounded by large depositors removing funds from secondary banks as they realized the banks' commitment to lending in the property market. Thus, whereas certain banks could normally weather temporary storms their ability to do so was severely impaired. The lifeboat scheme alleviated the strain by effectively sustaining the deposit base of many secondary banks.

The painful experience of the early 1970s, combined with various EEC directives suggesting a battery of controls, resulted in the White Paper on the Licensing and Supervision of Deposit-Taking Institutions in August 1976 and culminated in the 1979 Banking Act. The Consumer Credit Act of 1974 had already instigated a system of licensing of credit granting institutions while the 1973 Insurance Companies Amendment Act and the Policy-holders Protection Act of 1975 had increased statutory supervision of insurance companies, which were seen to be particularly prone to uncertainty due to the long-term nature of their commitments. A similar deposit protection scheme is to be implemented for the banking sector under the 1979 Act, whereby 75 per cent of the first £10,000 of a depositor's sterling deposits are guaranteed by the scheme.

One particular feature of regulation in the UK recently is the increasing reference by the Bank of England to liquidity and capital adequacy in the monitoring of banking activity and the granting of banking status. The American banking system has of course adopted capital adequacy and prescribed lending limits for a number of years but only lately has the Bank of England circulated papers concerned with liquidity requirements for banking and prescribed capital backing for risky assets. One of the important contributing factors to this development was the removal of exchange controls, which has exposed banks to exchange risks as well as the normal risks associated with domestic investment.

4 Regulation of non-banking institutions

A common feature of the legislation throughout the 1970s which applies to banks and non-banks alike is the increasing tendency to impose authorization requirements or minimum conditions upon new entrants to the financial services industry. For example, the 1979 Banking Act requires authorization by the Bank of England to become a 'bank' or a licensed-deposit taker. Similarly, the Stock Exchange has exacting requirements for stockbroking firms, licensed dealers in securities and investment trust companies. The latter had, until 1982, to provide a five year track record and were severely restricted in the percentage of gross assets which could be invested in unlisted (non-quoted) companies. The conditions have now been relaxed to encourage newcomers and the financing of small firms.

The 1974 Insurance Companies Act empowered the Department of Trade to enforce certain conditions upon firms operating in the insurance market and Lloyd's has for some time applied its own strict membership criteria. Because of certain upheavals in the Lloyd's market during the late 1970s a Lloyd's bill was presented to Parliament in 1981 in order to amend the criteria for membership which had remained virtually unchanged since 1871. The bill hoped to implement the recommendations of a committee chaired by Sir Henry Fisher, which had concluded that the Lloyd's market was wanting in most aspects of self-regulation.

The Lloyd's debacle illustrates the undoubted truth that unless professions regulate themselves then a government will eventually assume the responsibility for doing so. Another aspect of public authorization procedure which applies to the banks and insurance companies is the requirement that those who manage them should be 'fit and proper persons'. Such a value judgement is made by the Department of Trade in authorizing licensed dealers in securities and by the Bank of England in granting banking and licensed-deposit taker status.

The Insurance Companies Act provides the Secretary of State for Trade with similar powers in respect of insurance business. The Wilson Committee recommended that if the 1979 Banking Act were found to operate successfully in this respect, then the provisions should be extended to certain non-banking institutions. Like the banking institutions, certain non-banks are closely monitored by the use of balance sheet ratios. We have already seen that this applies to investment trusts. Insurance companies carrying on general business are required to maintain strict solvency margins, i.e. the excess of assets over liabilities. The Wilson Committee noted however, that no such specific requirements are applied to assurance business but this is expected to change in order to meet EEC obligations in the next few years. Nevertheless, the Policy Holders Protection Act effectively provides insurance for policy holders in life assurance companies. The banks, of course, have traditionally been subject to liquidity requirements as a natural part of monetary policy. However, other institutions are increasingly required to conform to certain minimum liquidity conditions in order to achieve a certain status. This is exemplified by the building societies which are required to maintain certain liquidity and reserve ratios to qualify for trustee status.

In recognition of the increasing importance of both institutions in the financial system, the Wilson Committee paid particular attention to the problems of regulating the building societies and pension funds. There is no doubt that the latter have assumed a dominant position in the investment market and can influence significantly the market for stocks and shares because of the massive funds that have accumulated. At the same time, there is an increasing need for the pension funds to become more professional in their approach to measuring their own investment performance. Indeed, measuring investment performance has become an industry itself, with pension consultants, financial publications and academics competing for the privilege of providing the most acceptable measurement techniques and monitoring procedures.

Pension funds

The Wilson Committee identified two basic problems associated with pension fund management to which statutory supervision should be directed. The first was that the assets may be badly managed by the manager of the fund to such an extent that it is unable to meet pension obligations. The second, related problem, is that inadequate funding provision may be made and accrued pension entitlements may be again at risk. The Committee recognized that supervision must address itself to these problems.

It was noted in Chapter 2 that pension schemes are invariably set up as trusts and as such are entrusted with assets which must be managed in the best interest of the beneficiaries. The Trustee Act of 1925 and the Trustee

Investment Act of 1961 lay down responsibilities and limit the type of investment and proportions of assets in this respect. As such, the law relating to trusts constrains the actions of pension fund managers as do the deeds under which the fund is established. It is expected that these will be supplemented by further measures when the Occupational Pensions Board completes a five year report, which began in 1977, on the security of occupational pension rights. It is to be hoped that the OPB report will have more impact than the 1975 report which had had limited response to date[5]. Although the National Association of Pension Funds, the spokesman for the industry, seeks to ensure the adoption of voluntary codes of practice, it cannot be regarded as a regulating body.

The Wilson Committee noted that statutory supervision of pension funds was not as comprehensive as that which existed for insurance companies and that, in this respect, the UK lagged behind the United States. Besides the supervision which arises naturally from the legislation mentioned above, the Superannuation Funds Office of the Inland Revenue administers the provisions in the Finance Acts of 1970 and 1971 which relate to the capital gains and income tax reliefs which are available to recognized financial institutions. Indeed, we have already noted that it is the translation of fiscal advantages bestowed upon such schemes into a greater rate of return or a greater degree of security which has contributed to the popularity of such contractual saving. However, the Inland Revenue is naturally concerned with the realistic assessment of taxable surpluses rather than the prudential management of assets *per se*. This leaves the prime responsibility for such supervision to bodies such as the Occupational Pensions Board. In 1975 the OPB concluded that there was not sufficient evidence to support the imposition of strict funding and investment controls upon schemes in addition to those already required of schemes contracted out. However, the OPB did make certain recommendations worth noting though, as already mentioned, the more contentious recommendations have not been taken up:

(i) Where managers of funds have not fully insured the benefits then they should be 'expressly required' to prepare annual reports and accounts. Auditors and actuaries should also take part in the monitoring process to ensure objectivity and professional guidance.

(ii) Information should be provided on request by managers to members of the scheme.

(iii) Members and other beneficiaries of a scheme should be entitled to pass the above information on to trade unions or other associations which represent their interests.

5 OPB report on the question of solvency, disclosure of information and member participation in occupational pension schemes, Cmnd 5904, Feb. 1975.

(iv) All schemes should be obliged to register 'with a control authority' to ensure conformity with rules concerning the provision of information.

(v) Easier methods of redress should be made available to members and other beneficiaries through legislation allowing cases for breach of trust to be heard in the county court.

(iv) Member's participation in occupational pension schemes should be encouraged to ensure a code of good practice.

Although a government reply to the report accepted several of the recommendations little action has been taken to date[6]. The Wilson Committee registered disquiet in this respect and considered that the piecemeal development of a regulatory system is insufficient to meet the increased responsibility of pension funds. However, this does not mean that the Committee supported the imposition of strict solvency regulations upon all schemes. The Committee was quite explicit that it regarded voluntary codes of practice inadequate and that the rules governing disclosure are not absolutely clear. The objective, they insisted, was that the members of a scheme should have access to reliable information in much the same way as shareholders in a company. Pursuing the metaphor, they concluded that a Pension Scheme Act, analogous to the Companies Acts should be initiated providing regular statutory information, member participation and with the duties and responsibilities of the parties involved clearly stated and monitored. Finally, the Wilson Committee encouraged the setting up of a registry of pensions along the lines of Companies House where the public can gain access to financial information.

Building societies

As with the pension funds the Wilson Committee considered the societies to have outgrown the regulatory arrangements which have remained virtually the same since 1962. The Committee highlighted the inefficiency which, in its opinion, had persisted in some smaller societies as a result of their shielding from normal commercial pressures plus the fact that an excess demand for mortgages created a comfortable operating climate. It has already been stated that the recommended rate system was beginning to crumble in the early 1980s[7]. However, it has also been shown that freer competition, if unmatched by improved supervisory arrangements, can impose considerable strain upon the financial system, exemplified by the secondary banking crisis.

The societies have operated under a strict supervisory regime since the

6 Occupational Pension Schemes: the role of members in the running of schemes, Cmnd 6514, June 1976.

7 See 'The Cartel Cracks Up', an *Investors Chronicle* special report, *Investors Chronicle*, May 22, 1981.

Building Societies Act of 1962. Accordingly, the problems of supervision arise from consideration of the appropriateness of supervisory arrangements formulated twenty years ago. Many of the provisions which apply to the activities of building societies have been reviewed and need not be repeated here. Various statutory investments have since amended the form in which the societies may hold liquid assets[8]. Presently, the first $7\frac{1}{2}$ per cent of society's assets must be held in the form of short-term public sector securities or bank deposits. A further $7\frac{1}{2}$ per cent can be invested in medium-term public securities and any assets beyond 15 per cent in longer term public securities with up to 25 years to maturity.

The conditions imposed upon the building societies by the legislation are scarcely comparable to those imposed upon the banks under the 1979 Banking Act. Furthermore, societies are not allowed to advertise in their first year of operation, which places an extremely difficult burden upon new societies to attract depositors. The Wilson Committee noted that, during the decade 1970–1980, twelve newly formed societies had ceased to exist as a result of this condition and the absence of the strict liquidity and reserve requirements imposed upon banking. Unlike the pension funds, the societies are closely monitored by the Registrar of Friendly Societies. The Building Societies Association, while it is a professional association comprising the major building societies, has no statutory controlling powers concerning the activities of its members. The Joint Advisory Committee on Building Society Finance (JAC), set up in 1973, provides the link between the BSA and the Government but provides a monitoring rather than supervisory function for the building societies.

The framework within which the societies are allowed to operate was dealt with in Chapter 3. However, the Wilson Committee pointed to the inadequacy of the present arrangements and recommended five amendments to the present system:

(i) The Registrar should be given the power to promote mergers between societies and be able to enforce the winding-up of a society if its members' funds were considered to be at risk.

(ii) The scope and frequency of contact between the Registrar of Friendly Societies and the building societies should be extended.

(iii) The cash flow statements presented by the societies, which are voluntary, should be made compulsory.

(iv) The Registrar's department should be restructured and reorganized in order to meet the increased burden of work as a result of (i), (ii) and (iii).

(v) The setting up of a statutory deposit protection scheme in line with other major financial institutions.

---

8 The present liquidity requirements are set out in the Building Societies (Authorised Investments) Order 1977, SI No. 2052, later amended by SI 1979, No. 1301.

The report noted that the societies had coped admirably with problems occurring in their ranks and had always attempted to act to protect their members. However, the fact that 100 societies were not members of the BSA had always posed a potential weakness in building society self-regulation which the Committee found unacceptable. Since one of the persistent recommendations of the Committee was the consistent treatment of financial institutions from the viewpoint of supervision it is natural that a compulsory deposit scheme should be supported. Furthermore, the Committee recognized the increasing importance of providing adequate safety measures for depositors if competition in the financial system is to be actively encouraged. Finally, the first European Community directive on credit institutions, which was adopted in December 1977, devised a system of authorization for the setting up of credit institutions, prescribing minimum conditions for their operation. The Banking Act effectively implemented the directive in the banking sector while its application to the societies was deferred. However, discussions concerning the application of the directive are taking place. Its requirements are concerned with ensuring that institutions have adequate funds, are managed by at least two fit and proper persons and provide the right of appeal against refusal to grant authorization. The directive does not specifically require minimum reserve and liquidity ratios, though this is likely to be a future development.

While the committee's recommendations are commendable, it is difficult to see how the problems which have beset the system of providing mortgage finance through building societies can be improved by the adoption of its recommendations. The movement of mortgage rates is notoriously sticky and, as a consequence, the housing market has been alternatively swamped with and starved of funds and house prices have reacted in sympathy. This has created the occasional need for Governments to interfere with the allocation of funds in this sector. The grounds for interference were that the house purchaser should be protected from the vagaries of the market. However, the mortgage rate had consistently increased throughout the 1970s in response to the changing monetary tactics of Governments. At the end of the decade there appeared to be a consensus of opinion that exposure to the vagaries of the market could not be any worse than recent experience and the call for greater competition within and between the societies and other financial institutions was encouraged.

The consequence of this new competitive spirit, plus the increasing popularity of the philosophy of fiscal neutrality, has been an invigorated Department of National Savings, the crumbling of collusion in the building society system and an increasing commitment by the banks to providing housing finance. These three factors which characterize the financial sector in the early 1980s are indicative of the new competitive spirit which, it is hoped, will bring greater efficiency in the allocation of money and credit in the economic system. From the point of view of the building societies, there is little doubt that exposure to increasingly severe competition in both their borrowing and lending activities will bring pressure to bear on the more inefficient societies. This in turn is likely to promote further merger activity and probably a higher general level of interest rates on mortgages for house purchasers. This is the price the economy must pay in the attempt to remove the famine and feast which has characterized the financing of house purchase throughout the past decade.

5 Monetary policy

The direct consequence of revising the competitive conditions under which financial institutions must operate are not always apparent and rarely predictable. The Wilson Committee Report, *inter alia*, implied an amendment to the mix of competition policy in so far as it attempted to make the balance between statutory and non-statutory forms of control more equal between different financial institutions. One of the problems faced in this respect is that certain bodies, such as the Stock Exchange, already have the authority vested in them which can regulate that market. Other financial sectors, such as the insurance and pension funds, have not the same allegiance to a professional controlling body and therefore require a degree of statutory intervention in their affairs in order to inject the source of authority upon which any regulation must rely. In cases where an existing regulatory body does not possess sufficient sanctions to enforce an agreeable code of conduct then conflict will arise, as in the case of Lloyd's insurers. The major conclusion of the Wilson Committee in this respect was that a joint review body should be established which would monitor the regulation of all parts of the financial system and react immediately to circumstances as they change.

Developments in the 1970s such as the oil crisis, the abolition of exchange controls, a varying savings ratio, and the general surge in the growth of the non-banking sector have influenced public attitudes to financial institutions. One of the principal features of the financial system in the 1980s is the dominant influence of the pension funds in redirecting funds from saving to investment opportunities. The upshot has been an increasing call for the supervision of these institutions and there is an increasing likelihood that the degree of statutory control upon their activities will increase, although the speed of change will depend upon the political administration in power.

As far as monetary policy is concerned, the implications of the changing pattern of the financial system are already apparent. Issues concerning the control of the money supply and the impact of the growing non-bank sector have been discussed at length. The adoption of PSL1 and PSL2 as subsidiary definitions of liquidity underpinning sterling M3 as the predominant monetary target shows recognition of the growing influence of the non-bank sector.

In the summer of 1981, a form of monetary base system was introduced in the UK; this was described in Chapter 5. This was another step in the refining process which has taken place since 1976 when monetary targeting was adopted. It is inevitable that once a target is chosen then its measurement will be continually revised until it can be hit with some degree of accuracy. The problem faced then is whether, after the passage of time, the target is still relevant. Nevertheless, in order to achieve accuracy in monetary control the 'monetary sector' has been revised to include the institutions described on page 117.

Obviously, the inclusion of the deposits of additional institutions to the monetary list inevitably caused a temporary upheaval in the money supply. It was hoped that control of the monetary aggregates would be strengthened by the new arrangements. More significant was the abandonment of the direct control of interest rates. The consequence of that policy was always that the direct control of interest rates distorted the flow of credit and hampered competition. It has already been noted that a direct result of the policy, and in particular the reserve asset system, was a stimulation in the creation of money substitutes which, in turn, impeded monetary control.

Since October 1979, when the Federal Reserve in the USA switched the emphasis of its monetary control to directly influencing the money supply, allowing rates of interest to react to the flows of money and credit, interest rates have been particularly volatile. The British financial system will take time to adjust to the increased volatility of interest rates and many institutions are likely to devise 'shock absorbers' to protect themselves from rapid variations in rates of interest. The impact upon the primary non-banking institutions will not be extensive. Since the abolition of exchange controls, most institutions have learned to operate investment portfolios in a climate of rapidly varying international exchange and interest rates so that the new monetary order should provide no real surprises.

In order to cushion the impact of the new system upon the money markets, the Bank of England has adopted an amended interventionist policy. Greater emphasis is placed upon open market operations and less upon lender of last resort lending (i.e. lending to the discount houses), though open market operations will still be operated largely through the discount market. In order to allow the financial system to learn to live with automatic interest rate adjustment to the supply and demand for money and credit, the Bank endeavours to keep short-term interest rates within an unpublished band. The Bank's activities now concentrate upon the provision of stabilizing flows of short-term funds from its banking department into the money markets, rather than deliberately creating shortages of money and quenching the demand on its own terms in order to determine interest rates. The latter was a feature of monetary policy in the late 1970s and in 1980. A feature of the rest of the present decade may be the increasing volatility of rates of interest, a tighter control over monetary aggregates, and increasing competition in the financial system. If the latter is achieved it will be the result of a decade of painful experience.

6 Summary and conclusions

This chapter has been concerned with the practical consequences of changes in the structure and composition of the UK financial system and the conditions under which financial intermediaries have had to conduct their business. Several factors have been identified as crucial in determining the nature of competition in the financial system:

(i) The measures adopted by monetary authorities in the conduct of monetary policy, which in turn will depend upon the extent to which Keynesian or monetarist views are reflected in official thinking.
(ii) The fiscal incentives provided for certain types of saving.
(iii) Legislative and non-statutory constraints upon the operating conditions of a financial institution, which can be prudential or discriminatory and may be explicit or implicit.
(iv) The incidence of legislative constraints upon both the lending and borrowing policies of financial institutions.
(v) Technological innovation, which may have the consequence of narrowing the spread between borrowing and lending rates of financial institutions and can be considered a proxy for efficiency.
(vi) The economic 'climate', including the prevalence of inflation, internationalism and general trends in saving, which combine to favour certain financial assets at the expense of others in the wealth portfolios of individuals and institutions.

Of course, the list is not exhaustive but it illustrates the major influences which serve to dictate the structure of any financial system and the conduct of those institutions comprising it. There is little doubt, for example, that the 'qualitative' guidance given by the Bank of England to the commercial banks has in fact virtually dictated their lending policies in favour of lending either to manufacturing industry or for exports and regional development. As a result, the lending policies of other deposit taking institutions have displayed a greater tendency towards personal lending.

The direct consequence of the natural bias bred into the lending policies of commercial banks by successive governments is that when monetary conditions are tight the first sector to feel the pinch is manufacturing. Such in-built inefficiency in the provision of finance for industry is precisely the problem the Wilson Committee was asked to examine.

Earlier chapters have examined the theoretical constructs which have been developed to explain financial intermediation in general and were later refined in order to explain the growth of non-banking institutions. After introducing the important institutions and considering selective comparative systems, Part Two broached the complex subject of the impact that the growth of non-banking institutions may have on certain theoretical relationships which serve to underpin much of traditional thinking in the field of monetary economics.

Two separate points of view were identified in this respect. There are those who believe that the increasing proliferation of non-banking liabilities has served to destabilize the demand for money, which leads them to conclude that wider measures of liquidity are appropriate as measures of expenditure capability, rather than the narrowly defined money supply. The opposite view contends that money is, and always will be, the deterministic variable in the financing of exchange. Credit institutions rely upon the existence and provision of money as much as the credit created by banks. Just as the credit creating capacity of banks is directly influenced by their access to short-term liquid funds, so is the activity of credit institutions.

It is clear that an assessment of the true function of non-banking institutions as brokers or creators of money, or as creators or transmitters of credit, is necessary in order to identify which of these views is correct. Ultimately, however, the importance of money lies in its ability to finance exchange and in this sense the distinction between money and credit becomes unclear. It is sufficient that the student of money and finance be aware of the possible policy implications of the different interpretations attached to the roles of banking and non-banking financial intermediaries. It is obvious that evidence to support many viewpoints can be provided. In the end the objective of the architects designing any financial system must be the efficient transmission of saving to productive uses.

Topics

1 Appraise the methods adopted to control the activities of any *two* non-banking institutions, distinguishing between prudential and discriminatory measures.
2 Define 'fiscal neutrality' and examine the consequences of the application of such a policy for competition in the financial system.
3 Examine the changing lending policy adopted by the commercial banks over the past decade. What factors have combined to generate this reaction?

4 Discuss the differing liquidity requirements of building societies compared with the banks.
5 Examine the relationship between the borrowing and lending policies of banks. Describe the competitive performance of the banks in both respects since the policy of Competition and Credit Control was introduced in 1971.

Glossary of technical terms

Contractual saving Saving whereby a fixed term of certain contributions is agreed between two (or more) parties. This is sometimes called non-discretionary saving.

Corset A ceiling on banking liabilities introduced at the end of 1973 and suspended in 1980.

Crowding out Where the fiscal benefits of certain savings methods serve to deprive other areas (usually the private sector), of funds, with the effect that industrial investment suffers.

Domino effect The disproportionate chain of banking failures caused by the initial collapse of a single bank.

Disintermediation The diversion of resources to some other financial activity as a direct result of official constraints imposed upon a particular area of financial activity. The situation where companies can borrow from the banks in order to place funds in the money market is known as 'round tripping' and is encouraged by the misalignment of interest rates in financial markets which occasionally results from untimely interest rate policy.

Eligible liabilities Sterling deposits of less than two years to maturity minus interbank lending and non-callable loans to discount houses plus net CDs issued.

Endowment effect The windfall effect on bank profits arising from a rise in interest rates not offset by a corresponding increase in the cost of administering non-interest bearing accounts and vice-versa.

Financial innovation The development by financial intermediaries of financial instruments which seek to combine income and capital certainty in a new way in order to exploit market opportunities.

Financial instruments Debt instruments issued by financial institutions which comprise the financial element in any individual's wealth portfolio.

Financial intermediary An organization or person who intervenes between saver and borrower in order to direct funds towards some specified purpose.

Gearing Usually associated with investment trusts, gearing refers to the extent to which a trust is financed by prior charge rather than share capital. The effect is to magnify the impact of the increasing value of investments upon the earnings per share of the trust.

High powered or superior money That money defined as forming the base of the monetary system. It is the source of bank money creation and therefore potent as the source of any increase in money supply.

Lifeboat scheme A scheme sent out by the Bank of England in 1974 in order to deter the domino effect which could have taken place as a result of the collapse in the property market. It operated via the depositing of Bank and clearing bank funds with threatened institutions.

Listed banks Those banks listed by the Bank of England which are required to submit returns and are entitled to use the name 'bank'.

Money at call (call money) Borrowing by the discount houses from the banks which can be called in when the banks are short of cash. This forces the houses to sell bills, possibly at the penal Minimum Lending Rate.

Money market The most liquid market in the City, dealing in cash which is exchanged for discounted bills or lent overnight between banks and other members of the market, the most important of which are the discount houses. The market may occasionally be short of funds and the Bank of England will discount bills at the rate it feels appropriate. This rate is then transmitted to the banking system through the money market.

Notional rebate The implicit yield obtained on a bank account bearing no explicit interest and set off against charges for operating the account.

Parallel markets Where the same intermediary function is undertaken by a replacement intermediary or money market other than the discount market in order to avoid controls.

Recognized banks Banks which are recognized by the Bank of England as eligible to deal in the treasury bill market and whose own bills are eligible for discount at the Bank. This now includes many foreign banks; a full list is available in the Bank of England's *Quarterly Bulletin*, September 1981.

Re-intermediation The reverse of disintermediation, where the removal of controls invites intermediation to return to its original economic agent.

Retail deposits Small denomination deposits repayable at short notice upon which there exists a fixed rate of interest.

Sight deposits Deposits repayable immediately on demand.

Substitutability The extent to which two financial assets can be used to replace each other in a wealth portfolio.

Switching The exchange of one asset or liability for another in an asset or liability portfolio. It can apply to switching from foreign currency to sterling or vice-versa, from banking to non-banking financial instruments or between similar financial instruments with differing maturity/yield characteristics.

Syndicated credits The formation of a syndicate of banks in order to pool resources to provide a line of credit which would imply too much risk for one single institution to bear.

Time deposits Deposits repayable after a specific time period has elapsed.

Universal banking A financial institution with banking status which provides every conceivable financial intermediary function to a community.

Velocity of circulation The speed with which money passes between economic agents in order to finance exchange.

Wealth portfolio The collection of financial assets chosen by an individual or fund manager containing the precise combination which corresponds most closely to the savings propensity/investment policy of the appropriate economic agent.

Wholesale deposits Large denomination deposits, usually exceeding £50,000, upon which the rate of interest is negotiable.

Bibliography

Lord Armstrong 'Challenges in the 1980s' in *The Banks and their Competitors*, The Institute of Bankers, London 1980.

Arrow, K. J. *Essays in the Theory of Risk*, Markham Economic Series, Markham Press Fund, Chicago, 1971.

Ascheim, J. A. 'Techniques of Monetary Control' *Quarterly Bulletin*, Bank of England, Sept. 1971.

Bank of England 'Money Supply and Dometic Credit', *Economic Trends* Vol. 183–194, May 1969.

Bank of England 'Competition and Credit Control', *Quarterly Bulletin*, Sept. 1981.

Bank of England 'The Importance of Money', in (ed.) H. G. Johnson, *Readings in British Monetary Economics*, Oxford University Press, 1972.

Bank of England 'The Domestic Financial Implications of Financing a Balance of Payments Deficit on Current Account', *Quarterly Bulletin*, Vol. 15, No. 1, March 1975.

Barrett, C. R., Gray, E. and Parkin, M. 'The Demand for Financial Assets by the Personal Sector', (ed.) G. A. Renton *Modelling the Economy* Heinemann Educational, London, 1973.

Bell, G. L. and Berman, L. S. 'Changes in the Money Supply 1954–1964', *Economica*, Vol. XXXII, No. 126, May 1966.

Bhattacharya, D. K. *The Demand for Financial Assets: An econometric study of the UK personal sector*, Saxon House, Aldershot, 1978.

Cagan, P. 'The Effect of Pension Plans on Aggregate Saving', Occasional Paper Series 95, National Bureau of Economic Research Inc., Cambridge, Massachusetts.

Carson D. (ed.) *Banking and Monetary Studies*, Irwin, Homewood, Illinois, 1963.

Christ, C. F. 'Interest Rates and Portfolio Selection Among Liquid Assets in the United States' in *Measurement in Economics: Studies in Mathematical Economics and Econometrics in Memory of Yehuda Grunfeld*, Stanford University Press, Stanford, 1963.

Clayton, G., Dodds, J. C., Ford, J. L. and Ghosh, D. 'An Econometric Model of the UK Financial Sector', *Issues in Monetary Economics* (eds) H. G. Johnson and A. R. Nobay, Oxford University Press, 1974.

Clayton, G. and Wood, D. 'British Financial Intermediaries in Theory and Practice', *Economic Journal*, Vol. LXX, 11 Dec. 1962.

Cleary, E. J. *The Building Society Movement*, Elek Ltd, St Albans, 1965.

Coghlan, R. T. and Jackson, P. M. 'The UK Savings Ratio: past, present and future', *Scottish Journal of Political Economy*, Nov. 1979.

Coghlan, R. T. and Sykes, C. 'Managing the Money Supply', *Lloyds Bank Review*, No. 135, Jan. 1980.

Crockett, A. D. *Money: Theory, policy and institutions*, Nelson & Sons Ltd, Walton-on-Thames, 1973.

Croome, D. R. and Johnson M. G. (eds) *Money in Britain 1959–1969*, Oxford University Press, 1970.

Dale, R. S. 'Prudential Regulation of Multinational Banking: The problem outlined', *Quarterly Review*, National Westminster Bank, Feb. 1981.

Dodds, J. C. 'The Demand for Financial Assets by the British Life Funds: A comment', *Oxford Bulletin*, Vol. 37, No. 2, 1975.

Dorrance, G. S. *National Monetary and Financial Analysis*, Macmillan, London, 1978.

Dorrance, G. 'Savings in the 1970s', *Lloyds Bank Review*, No. 138, Oct. 1980.

Dorrance, G. and Threadgold, A. R. 'Personal Savings: the impact of life assurance and pension funds', Discussion paper No. 1, Bank of England, 1978.

Duck, N. W. and Sheppard, D. K. 'A Proposal for Control of the UK Money Supply', *Economic Journal*, Vol. 88, March 1978.

Falush, P. 'The Changing Pattern of Savings', *National Westminster Bank Review*, Aug. 1978.

Farr, H. T. 'Definition of Money, some Theoretical and Empirical Issues', Special Studies Paper No. 16, Federal Reserve Board, Washington DC, Jan., 1971.

Farrar, D. E. 'The Investment Decision under Uncertainty', Ford Foundation prize (unpublished), University of Chicago, 1961.

Feige, E. L. *The Demand for Liquid Assets: A temporal cross-section analysis*, Prentice-Hall, Englewood Cliffs, New Jersey, 1964.

Feige, E. L. and Pierce, D. K. 'The Substitutability of Money and Near-money: A survey of the time series evidence', *Journal of Economic Literature*, Vol. XV, No. 2, June 1977.

Fisher, I. *The Purchasing Power of Money*, Macmillan, New York, 1911.

Friedman, M. *The Quantity Theory of Money: A restatement in studies in the quantity theory of money*, University of Chicago Press, Chicago, 1956.

Friedman, M. and Schwartz, A. J. *A Monetary History of the United States*, Princeton University Press, Princeton, New Jersey, 1963.

Friedman M. and Mieselman D. *The Relative Stability of Monetary Velocity and the Investment Multiplier in the United States 1897–1958*, Research study in stabilization policies, Commission on Money and Credit, Prentice-Hall, Englewood Cliffs, New Jersey, 1963.

Ghosh, D. *The Economics of Building Societies*, Saxon House, Aldershot, 1974.

Ghosh D. and Parkin, M. 'A Theoretical and Empirical Analysis Portfolio, Debt and Interest Rate Behaviour of Building Societies', *The Manchester School* (Journal), Sept. 1972.

Gibson, N. J. *The Significance of Financial Intermediaries for Economic Policy 1932–1965, 1967–70*, (Second edn), Hobart paper No. 39, Institute of Economic Affairs, 1970.

Goldfield, S. M. *Commercial Banks Behaviour and Economic Activity*, North Holland Publishing Co., Amsterdam 1966.

Goldsmith, R. W. *Financial Intermediaries in the American Economy since 1900*, Princeton University Press, Princeton, New Jersey, 1958.

Goldsmith, R. W. *Financial Structure and Development*, Yale University Press, New Haven, Connecticut, 1969.

Goodhart, C. A. E. *Money, Information and Uncertainty*, Macmillan, London, 1975.

Grantham, G, Velk, T. and Fraas, A. 'On the Microeconomics of the Supply of Money', *Oxford Economic Papers*, Vol. 29 No. 3, Oxford Univesity Press, Nov. 1977.

Greenbaum, G. and Haywood, D. 'Secular Changes in the Financial Services Industry', *Journal of Money, Credit and Banking*, (USA), Vol. 111, No. 2, Part 2., May 1971.

Griffiths, B. 'Competition in Banking', Hobart paper No. 51, Institute of Economic Affairs, 1970.

Gurley, J. F. and Shaw, E. *Money in a Theory of Finance*, Brookings Institution, Washington DC, 1960.

Harrington, R. L. 'The Importance of Competition for Credit Control', *Issues in Monetary Economics*, (eds) H. G. Johnson and A. R. Nobay, Oxford University Press, 1974.

Hawtrey, R. G. *Currency and Credit*, Longmans Green & Co., London, 1919.

Hicks, J. 'Liquidity', *The Economic Journal*, Vol. LXXII, No. 268, Dec. 1962.

Hicks, J. *Critical essays in monetary theory*, (especially lecture II in the two triads) Oxford University Press, 1967.

Hill, S. and Gough, J. 'Concentration and Efficiency in the Building Society Industry', Dept. of Applied Economics, UWIST, Sept. 1978.

Johnson, H. G. (ed.) *Readings in British Monetary Economics*; Oxford University Press, 1972.

Johnson, H. G. (ed.) *Further Essays in Monetary Economy*, Allen & Unwin, London, 1973.

Kaldor, N. and Trevithick, J. 'A Keynesian Perspective on Money, *Lloyds Bank Review*, Nol 139, Jan. 1981.

Katona, G. 'Private Pensions and Individual Saving', Survey Research Centre, University of Michigan, Ann Arbor, Michigan, 1980.

Kaufman, G. G., 'More on an Empirical Definition of Money', *American Economic Review*, March 1969.

Kern, D., 'Monetary Policy and C.C.C.', *National Westminster Quarterly Review*, Nov. 1972.

Keynes, J. M. *The General Theory of Employment, Interest and Money*, Macmillan, London, 1936.

Laidler, D. E. W., *The Demand for Money: Theories and evidence*, (2nd edn), Harper & Row, London, 1977.

Laumas, G. S. 'The Degree of Moneyness of Savings Deposits', *American Economic Review*, Vol. LVIII, June 1968.

Lee, T. H. 'The Substitutability of Non-Bank Intermediary Liabilities for Money: The empirical evidence', *Journal of Finance*, Sept. 1966.

Lewis, M. 'Rethinking Monetary Policy', *Lloyds Bank Review*, No. 137, July 1980.

Llewellyn, D. T. 'Do Building Societies take Deposits away from Banks?', *Lloyds Bank Review*, Jan. 1979.

Lomax, D. F. 'Reserve Asset and Competition and Credit Control', *National Westminster Quarterly Review*, Aug. 1973.

Markowitz, H. M. *Portfolio Selection*, Cowles Foundation Monograph No. 16, New York, 1952.

Mason, L. E. 'The Empirical Definition of Money: A critique', *Economic Inquiry*, Vol. XIV, No. 4, Dec. 1976.

Mathews, K. G. P. and Ormerod, P. A. 'St Louis Models of the UK Economy', *National Institute Economic Review*, No. 84, May 1978.

Munnell, A. H. 'Private Pensions and Saving: New evidence' *Journal of Political Economy*, Vol. 84 (5), 1976.

Newbould, G. D. and Doyle, P. 'Marketing Strategies for Building Societies', (unpublished), University of Bradford, 1974.

Newlyn, W. T. 'The Supply of Money and its Control'. *The Economic Journal*, Vol. 74, June 1964.

Oherlihy, C. St. J. and Spencer, J. E. 'Building Society Behaviour 1955–1970', *National Institute Economic Review*, Aug. 1972.

Parkin, M. 'Discount House Portfolio and Debt Selection' *Review of Economic Studies*, Nov. 1969.

Parkin, M. 'Where is Britain's Inflation Going?', *Lloyds Bank Review*, July 1975.

Parkin, M. 'A comparison of alternative techniques of monetary control under rational expectations', *The Manchester School* (Journal), Sept. 1978.

Patinkin, D. '*Money, Interest and Prices: An integration of monetary and value theory*', (2nd edn), Harper & Row, London, 1965.

Pesek B. and Saving, T. *Money, Wealth and Economic Theory*, Macmillan, New York, 1967.

Pierce, D. G. and Shaw, D. M. *Monetary Economics, Theories, Evidence and Policy*, Butterworth, London, 1974.

Pierce, J. L. 'An Empirical Model of Commercial Bank Portfolio Management', D. Hester and J. Tobin (eds). *Studies in Portfolio Behaviour*, Cowles Foundation Monograph No. 20, New York, 1967.

Pigou, A. C. 'The Value of Money', *Quarterly Journal of Economics*, No. 37, Nov. 1917.

Polakoff, M. E. *Financial Institutions and Markets*, Houghton-Mifflin, Boston, 1970.

Radcliffe Report 'Committee on the Working of the Monetary System', Cmnd 827, HMSO, London, Aug. 1959.

Revell, J. *The British Financial System*, Macmillan, London, 1973.

Robertson, R. M. *A History of the American Economy*, Harcourt Brace and World, New York, 1964.

Robinson, J. 'The Theory of Money and the Analysis of Output', *Review of Economic Studies*, 1933.

Rose, H. 'The British Financial Structure: Some underlying trends in the capital market and banking system, and some questions for the 1980s', *The Banks and Their Competitors*, Institute of Bankers, London, 1980.

Ryan, T. M. 'The Demand for Financial Assets by the British Life Funds', *Oxford Bulletin of Economics and Statistics*, Vol. 35, No. 1, 1973.

Ryan, T. M. 'A Rejoinder', *Oxford Bulletin of Economics and Statistics*, Vol. 37, No. 2, 1975.

Savage, D. 'Monetary Targets and the Control of Money Supply', *National Institute Economic Review* No. 18, Aug. 1979.

Sayers, R. S. *Modern Banking*, Oxford University Press, 1967.

Slovin M. B. and Suska, M. E. 'The Structural Shift in the Demand for Money', Working paper for the Division of Research and Statistics, Board of Governors of the Federal Reserve System, Washington DC, 1974.

Slovin, M. B. and Suska, M. E. *Money and Economic Activity*, Lexington Books, Massachusetts 1977.

Smith, A. *The Wealth of Nations*, 1776, Everyman, Dent, London, 1977.

Smith, D. 'The Demand for Alternative Monies in the UK 1924–1977', *National Westminster Quarterly Review*, Nov. 1978.

Stevenson, A. A. and Trevithick, J. A. 'The Complementarity of Monetary Policy and Prices and Incomes Policy: An examination of recent British experience', *Scottish Journal of Political Economy*, Vol. 24, No. 1, Feb. 1977.

Tew, B. *Monetary Theory*, Routledge & Kegan Paul, London, 1969.

Timberlake, R. H. Jr. and Fortson, J. 'Time Deposits in the Definition of Money', *American Economic Review*, March, 1967.

Tobin, J. 'Liquidity preference as behaviour towards risk', *Review of Economic Studies*, Vol. 25, Feb. 1958.

Tobin, J. 'Commercial banks as creators of money', in Carson (1963).

Tobin, J. 'The Theory of Portfolio Selection', in *The Theory of Interest rates*, (eds) F. Hahn and F. Brechling, Macmillan, London, 1965.

Tobin J. and Brainard, W. 'Financial Intermediaries and the Effectiveness of Monetary Controls', *American Economic Review*, Vol. 53, No. 2, May 1963.

Townend, J. C. 'The Personal Saving Ratio', *Bank of England Quarterly Bulletin*, Vol. 16, No. 1, March 1976.

Williams, L. 'A Competitor's View', in *The Banks and Their Competitors*, Cambridge Seminar, Institute of Bankers, London, 1980.

Wilson, Sir Harold, Committee to Review the Functioning of Financial Institutions, 1980. Volumes of evidence presented to Committee published by HMSO, London.

Wilson, K. W. 'A Note on the Further Implications of Competition and Credit Control: A structural shift in the demand for financial assets', *Scottish Journal of Political Economy*, Vol. 25, No. 3, Nov. 1977.

Index

The abbreviation 'NBFI' for 'Non-Bank Financial Institution' has been used in subheadings throughout this index.